Praise for Doug Moran
and *If You Will Lead*

"Doug Moran looks at the practice of leadership from a unique perspective—through the lens of a literary classic. It's a fascinating way for today's managers to think about their own leadership brand." —*Steve Arneson, Ph.D., President, Arneson Leadership Consulting*

"Although the problems we confront have changed, the fundamentals of leadership remain the same. Recognizing this enduring truth, Doug Moran has created a book that draws leadership lessons from some of history's greatest figures. *If You Will Lead* surely will help readers become better leaders." —*George Allen, former governor and U.S. senator, Commonwealth of Virginia*

"Few people are born leaders. The rest of us need a guide to help us gain both the courage and competence to lead well. Doug Moran's book provides the perfect blend of a thoughtful leadership framework and anecdotes from the lives of history's greatest leaders to help make his points come to life. *If You Will Lead* is a great companion for any aspiring executive. —*John Scanlon, EVP and CFO, Intersections, Inc.*

"Doug Moran has taken a complex and challenging subject and created lessons and a framework that can help leaders realize and leverage their strengths." —*Sanjiv Yajnik, president, Financial Services, Capital One*

"This book offers the opportunity to learn from some of history's greatest leaders, so we can replicate their success. Moran's masterful framework translates these historical lessons into a concrete and practical guide for today's leaders." —*Larry Klane, CEO, Korea Exchange Bank*

"This book captures the importance of leadership stamina."
—*Cdr. Paul Galanti (USN ret.), former POW*

"Doug Moran does a great job of tying essential leadership attributes to great, recognizable leaders. The attributes chosen are essential traits of good leadership and very well organized."
—*Vice Admiral Ed Clexton, USN (Ret), former commanding officer, USS Dwight D. Eisenhower*

"One of the great needs in our country and in our world is the need for capable and inspiring leadership. This book gives the reader a sense of the qualities of leadership that are so needed today. In my judgment this book is most worthwhile and sorely needed." —*Walter F. Sullivan, bishop emeritus of Richmond, Virginia*

"After 26 years on Wall Street, the last 20 of them leading people, I am more aware than ever of the need to level-set your actions and philosophies and always be adjusting to the fast-paced world we live in, where change is the only constant. Doug Moran has proven himself to be a forward-thinking leader in an increasingly complex and competitive business environment, who has a demonstrated track record of both creative, strategic thinking and successful tactical execution across multiple leadership roles in both the public and private sectors. As one fights off the temptation to become jaded and dismissive of those offering the latest recipes for leadership success, Doug has proven to be one of the few people whose opinions I seek out, knowing that I can count on candid feedback, spirited debate, and a collaborative partner when dealing with issues important to me both personally and professionally. *If You Will Lead* is an important addition to any leader's short list of practical business reading and will make an immediate positive impact on how readers tie effective leadership principles to the future success of their organizations." —*Chris Dupuy, managing director, Merrill Lynch Wealth Management*

If You Will Lead

ENDURING WISDOM FOR
TWENTY-FIRST-CENTURY LEADERS

Doug Moran

A B2 BOOK

AGATE

CHICAGO

Printed in United States.

Library of Congress Cataloging-in-Publication Data

Moran, Doug, 1965-
If you will lead : enduring wisdom for 21st-century leaders /
Doug Moran.
    p. cm.
Includes bibliographical references and index.
Summary: "Management guide that uses Rudyard Kipling's poem
"If--" to define leadership qualities. Uses great leaders of the past as
examples of these leadership principals"--Provided by publisher.
    ISBN-13: 978-1-932841-58-9 (hard cover)
    ISBN-10: 1-932841-58-X (hard cover)
    1. Leadership. 2. Leadership--Psychological aspects. I. Title.
HD57.7.M653 2011
658.4'092--dc22

                       2011008683

10 9 8 7 6 5 4 3 2 1

B2 Books is an imprint of Agate Publishing.

Agate books are available in bulk at discount prices.
For more information, go to agatepublishing.com.

CONTENTS

ACKNOWLEDGMENTS

In many ways, this book was more than a century in the making. Rudyard Kipling wrote "If—" in 1895, he published it in 1910, and it has been changing lives ever since. I want to acknowledge the timeless wisdom that he captured in "If—." These 32 lines of poetry inspired me to be a better man and a stronger leader.

I am thankful for the gift of family and friends, without whose support this work would never have been possible. I owe so much to my parents, who instilled in me the faith, hope, and love that define me. To my mother, who first introduced me to "If—" and who always believed in me, thank you for making me believe in myself. To my father, thank you for your life as an example of true leadership—often unsung but ever present. You taught me that leadership is about much more than title or position. Mary Kate and Max, you gave me my greatest title, Dad. You inspired me to change the world, starting with me. To my sisters, thank you for a lifetime of being my biggest cheerleaders.

I owe a special thank you to the teachers who instilled in me the love of history and to see it as a source of infinite wisdom. You brought history to life for me, and you helped me to see many of the lessons that this book contains. I also owe a debt of gratitude to the many leaders with whom I have worked throughout my career. Good leaders or bad, I learned so much from all of you. Thank you to all of my friends who allowed me to share their stories as everyday examples of the "If" Sixteen Leadership Attributes.

There were so many people who helped me create *If You Will Lead*. Thank you to the many colleagues who invested your time and energy to help me craft my message. Your guidance, mentorship, support, and encouragement have been invaluable. Thank you to the many friends who read drafts of the book and helped me to refine it. I especially want to thank Tim Evans, Mary Ruth Clowdsley, Bob Godfrey, Chuck Hansen, Laura Moran, and Michael Tice for the time and energy you invested in reading and editing my early manuscript.

Thank you to Doug Seibold, and everyone at Agate B2 Publishing. Doug, your confidence made *If You Will Lead* a reality. To my editors, Ewurama Ewusi-Mensah and Kate DeVivo, thank you for making my work so much better. Eileen Johnson, I appreciate your marketing guidance and wisdom. Thank you to Jim and Lynda O'Connor at O'Connor Communications for connecting me with Doug and Agate and for all your help promoting my work. Thank you to Maguire Neblett for your genius with a camera.

Most of all I want to thank Laurie, my wife, my best friend, my partner, my first and best editor, and my muse. Thank you for your love, your patience, your support, your advice, your guidance, and for your willingness to read anything I give you. You make everything I do better. You are my "summum bonum."

Rudyard Kipling as Leadership Guru

In 1910, Rudyard Kipling published the poem "If—" in a collection of short stories entitled *Rewards and Fairies*. The poem became his most popular work, and it remains so one hundred years later. It has been translated into twenty-seven languages, and tens of millions of copies have been sold in the past century. Generations of students have memorized it. Leaders quote it. Advertisers use "If—" to promote everything from financial services to sporting events. Comedians parody it, and Hollywood continues to weave the poem into television shows and movies. It appears on postcards, T-shirts, and posters. It is now the foundation of this book about leadership.

Rudyard Kipling remains a prominent figure in British literature, and he is best known for his children's tales, military and travel stories, and poetry. Kipling wrote "If—" to celebrate the Jameson Raid, a failed British attack led in 1895 by Dr. Leander Starr Jameson against a band of Boer guerillas in what later became South Africa. This unsuccessful military action was a major catalyst for the Second Boer War, and both the poem and the British press celebrated Jameson as a hero and helped stir up support for the war. While Jameson's Raid has become a minor footnote in history, the poem it inspired lives on. In a 1995 BBC poll, "If—" was selected as Britain's favorite poem.

What has kept this poem relevant for the past one hundred years? What lessons can we learn from it and from its author?

While Kipling did demonstrate many characteristics associated with leadership, we do not remember him for this. He is most remembered for what he did best—write. Still, his career as a writer—especially as a journalist—provided him with great opportunities to observe and understand leaders and leadership. Whether that makes him an authority on leadership is largely irrelevant. His writing has inspired many to find meaning in his words that may be well beyond what Kipling intended. Kipling believed that a reader should find the truth in a writer's words. He once said, "The true nature and intention . . . of a writer's work does not lie within his own knowledge."

Rudyard Kipling has been celebrated and criticized with equal passion. His supporters included literary great Henry James, who said, "Kipling strikes me personally as the most complete man of genius that I have ever known." In 1907, Kipling became the first British citizen to win the Nobel Prize in Literature, awarded "in consideration of the power of observation, originality of imagination, virility of ideas and remarkable talent for narration which characterize the creations of this world-famous author."

Much of the criticism leveled at Kipling is based on accusations of militarism, imperialism, and racism. His works often included derogatory comments about indigenous people under British rule. George Orwell, one of Kipling's most vocal critics, referred to Kipling as the "prophet of British Imperialism." According to critic Douglas Kerr, "He is still an author who can inspire passionate disagreement."

WHO WAS RUDYARD KIPLING?

Kipling's life provides interesting insights into his thoughts and writing. Born in Bombay, India, in December 1865, Kipling was the son of English expatriates. While he spent most of his life elsewhere, he always thought of himself as Anglo-Indian; India was an essential part of who he was. Among his greatest sources of inspiration were the people of India—indigenous Indians and his fellow colonials alike.

Kipling and his sister, Trix, left India to attend school in England when he was six and she was just three. This was a defining period in Kipling's life. He overcame the adversity of boarding with an abusive family while in England, and it was during this period that family began to emerge as the dominant force in Kipling's life. The extended absences from members of his family strengthened his bonds to them. Kipling often referred to the "family square," a military term that indicated the importance of his family to his emotional and spiritual strength and well-being. Family and close friends would remain Kipling's strongest influences throughout his life.

Kipling returned to India at the age of seventeen to pursue a career as a journalist. As the subeditor of the *Civilian and Military Gazette* in Lahore, India (now part of Pakistan), he learned about the business of journalism and gained valuable writing experience. This role also gave Kipling his first taste of leadership and its challenges.

As a budding Anglo-Indian journalist, author, and poet, Kipling began to explore and understand the nature of human relationships. He observed the effects of societal boundaries; he also began to understand the power of "boundary crossing." Kipling biographer Harry Ricketts devoted an entire chapter to this topic. Kipling excelled at seeing across the societal divides. He truly understood and appreciated those around him—regardless of culture, rank, or status.

Kipling's boundary crossing enabled him to create fictional characters who seemed real. This skill also gave him the ability to connect with those he was interviewing. Finally, it allowed him to bridge the cultural gap that typically existed between colonials and Indians. He used these skills to meet and befriend prominent leaders within the Indian and Anglo-Indian communities. These relationships exposed Kipling to many political, business, and military events that taught him valuable leadership lessons.

Having achieved a degree of literary success in India, Kipling returned to England in 1889. He wanted to test himself in London, then the center of the literary world. Kipling found immediate critical and popular success that continued to grow for the next twenty years. He wrote and published some of his best poems and short stories during those years, including such classics as the poems "If—," "Gunga Din," and "Recessional" and the books *The Jungle Book, Just So Stories, Kim,* and *Captains Courageous.*

Kipling's fame and wealth enabled him to travel extensively and live in many countries, and his travels were a major influence on his writing. Kipling's literary success and travels provided him access to many of the great leaders and celebrities of his time, including Theodore Roosevelt, Cecil Rhodes (South African leader and creator of the Rhodes Scholarship), Stanley Baldwin (future British prime minister), Mark Twain, and many other leading military, colonial, and political leaders of his day.

Kipling remained a celebrity for most of his life, but his critical success waned during his later years. Some blame a series of personal tragedies and ill health for his decline. The death of Kipling's son, Jack, hit him very hard. Kipling had used his influence to help Jack obtain an officer's commission in the British Army during the First World War. Jack died in combat, and Kipling blamed himself. Others attribute Kipling's decline to his decision in the early twentieth century to use his writing to advocate his political agenda. Regardless, Kipling continued to write for the remainder of his life. He died in January 1936 at the age of seventy.

INTRODUCTION

"If—," a Leadership Framework

A CRISIS OF LEADERSHIP

It is easy to become depressed reading or watching the news. Everywhere we look, we see crisis, disaster, and failure—the global financial crisis, inadequate responses to natural or man-made disasters, violent movements born out of religious extremism, corporate scandals, and political corruption. We face daunting challenges as we enter the second decade of the twenty-first century. All of these challenges have one thing in common: *a failure of leadership*.

We have come to accept leadership mediocrity. In turn, we exacerbate our leadership failures with our desire for quick fixes and our impatience to get ahead. We ignore opportunities to learn from our mistakes, because acknowledging failure might open us to criticism. God forbid we do anything that might delay our next promotions or jeopardize our bonuses. We lull ourselves into accepting simple answers to complex problems. We refuse to hold each other or ourselves accountable. Leadership excellence requires a lifetime of work. Instead, we often look for shortcuts. We throw our money into seminars promising immediate results, books that offer one-size-fits-all solutions, and degree programs that try to cram years of learning into months of study. Our search for simple answers is at the heart of this epidemic of leadership failures.

The good news is that we are aware of our leadership challenges. That you are reading this book reveals a level of awareness of the problems we face. Fortunately, many leaders are genuinely committed to closing our leadership gaps. This book provides a foundation that any aspiring or current leader can build upon.

THE LEADERSHIP PARADOX

What does it take to become a competent and effective leader? The answer is both quite simple and exceedingly difficult. That is the leadership paradox. Leadership boils down to two words and a life-time of experience and commitment. The two words—*awareness* and *choice*—are at the heart of all learning and growth. The words and concepts are simple. Living them is the challenge. Successful leadership requires a great deal of experience. Each problem we encounter, each failure we confront, and each success we achieve has the potential to make us a better leader. The key is being *aware* of the experiences and *choosing* to learn from them and grow because of them. Leaders excel by seeing and grabbing the leadership opportunities around them. Their awareness and choices build upon each other and form a virtuous cycle, one feeding another. Everything we do is a test of choices, beliefs, and determination. The value of these tests isn't to be right; rather, it is to learn and to grow.

Often our first leadership choice is simply deciding to lead. We may not be aware that we have this choice. Leadership is not about position or title. No one can force us to lead. Similarly, no one can prevent us from leading. Others may influence us, but the choice is ours. Once we decide to lead, we must learn to lead well. The more we learn, the more choices we see, and the cycle continues. Becoming a great—or even competent—leader is a *lifelong* journey. In the words of Aristotle, "You are what you repeatedly do. Excellence is not an event—it is a habit." This applies to everything we do, especially leadership.

Great leaders understand that leadership is a vocation that requires hard work and dedication. My grandfather understood this. He lived by the motto, "Anything worth doing is worth doing right." When I was a boy, my mother introduced me to his favorite poem, "If—." It has come to form the foundation of my approach to leadership. The poem's words have helped me begin to unravel the complexities and challenges of leadership.

RUDYARD KIPLING'S "IF—"

While Kipling wrote "If—" to celebrate the exploits of an overzealous British colonial leader, he published it as a guide for young men at the turn of the twentieth century. He intended to help them become better men and better leaders. His poem and his guidance described a perfection that was unattainable, and young men who were frustrated by the incredibly high bar that he had set for them often accosted Kipling. His words present today's leaders—men and women, young and old—with the same unattainable perfection. But leadership is not about attaining perfection. It is about knowing who we are and what we believe. It is about seeing things that others can't or won't see. It is about motivating others to attempt things they thought were impossible. It is about having a dream and working to attain it. The most important lesson the poem teaches is that one should have the boldness and courage to step up and lead. Kipling's words remain powerful and his wisdom enduring:

If—

If you can keep your head when all about you
Are losing theirs and blaming it on you;
If you can trust yourself when all men doubt you,
But make allowance for their doubting too:
If you can wait and not be tired by waiting,
Or being lied about, don't deal in lies,
Or being hated, don't give way to hating,
And yet don't look too good, nor talk too wise;

If you can dream—and not make dreams your master;
If you can think—and not make thoughts your aim,
If you can meet with Triumph and Disaster
And treat those two impostors just the same:
If you can bear to hear the truth you've spoken
Twisted by knaves to make a trap for fools,
Or watch the things you gave your life to, broken,
And stoop and build 'em up with worn-out tools;

If you can make one heap of all your winnings
And risk it on one turn of pitch-and-toss,
And lose, and start again at your beginnings
And never breathe a word about your loss:
If you can force your heart and nerve and sinew
To serve your turn long after they are gone,

And so hold on when there is nothing in you
Except the Will which says to them: "Hold on!"

If you can talk with crowds and keep your virtue,
Or walk with kings—nor lose the common touch,
If neither foes nor loving friends can hurt you,
If all men count with you, but none too much:
If you can fill the unforgiving minute
With sixty seconds' worth of distance run,
Yours is the Earth and everything that's in it,
And—which is more—you'll be a Man, my son!

AWARENESS, CHOICE, AND THE "IF" SIXTEEN

So, what leadership advice could a twenty-first-century leader possibly get—or want—from a hundred-year-old poem written by a poet who is most remembered for his children's stories? What can an Information Age leader learn from a Victorian poem?

"If—" describes a path we may choose to follow to become better leaders. This book is a guide along that path. "If—" is simply written and easy to read and understand. And, most important, the messages are direct and powerful. The poem is not a checklist that will guarantee success for an aspiring leader, nor should this book be seen as a recipe for successful leadership.

Each of the poem's sixteen couplets describes an essential leadership attribute. By incorporating the concept of "awareness and choice," they form a comprehensive leadership structure, the "If" Sixteen Leadership Framework. While each of the attributes is unique and essential, some may seem similar or even redundant. Many of the attributes share characteristics and manifest themselves in related behaviors; they are interconnected and interdependent. I recommend that you read this book with an eye toward seeing the distinctions associated with the various attributes while also recognizing the ties among them.

The "If" Sixteen Leadership Attributes help us answer four questions that define each of us as leaders:

- Who am I, and what do I believe?
- What do I want?
- How will I attract and motivate others?
- How will I earn and retain the privilege to lead?

The book is organized into four sections based on these questions. Each section includes four chapters, with each chapter focusing on one of the "If" Sixteen Leadership Attributes. All of the attributes can and will help us address more than one of the four questions. For the sake of clarity, each attribute appears in the section it best supports, rather than in the order of the poem's couplets. The order of the sections is important. Self-awareness is first because before we can lead others we must first know ourselves. That self-awareness leads to awareness of what we want. Only after attaining both forms of awareness can we begin to contemplate attracting others or earning their trust.

Part 1: Knowing Who You Are and What You Believe

The most fundamental aspect of leadership is self-awareness. Leadership begins with knowing who we are and what we believe; however, leadership is more than simple self-awareness. It also means sharing our values and beliefs with others. The first four chapters deal with attributes that help us define, express, and expose who we truly are. Part 1 focuses on the importance of self-awareness and the challenges of self-discovery. Our heightened awareness begins to reveal the choices we make. We can begin to see how well our actions reflect our beliefs, values, and principles. These first four attributes are interdependent, and each builds on the others.

➤ **Chapter 1, Character,** examines the idea that leaders must truly know themselves before leading others. At its most basic, character involves cataloging and understanding the traits and features that define us. Character means knowing who we are and what we believe and value. It means acting in ways that demonstrate these beliefs and values. **Ronald Reagan** showed the strength of his character throughout his efforts to fight and win the Cold War. He trusted himself when others doubted him, because he truly believed in the virtue of his actions.

➤ **Chapter 2, Authenticity**, delves into the need for leaders to be themselves regardless of the situation. We play many roles, and leadership means being genuine in all of them. By living and acting according to our beliefs, values, and principles, each of us can lead from a position of strength and power. **Theodore Roosevelt** epitomized authentic leadership. Whether he was president of the United States, an Amazonian explorer, a cowboy, a writer, or a soldier, he was always himself. He remained authentic, whether he talked with crowds or walked with kings.

➤ **Chapter 3, Integrity,** encourages leaders to have the wisdom to learn the truth and the fortitude to defend it. Speaking and defending the truth reveal who we are. But integrity goes far beyond truth. Integrity also involves remaining whole. Leading with integrity means that we remain true to ourselves in our many roles. It means leading with an awareness of the potential for conflict or contention among our various roles. **Michael Collins** revealed his integrity as he fought for Irish independence. He sought the truth and defended it from those who tried to twist it to their advantage.

➤ **Chapter 4, Self-Efficacy,** teaches that we must have the humility and confidence to learn from both triumphs and disasters. Self-awareness and self-knowledge give us the confidence and wisdom to learn and grow from every experience. **Winston Churchill** personified self-efficacy: He met with triumphs and disasters, but he never allowed them to define him. He always remained confident in himself and his destiny, even during the loneliness and rejection of his "wilderness years."

Part 2: Knowing What You Want

Once we know who we are and what really matters to us, we can begin to better understand the world around us. We can visualize the improvements we want to make in our world. Our self-awareness allows us to explore how we can truly effect change. The four chapters in this section speak to understanding and articulating what we want to achieve and acting to make it real.

➤ **Chapter 5, Ambition,** teaches the importance of first being aware of our "Earth and everything that's in it," and second choosing how big we want our impact to be. This chapter helps leaders become aware of both personal and societal ambitions. **Abraham Lincoln**'s primary personal ambition was to rise out of poverty, but his greater societal ambition was to preserve the Union. His ambition made him one of America's greatest leaders.

➤ **Chapter 6, Vision,** explores the external manifestation of character and ambition. Vision starts with telling the world what we believe and then what we want to accomplish. We do this by describing a world that reflects our ambitions and aspirations. Choosing to make our dreams known is essential to leadership. **Dr. Martin Luther King**'s vision transformed the civil rights movement. He had the courage to dream and think about positive change. He led, enlisted, and inspired others to share his dreams and vision.

➤ **Chapter 7, Boldness,** examines our ability to see opportunities that others don't. More importantly, it promotes the willingness to seize those opportunities, even when others say we should not. **Thomas Jefferson**'s boldness drove him to see and seize opportunities and "risk it [everything] on one turn" to make the Louisiana Purchase.

➤ **Chapter 8, Resilience,** introduces the concept of bouncing back from setbacks. Leading by knowing what we want means anticipating challenges and recognizing and overcoming the obstacles we encounter. **Harriet Tubman** showed extraordinary resilience in her struggle to gain freedom for herself and her fellow slaves. She used whatever "worn-out tools" she could find to continue her fight.

Part 3: Attracting Others and Motivating Them to Follow

Knowing who we are and what we want gives us a solid foundation from which to lead. Engaging and motivating ourselves and compelling others to choose to follow us requires more. This section will help leaders understand these challenges, as well as the needs and motivations of others.

➤ **Chapter 9, Inspiration**, investigates the ability to connect with and motivate others—both friends and foes. Our actions and words can inspire others to achieve extraordinary accomplishments. **Mother Teresa** had the ability to inspire others. She motivated both foes and loving friends to serve the neediest and most neglected.

➤ **Chapter 10, Courage**, examines how leaders respond when the risks they anticipate become reality. These difficult situations can be make-or-break moments for leaders. Courage requires leaders to force their "heart and nerve and sinew" and to put themselves in harm's way. **John Paul Jones** showed his courage when he engaged and defeated a superior force in America's first major naval victory. He understood the extreme risks, yet he did not shy from them.

➤ **Chapter 11, Selflessness**, examines the challenges and importance of putting our people and our cause ahead of our own interests. This requires a deep awareness, and it often requires difficult choices. **Nelson Mandela** remained selfless despite persecution, abuse, and "being hated." He would not "give way to hating" as he fought to end apartheid.

➤ **Chapter 12, Stamina**, focuses on the exhausting nature of leadership. Leading can be draining physically, psychologically, emotionally, and spiritually. Our ability to maintain our energy and persevere will inspire others to do the same. **Jim and Louise Mulligan**'s ordeal during the Vietnam War required tremendous stamina. Captain Mulligan's stamina as a POW in Vietnam enabled him to survive and lead in spite of horrific torture and abuse. His wife, Louise, endured despite the years of loneliness, public apathy, and mind-numbing bureaucracy. They both held on when there was nothing left but faith and will.

Part 4: Earning and Retaining the Privilege to Lead

Leadership is meaningless unless it produces action and delivers results. The final section of this book focuses on attributes that reveal our leadership capabilities through our actions and choices. Those we lead often judge us by how we respond to the challenges we confront and the opportunities we are given.

➤ **Chapter 13, Composure**, focuses on understanding how great leaders can turn a crisis into positive action by keeping their heads. Composure requires being fully aware of the situations we face. At the same time, composure is about making choices and taking action to restore calm. **George Washington** maintained his composure in the disastrous early days of the American Revolution. He kept his head when, to paraphrase Kipling, all about him were losing theirs and blaming it on him. Washington prevented a crisis from becoming a panic that could have ended the American Revolution in failure.

➤ **Chapter 14, Patience**, discusses the ability to know when we should act and when we must wait. Patience often means choosing to wait when others are pushing us to move. **John "Blackjack" Pershing** showed his patience when America entered the First World War. He led an army that was unprepared and ill equipped to enter the fray. Pershing understood the importance of waiting until America was ready. He had the resolve to "wait and not be tired by waiting."

➤ **Chapter 15, Enthusiasm**, examines how positive energy and passion are at the heart of innovation, creativity, and exceptional performance. Leaders who produce great ideas often possess extraordinary enthusiasm. **Thomas Edison**'s enthusiasm was the fuel for his innovation and creativity.

His passion for invention and creation gave him the energy to "fill the unforgiving minute."

➤ **Chapter 16, Accountability**, reveals the importance of choosing to take ownership, regardless of how things turn out. Our decision to be accountable helps define us as leaders. **Golda Meir**'s accountability following the Yom Kippur War restored her nation's confidence. She led Israel through one of its greatest challenges, only to resign, further proving her sense of accountability and her leadership. Meir taught us how to "lose, and start again" with honor.

Like choice and awareness, these sixteen words and concepts are simple at a surface level. The difficulty comes when we decide to put them to use. This book explores the challenges that these simple words pose to those who wish to lead. It will raise awareness, reveal choices, and provide examples of how you can apply the "If" Sixteen Leadership Attributes to your everyday issues and problems.

Notice that the primary focus of the "If" Sixteen Leadership Framework is upon the leaders rather than on those who are led. Although followers are essential, leadership starts with the leader. Before we can lead others, we must lead ourselves. Before we can challenge others, we must challenge ourselves. Before we can motivate others, we must first be motivated. This idea of focusing on oneself first seems to run counter to many leadership theories, but it has ancient roots. In the sixth century BC, Lao-tzu wrote, "He who controls others may be powerful, but he who has mastered himself is mightier still." Leaders understand that self-awareness precedes self-mastery, and both precede leading others.

Everyone has the capability to lead, but no one is born with the ability to lead well. Throughout our leadership journeys, we gain experience and perspective. This experience can foster growth and learning—but growing and learning are not certain. They require critical self-examination and a rigorous regular inventory of our skills. They also demand a strong curiosity and interest. Knowing the attributes we possess helps us expose those we lack. Understanding the "If" Sixteen Leadership Framework can help us become the leaders we wish to be.

Each of the book's four sections starts with a brief description of the attributes it discusses. This introduction highlights the similarities and distinctions among them and their relationship to one another. Each chapter begins with a short historical account of an event that illustrates one of the "If" Sixteen Attributes. These accounts examine the historical significance of the leader's actions and the possible implications of failure. I intentionally chose extraordinary events to shed light on these leadership attributes. Most of us will never experience anything approaching the challenges and obstacles faced by the leaders in these stories. The problems we encounter rarely involve the profound historical significance or extreme personal risk that these leaders faced. Most of the individual challenges we confront are relatively mundane, but they are real and they are important, especially to those we lead. Collectively, the problems and challenges we face—and how we respond to them—form the basis of our lives and careers. Each chapter includes practical lessons that we can use to nurture our leadership growth and ends with an everyday illustration of the attribute that I have observed in my own life. I hope these examples prompt you to notice leadership in your life, especially in places you might not expect it.

Leaders Learn from Everyone

Some of the best leadership lessons I have learned have come from some of the weakest leaders I have known. Often this was through learning from their mistakes. Other times, it was clear that they knew the right thing to do, but just didn't know why the things they were doing mattered. Had I failed to pay attention, I would have missed important lessons. There is wisdom all around us. It is up to us to choose to look for it and be open to it when it presents itself.

We do not have to like people or even respect them to learn from them. We may be fundamentally and passionately opposed to them and what they stand for. We may find their beliefs, values, or actions repugnant, but we can learn from them nevertheless. They can still help us become more effective and powerful leaders.

You may find some of the "If" Sixteen leaders to be unappealing or even objectionable. This is especially likely for the political leaders. I encourage you to put aside any political or philosophical biases. Ignore that voice whispering—or yelling—in your ear, "I can't believe he included ____! There is *nothing* I can learn from that person."

It is easy to learn from those we like and respect or those who resemble us or share our beliefs. The challenge lies in finding wisdom in those with whom we disagree. The "If" Sixteen leaders are diverse on many levels. I intentionally chose some leaders whom I did not agree with politically or philosophically. I chose them to test my own ability to find lessons from anyone. It was not always easy, but it proved to be a powerful way to learn and grow.

Whenever I talk with groups about leadership, I typically start by asking them to identify examples of effective and powerful leaders. Many of the "If" Sixteen leaders always come up. These are never surprising or controversial. Most people immediately recognize the opportunity to learn from them. Occasionally, a person will identify someone like Hitler, Stalin, or Mao. Whenever this happens, the reaction is always the same. The person who said it becomes embarrassed or defensive. Others in the audience become indignant or hostile. I always use this tension as an opportunity to highlight an important point—that we can and must learn from everyone. Leaders may be good or evil, but leadership is not. What one *does* with leadership will determine its relative virtue. Our ability to learn and use the lessons we encounter will determine our success.

Regardless of who looks at the list of the "If" Sixteen leaders, he or she can always find someone I missed. I typically acknowledge the omission, but I rarely feel that the omitted leader would better represent any of the attributes than the leaders I chose. There are a few leaders whose absence is more challenging, but in most of these cases, I felt that it would have been impossible to limit them to one attribute. Doing so for the "If" Sixteen leaders was difficult enough. So, please accept my humble apology for any omissions you find. Better yet, share those leaders' stories with the *If You Will Lead* community. Post a short summary of their leadership story at www.ifyouwilllead.com.

Using This Book

As you read on, consider your biggest leadership challenges. Spend some time reading and reflecting about leaders who excelled in areas you find difficult. As you read each chapter and think about the attribute it describes, contemplate these questions:

- Are there leaders you have known personally who have stood out using this attribute?
- What made them effective in leveraging this attribute?
- Have you missed opportunities to exhibit this attribute?
- What could you have done differently in those instances?
- How can you be better prepared to seize the next opportunity?
- What prevents you from using this attribute?

Talk about your findings with your manager, your mentor, your coach, or a leader you admire. Begin to incorporate the lessons into your personal development plans and objectives. You may choose to do additional reading on an attribute, leader, or event. Each chapter provides a list of books, websites, and other resources to facilitate your continued learning and exploration.

As you find yourself facing a leadership challenge, review the chapters that describe the attributes the situation demands. Consider how the "If" Sixteen leaders would have led if faced with a similar challenge. Be curious about the situation you are facing, and try approaching it from different angles. What lessons can you learn from those who have faced comparable challenges before you?

Remember, this book is not about quick fixes and easy answers. It is about increasing your awareness and opening up choices. Real leadership will come with the experience you gain through practice and experimentation. Every scientist knows that most experiments fail. Failure is essential to learning and growth. It takes a lifetime to become the leader you have the potential to be, and every setback and failure can help you along your leadership journey.

A Note to Historians

This is not a history text. Each story accurately highlights a leader's use of a specific leadership skill to achieve historically significant results. The leadership lessons that I have drawn from the stories reflect my personal observations and conclusions. The leaders may have been unaware that their actions reflected the lesson I've described. Each leader's story is complex and worthy of further reading. The bibliography and recommended resource section of each chapter include some of my favorite books about each of the "If" Sixteen leaders. I am neither a historian nor a biographer, so I have relied on professional biographers and historians for the research on which I have based my conclusions.

Knowing Who You Are and What You Believe

WHY SELF-AWARENESS MATTERS

If we are to become the leaders we have the potential to be, it is essential that we understand who we are and what we believe. While there is a great deal of self-awareness associated with all of the "If" Sixteen Leadership Attributes, these first four in particular, *character, authenticity, integrity,* and *self-efficacy*, provide a strong foundation for self-awareness.

This section will help answer the first of the "If" Sixteen Leadership Framework questions: *Who am I, and what do I believe?* While reading the next four chapters, focus on what truly matters to you. Think about the values and beliefs that define you and your actions. Consider what it would take to live and act in a way that truly reflects who you are. Strong leaders understand that the source of their power is the principles that define who they are. Our principles allow us to discern right from wrong. Abraham Lincoln said, "Important principles may and must be inflexible." Our principles form the foundation on which we build our personal brand of leadership. In order to know what our principles are, we must first know what matters to us. That is the value and importance of self-awareness.

This first question—*Who am I, and what do I believe?*—may seem extraordinarily self-absorbed. While it *is* very inwardly focused, this question is about self-awareness and self-knowledge, not egotism or self-absorption. There is a huge difference. Self-awareness helps us to know ourselves better for the sake of becoming leaders who are worthy of being followed. Self-absorption, on the other hand, is a preoccupation with oneself to the exclusion of others or the outside world. Many people in leadership roles are highly self-absorbed, and often this becomes an impediment to effective leadership. Conversely, too few leaders invest enough time and energy in the type of introspection and self-discovery required to become good—let alone great—leaders.

Some people would argue that self-awareness doesn't matter. Most of us can point out examples of people who have been highly successful without having invested any energy in knowing themselves. Typically, their accomplishments are a function of exploiting a set of extraordinary gifts and talents. Their raw intelligence, effective communications skills, or strong will may have been enough to produce meaningful change. While they may have a superficial knowledge of themselves, they may not have fully explored their beliefs and values. Their introspection is often limited to learning and understanding their skills, abilities, talents, likes, and dislikes.

It is true that leaders can be successful without deep self-awareness, but this lack of self-awareness limits them to transactional or event-driven change. Many people have built their careers on this type of change. They move from project to project—transaction to transaction—delivering results. They play important roles in their organizations. They are likely to develop dedicated and loyal followings based on their history of success and accomplishment. But regardless of the degree of success they achieve, they are unlikely to reach their fullest potential. This type of success is fine for some people, but many of us are looking for something more meaningful and fulfilling.

This book focuses on transformational leadership—leadership that drives lasting and fundamental change. Sea-change events such as the American Revolution, the end of apartheid, or the end of the Cold War provide examples of transformational leadership;

however, transformational leadership isn't limited to these bigger-than-life examples. We see it in everyday leadership as well, from the person who makes a radical career change to follow her passions to the company that chooses to focus on long-term profitability over short-term results. This type of leadership depends on leaders who know what is truly important.

Creating real and lasting change requires that we know ourselves and those we lead and that they know us. This self-knowledge is what enables us to remain true to ourselves regardless of the situations we confront. It is what gives us the ability to see and understand what we really want. Self-aware leadership does not mean virtuous leadership. Unfortunately, there are transformational (and, I am sure, everyday) leaders who have a perverse sense of what is truly important.

The heart of leadership is the connection between two individuals—a leader and a follower. Whether we are leading one person or thousands, leadership means creating an *individual* connection with each person we lead. Some would argue that this is impossible. Most of the people in this book personally knew only a small fraction of the people who were following them. By knowing themselves and sharing this knowledge openly, however, they allowed others to begin to know them. The follower makes the connection, not the leader.

By learning and understanding who we are, we can begin to share ourselves with others. This is critical because true leadership means attracting others so they willingly choose to follow us. We will explore this choice in part 3. Certainly, our positions or titles may enable us to impose our will on them, but real change happens when people freely choose whom they will follow. Most people will only decide to follow people they feel they know. We want to know our leaders, because we want to feel connected to them. We want to believe that they are worthy of our trust. As leaders, we must realize that before anyone can know us, we must first know ourselves.

Self-awareness has very tangible value. When we know ourselves, we know what we like and dislike, what we are good at, and what challenges us. We can begin to see and understand where we want to focus our development efforts. We can also recognize and accept that we may never be competent at certain things. This knowledge and acceptance allow us to seek help from others who are skilled in those areas.

Self-awareness is a key component of emotional intelligence. Emotional intelligence is increasingly recognized by social scientists, business leaders, and human resource professionals as a primary contributor to leadership success. Self-awareness is essential to the first three domains of emotional intelligence. According to Daniel Goleman, a pioneer in emotional intelligence, the domains are as follows:

1. Knowing your emotions
2. Managing your own emotions
3. Motivating yourself
4. Recognizing and understanding other people's emotions
5. Managing relationships

By knowing our values and beliefs, we can begin to understand our emotions. When we understand our emotions we can begin to manage them, and when we know what really matters to us we can see what inspires us and motivates us to act. It all starts with self-awareness.

UNDERSTANDING THE FIRST FOUR ATTRIBUTES: THEIR INTERDEPENDENCE AND DISTINCTIONS

The first four attributes—character, authenticity, integrity, and self-efficacy—play an important role in our ability to know ourselves. They also play a critical role in our ability to help others begin to know us. The next four chapters will explore these attributes. While you are reading the stories about Reagan, Roosevelt, Collins, and Churchill, you may notice the similarities and overlap among these four leadership attributes. Character, authenticity, and integrity, in particular, have a great deal in common. They may even seem redundant. For the sake of clarity and focused development, I have chosen specific definitions for each attribute. These definitions will help you see how each attribute stands alone while supporting the other attributes in this section and in the rest of the book. The distinctions matter because they offer us a greater precision in our understanding of leadership. This precision gives us the ability to pinpoint those areas that matter most to our personal leadership development.

Character

Just as leadership starts with self-awareness, self-awareness starts with character. We all know that we are at our best when our actions and behaviors reflect who we really are. Great leaders understand the necessity of living and leading in ways that are consistent and aligned with their beliefs and values. That is the essence of leading with character—knowing what we believe and value and then ensuring that our actions reflect those beliefs and values. According to *Webster's Encyclopedic Unabridged Dictionary*, *character* is "the aggregate of the features and traits that form the individual nature of some person or thing." At its most basic, character is simply an inventory and accounting of one's features and traits—our mental, emotional, and spiritual features and traits that define us as individuals and leaders.

It is important to remember that people are always observing and assessing leaders. We are under constant scrutiny. Do our actions and decisions align with what we say matters to us? Do the people we lead even know what we believe and value? Do they understand what we stand for? Often they think they do, but frequently they are unsure. Their uncertainty can be the source of tension, confusion, or even conflict, which in turn undermines our ability to lead.

In Chapter 1, the story of President Ronald Reagan illustrates the power of leading with character. While Reagan possessed and used many of the "If" Sixteen Leadership Attributes, I chose him to represent character, because it was such an important part of how he led. Reagan was as complex as any other leader described in this book, yet those close to him often spoke of the consistency of his character. He was an open book about his beliefs and values. One of his nicknames, "the Great Communicator," stemmed from this openness. When he spoke, his values and beliefs were always present through words like "I believe" and "I hope." He told his audience what he wanted, but more important, he told them why the things he spoke of mattered to him personally.

Authenticity

So, what does it mean to be authentic? How does authenticity differ from character? Authenticity involves being true to one's own personality, spirit, or character. *Webster's Encyclopedic Unabridged Dictionary* defines *authentic* as "not false or copied, genuine, real." Being authentic requires that we know who we are—we must be self-aware. As we inventory and account for those values, beliefs, and traits that define our character, we can begin to define what *real* means to us. This awareness also begins to reveal interesting truths about who we are. The chapter on character may give the impression that we are static and constant beings. In truth, we live dynamic and complex lives. Each of the many roles we play requires us to display a different combination of our features and traits, and each role reveals different parts of our character. Different situations require us to make subtle changes in how we act. Our character is not changed through this; we simply emphasize different traits depending on what we encounter. Regardless of these shifts in emphasis, authentic leaders remain themselves no matter what happens or whom they happen to be with. They are open and honest with themselves and others about the fact that they are dynamic and constantly changing. They recognize the importance of finding and maintaining the right balance so they can remain genuine.

I chose Theodore Roosevelt to illustrate authentic leadership, because his life was so complex. He was authentically himself in the myriad roles he performed. Whether he was a political leader, soldier, cowboy, athlete, father, son, husband, or explorer, he was always himself. The way he emphasized aspects of his character may have changed from one role to the next, but regardless of the situation, he remained authentic.

Integrity

How is integrity different from character and authenticity? In what ways is it similar? Do the distinctions among these three attributes really matter? The first two definitions of *integrity* in *Webster's Encyclopedic Unabridged Dictionary* are most appropriate for leaders:

> Adherence to moral and ethical principles; soundness of moral character; honesty
> The state of being whole, entire, or undiminished

Many people limit their consideration of integrity to the first definition. The chapter on integrity discusses the challenges and the obstacles that interfere with our ability to seek, embrace, and defend the truth—to maintain a sound moral character. The second definition—"the state of being whole"—presents a different set of challenges that are directly related to our character and our authenticity. Being whole means finding balance and making difficult trade-offs without eroding or diminishing ourselves. It is a matter of integrating all of our values and beliefs and all of the roles we play.

Being whole means that we are living and acting in ways that are consistent with who we are, regardless of the number and diversity of the roles we perform. It requires that we look for those situations where we are ignoring or violating some of our values and beliefs for the sake of others. Integrity is easy when we are making choices between good and bad or wrong and right. But what happens when our choices are not so clear? There may be times when doing something violates one of our values and failing to do the same thing violates another value. Political leaders are often accused of vacillating on issues or being inconsistent for this very reason. Wholeness requires reconciling these difficult decisions and being open about why we made them. Unfortunately, people may not have the patience or willingness to listen to or understand our internal conflicts or the rationale for our decisions.

Michael Collins, the Irish revolutionary and political leader, represents integrity for one overarching reason. He demonstrated an aspect of integrity that is uncommon today: he changed his mind about a fundamental issue of his day. He had known and defended one truth for most of his life, but when he learned new facts and gained a different perspective, he realized that he had been wrong. He recognized a new truth. His principles and character remained unchanged and whole. Only his position changed. This change in position earned him the disdain and contempt of many of his friends and colleagues, and it ultimately cost him his life. Collins knew that integrity meant seeking the truth regardless of the price.

Self-Efficacy

Finally, there is self-efficacy. Dr. Albert Bandura, the psychologist who first described and studied self-efficacy, defines it as "the belief in one's capabilities to organize and execute the courses of action to manage prospective situations." Highly self-efficacious people know themselves extraordinarily well. They possess a genuine confidence in their own abilities. They have to. In order to truly believe in our abilities, we must know what they are. Just as character requires that we continuously inventory and understand our values and beliefs, self-efficacy requires that we do the same thing with our skills, abilities, and preferences.

Self-efficacy's connections to both authenticity and integrity are extremely important. Authentic leaders do not try to be people they are not. Authentic and self-efficacious leaders understand which capabilities they possess and which they lack. This gives them the confidence both to take on new and challenging roles and to ask for help when they need it. This requires a great deal of integrity and means being truly honest with oneself. As with integrity, it means seeking the truth even when that truth may be unpleasant.

The greatest tests of our self-efficacy are our failures. In the fourth chapter, Winston Churchill illustrates the power of a high level of self-efficacy. Despite catastrophic failures throughout his life, Churchill never doubted his destiny to be prime minister. His supreme confidence was rooted in his belief that he possessed the skills and ability to accomplish the goals he set for himself. He knew himself and what he was capable of.

The Power of Self-Awareness

Gandhi once said, "We must become the change we want to see." He understood that without intimate self-knowledge, we cannot begin to understand what we truly want. Gandhi devoted a great deal of time and energy to the pursuit of full self-awareness. His awareness helped him see what mattered most. It allowed him to recognize what he had to do to live his values and beliefs.

Imagine knowing yourself so completely that you can trust yourself, even when everyone else doubts you and believes you are wrong. Imagine being comfortable enough with who you are that you can be yourself, regardless of the situation. How would it feel to have the integrity to always seek and defend the truth, regardless of how unpopular it is? What would it be like to have the self-efficacy to confidently take on any task set before you?

Everyone has the ability to live and lead like this. It requires a great deal of hard work and self-examination. It demands extraordinary resolve and commitment. Most of all, it means becoming and remaining truly self-aware. Self-awareness is not developed via a onetime activity. It requires constant introspection. It demands openness to feedback and criticism and a willingness to seek the value and truth they may contain.

Leadership also requires us to distinguish between individual self-awareness and organizational self-awareness. We must understand our own values and beliefs and those of the organizations with which we are affiliated. Most of us want to join groups or organizations that share our values. We desire to work for organizations with whom we are philosophically aligned. Unless we take the time to become aware of who we are—as well as who our associates are—this type of alignment is impossible.

As you read the next four chapters, think about each attribute independently, but also consider how they can work together to enable you to truly know yourself. The lines separating character, authenticity, integrity, and self-efficacy may become blurred, because these attributes are interconnected. They share similar characteristics, and our behaviors will reveal multiple attributes simultaneously. Together they allow us to better know who we truly are and what really matters to us. This knowledge is the first step toward true leadership.

CHAPTER 1

Ronald Reagan's Character: The Value of Trusting Yourself

If you can trust yourself when all men doubt you,
But make allowance for their doubting too

REAGAN'S CHARACTER

When Character Was King, Peggy Noonan's biography of President Ronald Reagan, captures with its title his most compelling leadership trait. Reagan's character defined him and his presidency. His beliefs and principles defined his actions and decisions. His politics, policies, and decisions were often unpopular. Even today, "Reaganomics" is a term of derision and contempt among many. His obstacles were great, and his path was often difficult. Despite the obstacles and criticisms, Reagan led America out of economic crisis and to victory in the Cold War.

Like many who enter politics from nontraditional fields, Reagan was criticized for being unprepared to lead. His critics chided that he was just an actor. Many accused him of being ignorant of the issues that confronted America. But by remaining true to his principles, he led with conviction and strength. Many doubted him, but he trusted himself. Fredrick J. Ryan captures this aspect of Reagan in the foreword for *Ronald Reagan: The Wisdom and Humor of the Great Communicator*. He writes, "He [Reagan] did not adjust his beliefs to conform to the prevailing political winds or to better fit someone else's view of political 'correctness.'" That doesn't mean he didn't change his positions on issues, but who he was and his core principles never changed. He had character; and, more important, he *led* with character.

The triumph of the West over the Soviet Union was, in part, a product of Ronald Reagan's character. Despite overwhelming opposition to his foreign policy, Reagan prevailed. In 1980, when he was elected president of the United States, the common worldview was that passive coexistence was the only way to deal with the Soviet Union and the spread of communism. The opinion shared by most mainstream American and European intellectuals and political leaders was that communism was an unstoppable force. At best, the West could slow its advances. The communist successes in Southeast Asia, Africa, and Latin America simply reinforced this belief.

Reagan's views on communism were seen as so misaligned with this perceived reality that many of his critics, and even some of his friends, felt it undermined his competence to serve as president of the United States. People described him as "geopolitically naive," "dangerous and destabilizing," and a cowboy. Many of his detractors feared that his provocations would lead to World War III. Reagan had few allies among world leaders, and his party was in the minority in both houses of Congress for most of his two terms in office. So, how was Ronald Reagan able to convince those who doubted him to fight the Cold War according to his rules?

Reagan was absolutely convinced that the spread of communism could be stopped and reversed. He believed that communism was a doomed ideology and economic model that was destined to collapse under its own weight—and he believed that it was inherently evil and dangerous. He felt that the United States and its allies had an obligation to hasten this collapse.

Reagan's beliefs were built on one overarching principle: human freedom. According to historian Peter Schweitzer, "The 'one big thing' that Reagan knew was the power and value of human freedom." Reagan saw communism as the single greatest threat to that freedom. His commitment to freedom and opposition to communism became the essence of his entire public career.

Reagan's public fight started in 1947 with his confrontations with communists in Hollywood. Reagan became increasingly active in politics during the 1950s and 1960s. He was determined to reverse the growth in government that had started with the New Deal. His two terms as governor of California from 1967 to 1975 reinforced his belief that limited government was essential to human freedom. He made an unsuccessful bid for president in 1976. His election as president in 1980 marked a fundamental shift in American politics and government. During his two terms as president, Reagan fought two fights: stopping communism and limiting the size, scope, and reach of the federal government. While he was less successful in the latter, his fight against communism culminated with the destruction of the Berlin Wall in November 1989.

Reagan spent more than forty years forming and refining his vision for fighting communism, but he spent his entire life building his character. He knew that freedom could not be taken for granted. As the son of an Irish American, he had seen how discrimination and prejudice had deprived his father of economic freedom. He had read the signs, "HELP WANTED—NO IRISH NEED APPLY." He had seen the political cartoons that stereotyped the Irish as drunken, ignorant miscreants. He experienced how discrimination and hatred had denied people their most basic freedoms. As an adult, Reagan witnessed the horrors that stemmed from fanatical ideologies like fascism and communism. He saw how tenuous freedom was, and he understood the importance of fighting for that freedom. Reagan's commitment to freedom was tempered by his belief in personal responsibility. Left unchecked, unfettered freedom can lead to anarchy. Reagan's beliefs were unshakeable, because his character and principles were the foundation on which they were built.

Reagan's awareness of his own principles enabled him to better understand the views of others. This awareness gave him the ability to, as Kipling writes, "make allowance for their doubting too." He appreciated and accepted others' beliefs. Even when he didn't agree with someone, he would try to understand his or her point of view. For example, many of those who doubted Reagan's foreign policy were motivated by a desire for peace. Pope John Paul II shared Reagan's opposition to communism, but they differed in approach. The pope believed Reagan's policies were often too confrontational. Reagan shared the pope's desire for peace, so he could appreciate the fears that his policy created. By appreciating others' positions and making allowances for their doubting, Reagan was better able to try to allay their concerns. He exhibited this in many speeches and statements. In late 1982, while speaking to the American people on nuclear deterrence, Reagan said, "We desire peace. But peace is a goal, not a policy. Lasting peace is what we hope for at the end of our journey." Reagan made many similar declarations committing

America to peace. He was equally firm that peace could only be achieved through strength.

Reagan knew that open and direct war between the United States and the Soviet Union would have apocalyptic ramifications. Accordingly, he understood the fears that many had about his policies and actions. One of the most controversial policies and best demonstrations of his character in action was the Strategic Defense Initiative (SDI). Reagan believed that SDI, a defensive shield against nuclear attack, could end the threat of nuclear war. His belief in SDI as a tool to end the Cold War and as a lever that would bankrupt the Soviet economy was absolute. While others saw SDI as the ultimate bargaining chip in negotiations with the Soviets, Reagan believed that SDI offered hope to eliminate the threat of nuclear war while achieving his goal of bringing freedom to those suffering under communism. Throughout Reagan's presidency, SDI remained only a theory, which had yet to be proven viable. Many scientist and foreign policy experts doubted that SDI would work, and they doubted Reagan himself for having confidence in it.

But Reagan never let the doubts of others cause him to doubt himself. He recognized that freedom and lasting peace required true change. If SDI were to be the tool that would enable this change, it had to be more than a bargaining chip. He had to create a belief within the Soviet leadership that SDI was real and attainable. By creating this threat, Reagan knew that the Soviets would feel compelled to try to keep pace with America's innovations; otherwise, SDI would make their military obsolete and undermine their position as a world power. Ultimately, the Soviet Union's decision to try to compete helped lead to the nation's collapse. The Soviets simply lacked the economic and technological capability that the race demanded.

Reagan's victory over communism was not an accident. He was successful because he knew what he believed, and he stayed true to his beliefs. His path to the White House reflected his character. His policies and platforms were not built on the latest public opinion polls. After he was elected president, he governed the same way. His beliefs and his principled leadership enabled him to first win the election of 1980 and then to accomplish a great deal in the face of constant doubt. Reagan's character drove him to overcome his opponents' objections and implement real change. Character was king.

RONALD REAGAN TIMELINE: CHARACTER DEFINED

- **1911:** Born in Tampico, Illinois
- **1930s:** Recognized the oppression associated with fascism and communism
- **1947:** Elected to the first of five terms as president of the Screen Actors Guild, the start of his political career and public fight against communism
- **1966–1974:** Served two terms as governor of California
- **1970s:** Communist expansion in Africa, Asia, and Latin America solidified Western strategy of containment and coexistence
- **1976:** Reagan ran an unsuccessful campaign for president of the United States
- **1980:** Elected fortieth president of the United States
- **1982:** Criticized for speech predicting that "the march of freedom and democracy . . . [would] leave Marxism-Leninism on the ash heap of history"
- **1983:** Further inflamed critics with his "evil empire" speech warning of Soviet aggression and unveiling SDI
- **1984:** Called for a return to arms talks with the USSR; reelected to a second term as president of the United States by an overwhelming margin
- **1985:** Met with Soviet Premier Mikhail Gorbachev at the Geneva and Reykjavik summits; both summits end without agreement; Reagan is criticized for increasing tension and risk of nuclear war
- **1987:** Delivered Brandenberg Gate speech ("Mr. Gorbachev, tear down this wall."); with Gorbachev, signed the INF Treaty, the first US–Soviet treaty to provide for destruction of nuclear weapons

➤ **1989:** Retired at the end of his second term; Germany reunified after the fall of the Berlin Wall

➤ **1991:** Formal dissolution of the Soviet Union

➤ **2004:** Died at the age of ninety-three in Los Angeles, California

THE NATURE OF CHARACTER

We often describe great leaders in terms of their character. What exactly do we mean by character, and why does it matter? The fact is character can be extremely discomforting to discuss. Character is rooted in very personal—and sometimes polarizing—factors: our values and beliefs. When we talk about our character, it is easy to come across as either self-righteous or irresolute. The self-righteous are too certain and the irresolute are unsure of what their beliefs really mean. Both extremes make for weak leadership. That said, and for the very same reasons that make it a difficult subject, character is an essential leadership attribute.

Kipling writes, "If you can trust yourself when all men doubt you, yet make allowance for their doubting too." This challenge requires a great deal of courage and self-confidence, but most of all it takes character. Standard dictionary definitions of character do not distinguish between good character and bad; they simply describe character as an inventory or accounting of one's features and traits. Typically, when we talk about a person's character, the definition of British writer and politician Thomas Babington Macaulay resonates: "The measure of a man's character is what he would do if he knew he never would be found out." Another great description of character comes from the *United States Air Force Academy Code of Conduct*: "We define character as the sum of those qualities of moral excellence that stimulate a person to do the right thing, which is manifested through right and proper actions despite internal or external pressures to the contrary." Both of these definitions speak of character as a positive attribute. These definitions point out an important truth: real leadership is built on the foundation of virtuous character.

How we conduct ourselves shows our character to those around us. What we claim to value is often less important than what our actions reveal to the world about what matters to us. When we describe leaders as having strong character, we acknowledge that their actions reflect their expressed values and beliefs. Conversely, leaders demonstrate weak character when they say one thing and do another or act in ways that do not convey a consistent message about who they are.

Strong character comes from knowing and trusting oneself. It is an essential attribute for earning and maintaining the trust of those we lead. The development of character starts with investing the time and energy to know ourselves fully—coming to understand what we believe and value, as well as why we believe and value what we do. It means identifying our skills and abilities, our strengths and weaknesses, and our likes and dislikes. Knowing ourselves this well requires ongoing introspection and critical self-analysis. This is a lifelong process that will allow us to become more and more self-aware regarding our true character. Unfortunately, complete self-knowledge is difficult, if not impossible. Even the most self-aware are unable to articulate a complete inventory of their beliefs. Life is an ongoing process of self-discovery. Like our leadership style and skills, our character matures and evolves as we grow and learn.

Character guides us to do what we know is right. The more we reveal the strength of our character—by ensuring that our words and deeds are consistent with our beliefs and values—the stronger the trust grows between us and those we lead. Character is not moral superiority or sanctimony. It's about doing what we believe is right, regardless of the opinion of others. It means doing what is right, even when no one ever knows.

One of the most important parts of Kipling's guidance on character is the role that doubt plays in building and testing our character. Character means having the confidence to accept the doubts of others. It means being open and curious to understand fully what is causing their reservations. When Kipling writes, "make allowance for their doubting too," he is advising his readers to seek to understand the source of others' doubts. When colleagues express misgivings about our actions or decisions, they are giving us the opportunity for self-examination.

It is important to remember that doubt is not inherently good or bad. In some cases, doubt may simply reveal that we are challenging the status quo. In other cases, it may reveal that we are doing something that is contrary to our core beliefs or creates conflict between two or more core beliefs or values. This is not uncommon. Our values and beliefs are as complex as we are. How could they not conflict occasionally? For example, a CEO may believe strongly in maintaining an open and honest work environment, yet he may be compelled to withhold sensitive information from employees. His values are in conflict, and he must choose which is more important.

Reagan understood the importance of changing his position to fit the reality of the situations he confronted. He understood compromise. He would not compromise his principles, but he would seek compromises that were consistent with his values. Reagan once told a reporter, "I have never believed in jumping off the cliff with the flag flying." When negotiating or dealing with difficult choices, he would rather get most of what he wanted rather than none. This required that he develop the ability to quickly and accurately assess the strength of his positions. It also meant understanding how far he could yield without violating his character. At times during his negotiations with Mikhail Gorbachev over arms control, Reagan seemed to walk away with nothing. His diary reveals that he knew that these were temporary setbacks and that the Soviet Union would eventually agree to his terms. Ultimately, he was proved correct, but at the time, many critics accused him of obstinacy for not compromising.

Everyone faces doubt. Self-doubt is among the most common and destructive forms of it. We regularly take on responsibilities for which we are ill prepared, and these situations can cause uncertainty and self-doubt. But character, our moral fiber, enables us to trust ourselves even in the face of self-doubt.

Of course, those we lead will also face doubt. As leaders, we must help them to trust themselves. When we challenge others to step up to new opportunities, they will likely make mistakes as they learn. Their failures have the potential to erode their confidence and create further self-doubt. Effective leaders recognize this risk and take steps to restore confidence and trust after failures.

Finally, it is essential to understand the difference between simply having character and *leading* with it. Our ability to lead is in large part based on our ability to inspire trust in others. Those we lead want and need to trust us. And to trust us, they must know us. Thus we must allow them to get close. We must share and expose our beliefs and values. Leading with character requires that we make ourselves vulnerable. In essence we give others insight into our souls. This can very uncomfortable, especially for those who have not fully explored their own beliefs.

REAGAN'S LESSONS

Ronald Reagan's character enabled him to lead powerfully and with absolute conviction. His beliefs and values were straightforward and clear, and his actions reflected who he was. I chose Reagan as the model for character, because he was open, honest, and consistent about who he was and what he believed. A close friend of Reagan's once said, "Nothing ever changed him. He was always the same." What lessons can we learn from Reagan about developing our character? How can we lead others by showing our character?

1. **Ronald Reagan taught that character matters.** Leaders know who they are and what they stand for. Reagan's "one thing" was human freedom. Each of us must learn what our "one thing" is. Understanding the value that matters most is essential to our self-awareness. Our actions will reveal our character, so our actions must be deliberate and intentional. Country singer Aaron Tippin sings, "You've got to stand for something, or you'll fall for anything." Reagan understood this, and his self-confidence reflected the stands that he took. The simple act of deciding that character is important will elevate our awareness of how well (or how poorly) our actions and beliefs align. Truly understanding our beliefs and values requires us to invest time and energy to explore them.

2. **Reagan's beliefs were grounded both in principles and in morality.** Reagan demonstrated the importance of having a strong

moral foundation for our beliefs. His fundamental belief in human freedom was important to him personally, and it was good for those he wished to lead. Principled leadership without morality can be dangerous and destructive. History is full of despots and tyrants whose beliefs were clearly based on principles that were either misinformed or morally flawed. Terrorism, genocide, and slavery have all been justified and rationalized through the misinterpretation or manipulation of the Bible, the Koran, or other religious texts. A true leader maintains a strong moral compass in order to distinguish between truth and misinterpretation or manipulation. As trite and simplistic as it sounds, the Golden Rule provides the best standard for assessing the morality of one's principles. Twenty-one religions, including Christianity, Islam, Hinduism, Judaism, and Shintoism have as a fundamental tenet the direction to "do unto others as you would have them do unto you." Reagan believed that ending communism would be good for all. His actions were driven by his principles, not by public opinion or conventional wisdom.

3. *Reagan kept his actions and decisions aligned with his beliefs and values.* Reagan's policies, actions, political affiliations, and even his friendships revealed his character. He knew that what he did mattered far more than what he said. Similarly, our character and principles will influence the people and organizations we associate with and how we operate within them. A leader articulates a vision, a strategy, and objectives that reflect his or her character and beliefs. Leaders create cultures and values that reflect their principles and character. Everything from an organization's vision to its mission, values, strategic plan, operating plan, budget, policies, and actions should reflect the leader's character.

There will be times when our values and beliefs clash with those of others with whom we work and associate. This is not unusual because our values and beliefs are both personal and important. Conflict is as natural as it is difficult, and these situations test our character. Our response to each conflict depends on the degree of disagreement. In an extreme situation, we may choose to sever a relationship or publicly denounce the action that caused the conflict. If the conflict is with an employer, we may choose to quit, or we may be fired because our actions challenge the status quo. Fortunately, these situations are rare. Our ability to recognize them and respond appropriately will be dependent largely on our character. The greatest challenge is admitting when we have violated our own principles. Reagan's allowance for the doubt of others gave him the ability to see his mistakes and to change course. The Iran-Contra scandal provides an outstanding illustration of this. Reagan's diary reveals much about his character. As the scandal raged, he focused on regaining control and restoring confidence. He started by taking personal accountability for the scandal. Then he fired those who had misused their power. Finally, he reminded the American people and himself who he was and what he believed. He reasserted his character.

4. **Reagan tested his actions and decisions to ensure alignment with his principles and character.** Our lives are increasingly complicated. Our actions and decisions have consequences—both intended and unintended. At times, we may not even be aware that we have violated our beliefs and values, even when we are vigilant. Testing and critical self-assessment can help us stay true to our character. Leadership requires assessing and reconciling the misalignments between our principles and our actions.

Anyone who has ever driven a car with tires that are out of alignment knows how important this is. The misaligned tires pull the car off course. The greater the misalignment, the harder we must work to stay on the road. The same is true with misalignment between our actions and our principles. By looking for our own misalignments, we open up the opportunity to address them. This can be challenging and uncomfortable. We may have to do things that we don't like, and unfortunately, there are rarely perfect answers.

Reagan understood this. He struggled with the decision to supply arms and support to the mujahideen in Afghanistan. Reagan knew that they were fundamentally opposed to the type of freedom to which he was committed, but he accepted the trade-off because he believed the Soviet Union posed the greater threat. It is important to remember that those around us know when we are not living and acting in a way that reflects our principles. Even if we haven't expressed our principles publicly, people will sense the tension and anxiety that misalignment causes.

5. ***Reagan showed that leading with character requires being open and public about our beliefs and values.*** Reagan was comfortable with who he was. He was an open book about his beliefs and values. His friends and enemies all knew what he believed and valued. Some used this knowledge to support him. Others used it to advance their own agendas or to attack him. Still, Reagan knew that the benefits of being open outweighed the risks. By leading with character, he built a dedicated following. His supporters enabled him to achieve exceptional results. Similarly, we have the same opportunity. Certainly, exposing our values and beliefs can be risky. People may choose to exploit this knowledge for their own gain. Regardless, our willingness to knowingly take that risk will build the confidence of those we lead.

Leaders trust themselves while encouraging others to trust themselves. Reagan had a strong faith in himself, but he also had enduring trust in the American people. His faith and trust were rooted in his character and his belief in the character of those he led. Despite our hard work and the quality and strength of our character, others will doubt us, and at times we may even share their doubt.

Success in the face of doubt requires that we remain true to our principles and beliefs. That starts with knowing what they are. Failures will occur, and we will make mistakes. In those moments, remember Kipling's words: "If you can trust yourself when all men doubt you, but make allowance for their doubting too." By trusting ourselves while allowing for the doubts of others, we display our true character.

Everyday Character

We often expose our character through small acts and in seemingly insignificant ways. Individually, they often just feel like the right thing to do. Collectively, they have a huge impact.

The day my father died, I witnessed one of these seemingly minor acts. I called Scott Rodgers, one of my oldest and closest friends, to tell him the sad news. He offered his deepest condolences, and then he said, "I'll see you in a couple hours." Later that morning he arrived and spent the day with me and my family. He knew that we needed him there, so he dropped everything to drive two hours to our hometown.

Later I learned that some of Scott's subordinates had become upset that he was going to miss an important client meeting. Scott acknowledged the meeting's importance, but he told his team, "This is more important." He explained that his mentor had died, and he needed to be there. Scott had only been in his position for a couple of months—not long enough to feel totally secure of his footing at the company—yet he chose to put his values ahead of short-term results. What effect did that action have on Scott's team? They were probably disappointed or angry for a day or so, but I believe that Scott's actions helped to build long-term commitment and dedication. Seemingly minor actions by leaders like Scott reveal our character in ways that make people want to follow.

RECOMMENDED RESOURCES

Resources about Ronald Reagan:

Ronald Reagan: How an Ordinary Man Became an Extraordinary Leader by Dinesh D'Souza
When Character Was King: A Story of Ronald Reagan by Peggy Noonan

The Reagan Diaries by Ronald Reagan, edited by Douglas Brinkley
Ronald Reagan: The Wisdom and Humor of the Great Communicator
    by Fredrick J. Ryan

Resources about Character:

*Questions of Character: Illuminating the Heart of Literature Through
    Leadership* by Joseph Badaracco
The Force of Character: And the Lasting Life by James Hillman
*The Road Less Traveled: A New Psychology of Love, Traditional Values
    and Spiritual Growth* by M. Scott Peck
A Business and Its Beliefs: The Ideas That Helped Build IBM by
    Thomas J. Watson and Courtney C. Brown

CHAPTER 2

Theodore Roosevelt's Authenticity: The Resolve to Always Be Yourself

If you can talk with crowds and keep your virtue,
Or walk with kings—nor lose the common touch

ROOSEVELT'S AUTHENTICITY

President Theodore Roosevelt. Teddy. Teedie. T.R. Colonel Roosevelt. The Rough Rider. The Trust Buster. The Bull Moose. These were among the many names for one complex leader. His numerous monikers reflect his many distinct identities. But, regardless of what others called him, he was always himself.

Most historians rank Theodore Roosevelt among the most effective presidents in US history. His presidency produced great change. As president he launched the building of the Panama Canal, brokered peace treaties in Asia and Africa, modernized the United States Navy, vastly expanded America's conservation efforts, aggressively fought monopolies and corruption, and strengthened consumer protection and workers' rights. One could argue that his tenure in office was sufficient to define Roosevelt and his life. Historians have noted that he was proud of the accomplishments of his presidency; they also noted that he believed that it only defined a small part of who he was.

Roosevelt felt comfortable with whomever he met because he was comfortable with himself. He always remained authentically himself. Roosevelt biographer Edward Wagenknecht described Roosevelt's life as "one of the most crowded and varied lives of which we have any record." In his biography of Roosevelt, *The Seven Worlds of Theodore Roosevelt*, Wagenknecht describes the many facets of this complex man. He reveals how Roosevelt talked with crowds and walked with kings with equal ease. He also reveals how Roosevelt's authenticity made crowds and kings equally comfortable with him. Those with whom he interacted could sense that he was always genuine.

Roosevelt was many things—politician, cowboy, author, hunter, naturalist, explorer, bureaucrat, soldier, father, husband, and family man. Today we might call him a Renaissance man, but that description would be incomplete. Renaissance men dabble in many activities. In contrast, Roosevelt never played at anything he did. When he was on his ranch in North Dakota, he was a cowboy. When he led troops during the Spanish-American War, he was a soldier. Whatever he did, that was who he was. He embraced each role fully, and each role was integral to his identity. Those who knew him in any of his many worlds thought of him as one of their own. Roosevelt's ability to connect with a wide variety of people stemmed from his authenticity.

Roosevelt's authenticity was also apparent in whom he was not. He was uninterested in a variety of topics, and he readily ignored or delegated tasks related to those areas. For example, he knew very little about finance, either personal or governmental. Much of the administrative work in his life bored him. "Prepare me a paper" was one of his favorite expressions. There were many issues requiring Roosevelt's attention throughout his life on which he had no opinion. In those cases, he would direct others to tell him what his opinion should be. Elihu Root, Roosevelt's secretary of state, described him as "the most advisable man I ever knew." Roosevelt knew what mattered to him and what did not.

Two events in Roosevelt's life serve to highlight his ability to be authentically himself in radically different situations. First was his role in negotiating the end of the Russo-Japanese War in 1905. The second was his exploration of the River of Doubt in Brazil in 1914. The first shows his ability to walk with kings while the second shows his common touch.

As an emerging world power, America had a stake in resolving the Russo-Japanese War, which threatened to destabilize the western Pacific. The region was becoming increasingly important to America's commercial and diplomatic interests. Roosevelt's stake in the war went beyond his interest as president. The human costs appalled him: hundreds of thousands were being killed or wounded. Millions more were threatened.

During the war, Roosevelt made three offers to broker a peace treaty: first, at the outbreak of hostilities in 1904, again in January 1905, and successfully later that summer. This final offer led to the Treaty of Portsmouth, which ended the war. Roosevelt's successful mediation demonstrated his ability to communicate with and lead the monarchs of Europe and Asia. Russia's czar and Japan's emperor ruled countries steeped in hierarchy. Each believed he was divinely ordained to lead. Roosevelt may have been a fellow head of state, but to the emperor and the czar he was a mere mortal. Had he shown any uncertainty or lack of confidence, both rulers would have dismissed his offers to arbitrate their dispute.

Successful mediation between the Japanese and the Russians required sophistication and decorum. It demanded tenacity and patience. It also required understanding the cultures of honor that were essential to both parties. These characteristics were second nature to Roosevelt. Having grown up among the American and European elite, Roosevelt was at home with any world leader. In Roosevelt's view, he was their equal, regardless of their view of him.

Roosevelt's authenticity enabled him to excel as a peacemaker. He knew that what he was doing was right. He knew that he was uniquely qualified to end the bloodshed. Roosevelt's public life had established his reputation for fairness, giving him credibility. Both countries trusted him. Like Reagan in the previous chapter, Roosevelt understood the importance of principled leadership. Above all else, Roosevelt believed in fairness. During his life, he had based most of his fights on a sense that he needed to correct a wrong. The Russo-Japanese War felt wrong to him, thus he felt compelled to act.

The second event underscoring Roosevelt's authenticity, his exploration of the River of Doubt, provides a striking juxtaposition to his role in ending the Russo-Japanese War. In 1913, less than two years after his unsuccessful attempt to return to the White House, Roosevelt was invited to lead an expedition to survey the river. This was a rare opportunity to explore an uncharted river in a remote and pristine part of the Amazon.

The River of Doubt expedition proved to be one of the most challenging undertakings of Roosevelt's life. It required extraordinary leadership and fortitude. The problems began almost immediately. Insects, disease, accidents, injuries, food shortages, and inadequate and improper equipment were among the expedition's many and most pressing challenges. The River of Doubt's falls and rapids were more treacherous than anticipated, and the expedition's dugout canoes were ill suited to their needs. Hostile Amazonian communities were a constant threat. By the time they had traveled only one-quarter of the way down the river, they were exhausted and starving. Roosevelt was near death, having suffered an injury that had become infected. All of these factors weighed heavily on each member of the expedition.

As the expedition's coleader, along with Colonel Candido Mariano da Silva Rondon of the Brazilian army, Roosevelt felt it his duty to bring the expedition home safely. He led the group by sharing their burdens and hardships. Several members of the expedition had feared that this aging former president would simply play the role of explorer; they worried that he would be a burden. Roosevelt quickly put those fears to rest. He proved that he was a true member of the expedition, not a guest they should pamper. Although he had been the president of an emerging world power, at that moment Roosevelt was a true explorer and *their* leader. The injury that nearly cost him his life involved an accident in which a canoe had become entangled in some rapids. Rather than sitting back while his subordinates resolved this inconvenience, Roosevelt had literally jumped in to help. His commitment to the expedition enabled them to stay alive and achieve their goal. On April 15, 1914, Roosevelt and his team became the first non-Amazonians to descend the River of Doubt.

Whether mediating disputes between world powers or exploring an uncharted river, he was comfortable in his skin. He knew who he was, and he behaved accordingly.

THEODORE ROOSEVELT TIMELINE: THE MANY ROLES OF AN AUTHENTIC LEADER

- ➤ **1858:** Born in New York, New York
- ➤ **1880:** Graduated from Harvard and married his first wife, Alice Hathaway Lee
- ➤ **1881:** Began his political career; elected to the New York State Assembly
- ➤ **1882:** Published the first of eighteen books, *The Naval War of 1812*
- ➤ **1883:** Began his career as a rancher with the establishment of his first ranch
- ➤ **1889–1897:** Entered public service; appointed US civil service commissioner, NYC police commissioner, and US assistant secretary of the navy
- ➤ **1898:** Spanish-American War; appointed colonel of the Rough Riders regiment
- ➤ **1898:** Elected governor of New York
- ➤ **1900:** Entered national politics; elected vice president of the United States
- ➤ **1901:** Became president of the United States following President William McKinley's assassination
- ➤ **1903:** Sponsored construction of the Panama Canal
- ➤ **1904:** Reelected president of the United States
- ➤ **1905:** Negotiated end to the Russo-Japanese War
- ➤ **1906:** Won the Nobel Peace Prize
- ➤ **1907:** Launched the navy's Great White Fleet, establishing America as a world power
- ➤ **1909:** Left office after his second term as president
- ➤ **1912:** Founded the Bull Moose Party and ran unsuccessfully for president
- ➤ **1913:** Launched exploration of the River of Doubt in Brazil

➤ **1914:** Returned to the United States after successfully descending the River of Doubt

➤ **1919:** Died of an embolism at the age of sixty-one, in Oyster Bay, New York

THE ESSENCE OF AUTHENTICITY

Bill George, the former Medtronic CEO turned author and professor, writes in his book *True North*, "After years of studying leaders and their traits, I believe that leadership begins and ends with authenticity. It's being yourself; being the person you were created to be." George points out that this aspect of leadership is often ignored by aspiring leaders and leadership texts.

So, what does it mean to be authentic? *Webster's Encyclopedic Unabridged Dictionary* defines authentic as "not false or copied, genuine, real." It means being oneself no matter what happens or whom we are with. As with many other attributes examined in this book, authenticity requires us to know who we are and what we believe. Authenticity is about remaining true to oneself and one's character.

Leaders understand that the path to leadership is a journey of discovery. Authenticity comes from self-discovery and self-awareness. It comes from investing time and energy to learn about ourselves. We are dynamic and ever-changing creatures. We are complex beings who play many roles in our lives. We are also constantly growing and changing. As we mature, we learn new skills and acquire new competencies. We discover things about ourselves that we never knew, and we rediscover things we may have forgotten.

The process of self-discovery will also help to reveal who we are not. Just as a snake or crab must shed its skin to grow, our self-discovery may force us to let go of things that are preventing us from becoming our true selves. By shedding its skin, the snake does not fundamentally change. It gives itself the opportunity to become larger and stronger. Its pattern remains the same, but nuances and subtleties may become more apparent. The faster the snake grows, the more frequently it sheds. The same is true with authentic leaders. Embracing authentic behaviors while letting go of inauthentic behaviors makes us stronger leaders.

When we observe effective leaders, we may try to act like them by mimicking them or their behaviors. This is likely to fail. While it is important to observe and learn from leaders we respect, it is essential that we go deeper than imitation. We must seek to understand how their behaviors reflect who *they* are.

Authenticity means recognizing the complexities of our lives and being aware of how we may change from one role to the next. Kipling understood this complexity. When he writes, "If you can talk with crowds and keep your virtue, or walk with kings—nor lose the common touch," he acknowledges the difficulty of remaining true to oneself, given the variety of roles we play. Authentic leaders also recognize that we face a genuine risk of becoming inauthentic if we fail to find the right balance and priority among our beliefs and values as we move from one role to the next. This doesn't mean that our values and beliefs should change or disappear. We simply must emphasize those values that are appropriate to the particular roles we are playing at any given moment.

In my role as a father, my priority is on the values and behaviors associated with nurturing and fostering growth and learning, and my spiritual values are displayed openly and without filter. In my work settings, I may emphasize other values, such as intellectual rigor, but my spirituality is more subdued. What happens when we are performing different roles at the same time? For example, our roles as leaders or managers require a different emphasis from our roles as colleagues or subordinates, yet we may find ourselves playing these roles at the same time. We therefore have the potential to be viewed as inauthentic or inconsistent. This can create conflict or confusion, unless we are aware of our actions and behaviors and are explicit about them to those around us. The risk of being viewed as inauthentic is heightened when our shifting roles require a great degree of change in the values we are emphasizing. For example, Roosevelt would have seemed inauthentic to the czar and emperor had they seen him on the River of Doubt expedition. Radical shifts or erratic behavior can create the impression that our values are changing or ill defined. But the greatest risk to our authenticity is allowing societal pressure or other influences to cause us to ignore or repress our values or beliefs.

ROOSEVELT'S LESSONS

Much of Theodore Roosevelt's success came from his authenticity. He is the ideal model for authentic leadership because of the diversity of the roles he played. His commitment to being true to himself—regardless of the situation he was in or the people around him—allowed him to remain real and genuine. He knew who he was and who he wasn't, and this awareness defined his leadership. What lessons can he teach us about our own leadership? How can we be more authentic?

1. *Roosevelt built his authenticity on a solid foundation—his character.* Theodore Roosevelt was his own person. He often took and held positions that were unpopular. He was willing to defy friend and foe alike because he knew who he was and what he believed. At the center of Roosevelt's character was a deeply felt sense of fairness. Fairness was at the heart of his most controversial actions. Many of his greatest successes can be directly linked to his doing what he believed to be fair and right. His influence and power came from his character.

2. *Roosevelt demonstrated the importance of knowing who we are at any given moment.* Roosevelt committed himself to whatever he undertook. He was a cowboy on his ranch, a statesman in the White House, a soldier on the battlefield, and a father in his home. Like Roosevelt, we are all many different people: employee, boss, colleague, parent, spouse, sibling, friend. Being who we are in the moment requires awareness and commitment. These roles compete for our time and attention. Consider the many distractions that can take us out of the moment and prevent us from being authentic. Technology allows us to jump from one role to the next, yet these tools can challenge our authenticity. When I focus on my Blackberry rather than pay attention to a conversation with my children, I don't speak and act in ways that reflect what matters most to me.

3. ***Roosevelt showed the connection between authenticity and commitment.*** The Russo-Japanese mediation and the River of Doubt expedition revealed Roosevelt's ability to commit himself to an undertaking. His biographies are full of stories that highlight this trait. One of Roosevelt's favorite pastimes, the point-to-point walk, provides a great example. He would lead his family, friends, or colleagues on hikes from one point on a map to another. The purpose of these walks was to instill a sense of commitment—to stay the course regardless of the obstacles. If they encountered an obstacle, they could go over, under, or through it, but they could not go around it. Through these walks, Roosevelt tested himself and others.

What are the obstacles that undermine our commitment? How do they keep us from being authentic? Are they our reputations, friendships, insecurities, money concerns, or fears? When we choose to be our authentic selves, we must work to overcome the obstacles that may derail our authenticity.

4. ***Roosevelt's authenticity enabled him to build and maintain a diverse set of friends and associates.*** These relationships played an important role in making Roosevelt the leader he was. They ranged from royalty to common laborers, and they helped Roosevelt extend his reach through others. As with Roosevelt, our authenticity helps us build genuine relationships. These relationships can create leverage in our lives. Authenticity builds trust and makes us more attractive and compelling leaders. Conversely, authenticity may impede other relationships and even create adversaries. Roosevelt had many friends, but he also created many enemies. He showed that leadership is not a popularity contest. Leadership can be very lonely, especially when we take unpopular positions. Many of the leaders in this book experienced this unpleasant reality.

5. ***Roosevelt's actions revealed the importance of knowing who we are not.*** Knowing who we are also means learning who we are not. "Prepare me a paper" says so much. Roosevelt never tried

to be what he wasn't. This does not mean that he ignored those gaps or shortcomings. Rather, he surrounded himself with people he trusted who were competent to inform and advise him. As leaders, we will constantly face situations or challenges for which we are ill suited. I once spent two years in a role that was antithetical to my strengths and talents. It was exhausting and frustrating, and those were the longest two years of my life. It was also early enough in my career that I didn't initially realize the degree of mismatch—I was still learning who I wasn't. That experience taught me to value others who are what I am not. But that doesn't mean that we can simply dump the garbage on subordinates. It means building a team that leverages each member's strengths and passions.

Theodore Roosevelt was always himself. He demonstrated the power of living authentically, and he lived his life to the fullest. Early in his life, he learned that he had the power to define who and what he was. As a boy, Roosevelt suffered from chronic debilitating asthma. His parents and doctors told him that he would never live a normal life and that his frail body would not support his ambitious mind and spirit. He chose to change himself physically. Through strenuous exercise and hard work, Roosevelt remade his body. This act proved telling. He became a great leader through constant self-awareness and choice. He never forgot who he was. He never tried to be someone he wasn't. His famous "Man in the Arena" speech captures the essence of Roosevelt's authenticity:

> It is not the critic who counts; not the man who points
> out how the strong man stumbles, or where the doer
> of deeds could have done them better. The credit be-
> longs to the man who is actually in the arena, whose
> face is marred by dust and sweat and blood; who strives
> valiantly; who errs, and comes short again and again,
> because there is no effort without error and shortcom-
> ing; but who does actually strive to do the deeds; who
> knows the great enthusiasms, the great devotions;

who spends himself in a worthy cause; who at the best knows in the end the triumph of high achievement, and who at the worst, if he fails, at least fails while daring greatly, so that his place shall never be with those cold and timid souls who know neither victory nor defeat.

Roosevelt knew that whatever the arena, he was not an actor. He was authentically himself.

Everyday Authenticity

We show the world who we are every day. Our actions reveal our authentic selves. I once had a boss who was a phenomenal internal salesperson. He could sell an idea or project to senior management better than anyone I had ever met. I spent hours observing his behavior to learn his secrets. The more I observed, the *less* I understood what made him so successful. He could be socially awkward. At times, he was abrasive. He was smart, but the company was full of smart people. Finally, I asked him what made him so successful. How had he become so compelling? The simplicity of his answer amazed me. He said, "I am reliable." He had built a reputation for always delivering the results he committed to. Therefore, his secret wasn't that he could sell better than others. His secret was that he had built and nurtured his reputation. More than that, he had built his reputation by being himself: by being authentic. So even when he brought highly speculative initiatives forward for approval, he was able to garner the support he needed. He never tried to be a great salesperson or great influencer. That wasn't who he was. He was reliable, and that made him great at much more. He taught me that we are at our best when we are ourselves.

RECOMMENDED RESOURCES

Resources about Theodore Roosevelt:

Theodore Rex by Edmund Morris

The River of Doubt: Theodore Roosevelt's Darkest Journey by Candice Millard

The Seven Worlds of Theodore Roosevelt by Edward Wagenknecht

Resources about Authenticity:

Authentic Leadership: Rediscovering the Secrets to Creating Lasting Value by Bill George
True North: Discover Your Authentic Leadership by Bill George
Leading Out Loud: Inspiring Change Through Authentic Communications by Terry Pearce

CHAPTER 3

Michael Collins's Integrity: Knowing and Defending the Truth

If you can bear to hear the truth you've spoken
Twisted by knaves to make a trap for fools

COLLINS'S INTEGRITY

On December 6, 1922, after more than 700 years under British control, the Irish Free State made Ireland an independent nation. It also marked the end of the Irish War of Independence, which had started on Easter Monday 1916. Michael Collins, a thirty-two-year-old former postal clerk, led the treaty negotiations that made this day possible. Biographers have called Collins "the man who made Ireland" and "the man who won the war." No one person won the war or made Ireland free, but Collins's contributions were extraordinary. His leadership was essential to Ireland's victory.

Michael Collins was born in County Cork, Ireland, in 1890. He became active in nationalist causes at the age of fifteen. The 1916 Easter Uprising was the pivotal event of Collins's life, as it was for many Irish nationalists. The British imprisoned him after they put down the uprising. Collins's strong personality and organizational skills made him a leader among the Irish prisoners. He was one of the first prisoners released in late 1916, and he immediately returned to his nationalist activities.

In early 1919, hostilities between the Irish and the British resumed. During the war, Collins served in important leadership positions. He founded the Irish Republican Army—not to be confused with the Provisional IRA that terrorized the United Kingdom from 1969 to 1997—and he served as its head of intelligence and head of operations. Collins was the first minister of finance for the Dail Eireann, the Irish parliament. Collins's leadership skills, quick mind, and high energy made him a key leader during the war.

As head of intelligence, Collins established an espionage network that devastated England's many attempts to infiltrate and destroy the Irish rebellion from within. Previous Irish uprisings of the eighteenth and nineteenth centuries had failed, due largely to England's successful use of spies, traitors, and informers. Collins understood this and worked to use these same tools against the British. His efforts virtually blinded the British military and police force.

Collins also established much of the IRA's military capabilities. He created training and logistical capabilities that enabled this small, poorly equipped rebel army to defeat the most powerful military of the day. All of these factors made Collins a primary target for the British. For much of 1920 and 1921, many newspapers described Collins as the most wanted man in Europe.

Michael Collins exhibited many leadership attributes, but his integrity stands out among the rest. The greatest test and demonstration of his integrity was his leadership of the Irish delegation at the Anglo-Irish Peace Conference in the fall of 1921. Collins did not want this role, and as head of intelligence, he had many good reasons to decline the appointment. He had learned from his spies and informants that many of the Irish demands were unacceptable to the British. He feared that the negotiations were doomed before they started because both sides were unwilling to bend on key issues. Collins had learned from his sources that the British were planning to escalate hostilities if negotiations failed. They would crush the rebellion without regard to civilian casualties, and Collins questioned his ability to lead effectively if hostilities resumed. He had spent the war hiding in plain sight. Despite his most-wanted status, he had operated openly. He rarely wore disguises, and he moved about Dublin on bicycle. Collins's success at evading arrest and assassination was a result of the British inability to obtain photographs or accurate descriptions of him. His participation in the Irish delegation would give the British many opportunities to photograph him and learn his habits and behaviors. He knew that this exposure would force him underground, which would undermine his ability to lead effectively. But in spite of his reservations, Collins accepted the appointment to serve on the Irish delegation for two primary reasons. First, he was a soldier: he was compelled to follow the legitimate orders of his commander, President Eamon de Valera.

More importantly, he came to see that his knowledge, experience, unique perspective, and access to information would prove useful during the negotiations.

Publicly, the Irish delegates were tasked with obtaining a treaty with audacious and unrealistic goals. They sought an independent and unified Irish republic with no connection to Great Britain. Privately, the Dail and President de Valera had charged the delegation with getting the best deal they could. Collins saw his primary goal as negotiating a treaty that would end the war and create an independent Ireland. Early in the peace conference, the Irish delegation recognized that many of their initial demands were not viable. The British made it clear that they would be taking a hard line. The Irish delegates quickly realized that the best Ireland could hope for was something akin to the dominion status that Canada and Australia had at the time.

Early in the negotiations, Michael Collins proved to be as effective a negotiator as he was a revolutionary. This poorly educated former postal clerk was negotiating a treaty with a group of international heavyweights, including Prime Minister David Lloyd George and Winston Churchill. Although they were diplomatically outclassed, Collins and the Irish delegation brought home a treaty that created the Irish Free State, a remarkable achievement. It gave the Irish much of what they wanted but contained a few significant losses. While the Irish would gain the right to self-government, and British military would leave Ireland, Ireland would remain a part of the British Empire; the British monarch would be the Irish head of state; members of the Dail would have to swear allegiance to the king; and finally, Northern Ireland would have the right to withdraw from the Irish Free State. The Irish delegation had accomplished its mission: they had gotten the best deal they could. By accepting a treaty that was imperfect, they had achieved peace.

However, for many Irish, the peace accord and the Free State were unacceptable compromises. They felt it betrayed the promises and sacrifices of the Easter Uprising and its leaders. Their passions clouded their judgment and blinded them from seeing the reality of the situation. Collins and the other Irish delegates believed that President de Valera and the Dail leadership were equally aware of these facts. However, they knew that many of their comrades would repudiate the treaty and seek a return to war—a war that Collins knew meant certain defeat for the IRA and horrific suffering for the Irish people.

Collins did what he knew was the right thing to do: he signed and defended the treaty. He recognized the danger of his decision, knowing that his words and deeds would be twisted and used against him. Shortly after signing the accord, Collins told a colleague, "Think— what have I got for Ireland? Something which she has wanted these past seven hundred years. Will anyone be satisfied at the bargain? Will anyone? I tell you this; early this morning I signed my death warrant."

Michael Collins never lost his commitment to complete independence, but he knew that this compromise was the best he or anyone else could get for the Irish people. He put his personal feelings aside and did his duty for those he led. He expected the other Irish leaders to do the same, but he also knew many would not. Many of his friends and comrades turned against him, but Collins remained committed to the peace accord. He effectively campaigned for the treaty and the Irish constitution that supported it. The Dail ratified both, and the constitution won a majority vote of the Irish people.

Collins had argued that the Free State was the first step toward total independence and a united Ireland. During the treaty debate Collins stated, "In my opinion it gives us freedom, not the ultimate freedom that all nations desire . . . but the freedom to achieve it." While today Ireland remains divided, it achieved total independence from Great Britain in 1937.

The hate and mistrust created during the peace negotiations and constitutional debates led to the Irish Civil War, which lasted from May 1922 until June 1923. Nearly 4,000 died, far more than were killed by the British during the War of Independence. Among those was Michael Collins, dead from an assassin's bullet nine months after signing the treaty. Antitreaty forces ambushed him near his home in County Cork. The leader of the ambush, Liam Deasy, was a former subordinate of Collins's. He later admitted that he "profoundly regretted" Collins's death. Collins was thirty-two. One can only speculate what else he would have accomplished had he been able to devote himself to the task of building a peacetime government. His integrity—his unflinching commitment to speaking and defending the truth—cost him his life. But his integrity earned something more valuable, a free Ireland.

MICHAEL COLLINS TIMELINE: A PATH TO THE TRUTH

- **1890:** Born in County Cork, Ireland
- **1906:** Moved to London to become a post office clerk; joined a variety of Irish nationalist organizations
- **1916:** Returned to Ireland in January; participated in the Easter Uprising in April; imprisoned by the British from April to December
- **1917:** Assumed leadership positions in Sinn Fein, the Irish Republican Brotherhood, and Irish nationalist organizations
- **1918:** Coordinated Sinn Fein's parliamentary electoral efforts, electing seventy-three members including himself

January 21, 1919–July 11, 1921: Irish War of Independence

- **1919:** Appointed finance minister of the newly formed Irish parliament, Dail Eireann; elected president of the Irish Republican Brotherhood; named director of intelligence of the Irish Republican Army; masterminded assassinations and guerilla campaigns
- **1920:** Ordered increased assassinations and acts of sabotage against the British; dubbed the most wanted man in Europe by British newspapers after the British government offers £10,000 reward for his capture
- **1921:** Truce declared ending hostilities in July; Collins named deputy head of the Irish treaty delegation and became its de facto head from October to December; signed Anglo-Irish Treaty officially ending the war and creating the Irish Free State in December; predicted his own assassination

➤ **1922:**

  ➤ **January:** Led efforts to defend the treaty and Free State as a stepping-stone to the creation of an independent Irish republic; Dail Eireann ratified the treaty; the British government transferred control of the Free State to the provisional government with Collins as president; radical Dail members, including many of Collins's closest friends and colleagues, resigned in protest over the treaty

  ➤ **April:** Start of the Irish Civil War between antitreaty forces and the pro-treaty National Army, led by Collins

  ➤ **August:** Assassinated by antitreaty forces near his birthplace in County Cork

➤ **1923:** End of the Irish Civil War in May following the surrender of the antitreaty forces

➤ **1937:** Republic of Ireland established by the Irish constitution, fulfilling Collins's 1922 prediction

THE ESSENCE OF INTEGRITY

Former United States senator Alan Simpson once said, "If you have integrity, nothing else matters. If you don't have integrity, nothing else matters." But what exactly is integrity?

Kipling's words ("If you can bear to hear the truth you've spoken twisted by knaves to make a trap for fools.") remind us of the importance and cost of integrity. Integrity means speaking the truth regardless of the risk or traps. By speaking aloud what we believe to be true, we reveal who we are. This act can make us vulnerable. The more our words—our truths—are a reflection of our authentic character, the greater the harm we will feel when they are twisted, manipulated, or criticized. We are likely to feel that our moral and ethical principles are under attack. We may also feel diminished, as if someone has taken part of us away.

Integrity requires much from a leader. Above all, it requires honesty and courage. Honesty seems obvious, but it means far more than not telling lies. It means telling the whole truth, regardless of how unpopular or unpleasant it may be. It means performing the due diligence to learn the truth. It means encouraging others to be honest. Integrity requires courage, because it often means sacrifice. Consider the fate of many whistle-blowers. They often find themselves pariahs within their organizations.

Integrity forces us to acknowledge the complexities discussed in the previous chapter on authenticity. Being authentic means accepting and embracing the many roles and situations in which we find ourselves. It means reconciling the fact that certain beliefs and values are more important in different situations and roles. Integrity, remaining whole, means that we remain true to our character, regardless of the complexity. It means looking for inconsistencies between our character and our actions. It also requires us to be open to hearing criticism from others.

Our integrity becomes most apparent when others try to exploit our vulnerability by twisting our words or beliefs. Despite this risk, leaders cannot shy away from the truth. On the contrary, they must speak it and defend it. Those without integrity will avoid the truth. Worse, when they hear it, they may manipulate it to achieve their own ends. These are the "knaves" Kipling was referring to. While the term is no longer used, Kipling used it to describe a deceitful person.

Integrity comes from the same root word as *integrate*, to bring together or incorporate into a whole. This presents a new and difficult challenge for leaders. Leading with integrity means accepting new information that may require us to change our stances. Despite how strongly we have believed in something or how long we have fought for and defended it, new information may show that we were wrong. Integrity means having the courage and will to accept this new truth and change. Consider Copernicus or Columbus. They both introduced new truths to the world. However, Copernicus and Columbus first had to change and accept these new truths themselves. Copernicus was educated to believe that the earth was the center of the universe. Columbus was taught that the earth was flat. Both men gained new perspectives that allowed them to change their definitions of the truth. They were criticized and persecuted for their beliefs, but they ultimately succeeded in revealing the truth.

We often find ourselves frustrated with politicians and leaders who change their positions on important issues or refuse to speak the truth clearly and forcefully. It is easy to become cynical and believe that these changes are unprincipled or merely vacillation. We see their refusal to take stands as an unwillingness to reveal the truth about themselves and their positions and beliefs about important issues. Some of our cynicism is certainly warranted. Many public figures fear being held accountable for their beliefs, so they speak in platitudes that give them room to spin their messages to suit whatever audience they are addressing.

Some rare political leaders may demonstrate true integrity. Like Copernicus, Columbus, or Collins, great leaders have the ability to integrate new information that allows them to make fundamental changes on important issues. They willingly and openly take strong stands on controversial subjects. They are unafraid to expose their beliefs to scrutiny. They speak frankly and honestly because they know who they are and what truly matters. The challenge for us is to distinguish those rare leaders from the knaves.

Integrity means consistently doing the right thing, and that takes practice. Every time we show integrity about the small things, we are practicing for the big tests. Others will look for a consistent pattern of behavior that reflects a true commitment to integrity. Our actions will build respect—self-respect and the respect of others. By living by our principles and speaking the truth, we show our self-respect, and by trusting others to hear the truth, we reveal our respect for them.

COLLINS'S LESSONS

Michael Collins showed what it means to lead with integrity. It cost him his life, but it also enabled him to achieve his life's ambition. For most of us, the price will not be nearly so high. No one expects us to make that level of sacrifice. However, those we lead do expect us to speak and defend the truth. So what lessons can we learn from Michael Collins and his integrity? How can we use his integrity as a model to help us build our own? We start with a strong foundation of beliefs and principles and a reputation of speaking and acting with honesty. These lessons build on that honesty to create true integrity.

1. ***Michael Collins showed that the truth might be different when viewed from another perspective.*** For most of Collins's life, he was a passionate believer in the creation of an Irish republic, and he rejected the notion of any relationship with Great Britain akin to the Free State that he ultimately agreed to and defended. During the months that preceded the Anglo-Irish Peace Conference, he came to realize that a true republic was a pipe dream in the near term. He recognized that the best path to his desired end, a free Irish republic, was a series of incremental moves. He also came to see that his passion, youth, and lack of perspective had clouded his judgment. Reality was different from the truth he had believed. Similarly, we must also be willing to reevaluate our own truths. Perspectives change as new information becomes available to us. This doesn't mean that we compromise our principles, but we must be willing to change our opinions as new facts reveal the truth to us. As leaders we must not simply accept things at face value. We must take the time to gather the facts and truly understand a given situation. If our understanding of the facts changes the truth, as it did for Collins, we must change our position and defend the new truth. Others may criticize us either for being irresolute or for our failure to see the truth sooner. We must accept this as one of the costs of integrity.

2. ***Collins's actions showed the consequences of speaking and defending the truth.*** Michael Collins knew the risks he would take by speaking the truth. He also recognized that there were some nonnegotiable truths. Lord Birkenhead, a member of the British negotiation delegation, expressed his personal concerns about the Anglo-Irish Treaty by saying, "I have just signed my political death warrant." Collins responded that he had just signed his actual death warrant. It is important for us to understand the risks we take by speaking the truth.

Doing so allows us to decide whether we can accept the risks. Deciding where we draw the line is a matter of character and priorities. Leadership is also about picking our battles. Integrity doesn't mean we become Don Quixote tilting at every windmill. If an issue is truly important, we need to stand up. At other times we may decide an issue doesn't matter. The lines are rarely black and white, but it is essential that we remain consistent and open about what we stand for.

3. *Collins knew who the knaves were who would twist his words.* Some of Collins's closest friends and allies during the Irish War of Independence turned against him because of the treaty. He knew all along that the radicals would oppose him. But other opposition surprised him. Collins's keen knowledge of who opposed him enabled him to maneuver the treaty through the ratification process. Like Collins, if we know who opposes us—or is likely to—we can more effectively defend the truth. Whether driven by fear or malice, the knaves may twist our words. We must be prepared to defend them. The greater the change our truths call for, the greater the opposition we will experience.

4. *Collins failed to consider the perspective of the knaves.* One of the biggest mistakes Collins made was not thinking about his opponents' points of view. He failed to recognize that his unique perspective had helped him to see things that his opponents could not. Had he acknowledged this differing perspective, he might have been more effective in enlisting their support. As leaders we cannot force others to accept and embrace our truths. Leadership means having the ability to see things from many angles and encourage others to do the same. What opportunities exist for us to invite others to consider things from our vantage points? How might that sway them to our opinions?

5. *Collins demonstrated the need to repeat the truth often and consistently.* Michael Collins had to build a solid base of support

for the treaty. He had to engage several disparate constituencies with unique priorities, including the members of the Irish political leadership; the Irish combatants who had been waging war for more than six years; and the various nationalist groups who had been supporting the war. Ultimately, he knew that he would need to gain the support of the Irish people. In the end, this group mattered most. His ability to speak and lobby for the treaty in a clear and consistent way was vital to his success. Those opposing him would have used any perceived inconsistency to undermine his efforts. Like Collins, we must continue to speak the truth to our stakeholders. Our consistency and clarity will not guarantee our success in convincing others, but it will give our opponents less opportunity to twist our words.

Integrity is the characteristic people desire most in a leader. In the book *The Leadership Challenge,* James Kouzes and Barry Posner reveal that 88 percent of survey respondents felt that honesty was an essential leadership trait. While integrity goes well beyond honesty, their research reveals the importance of integrity in leaders. Most of us look for integrity in those we choose to follow. It is imperative that we keep this in mind as we lead. When we act with integrity, we give people an important reason to follow us.

Michael Collins led by demonstrating his integrity. He spoke and defended the truth—and he invested himself in finding and understanding the truth. Ultimately, he showed that there are truths for which we must be willing to make sacrifices.

Everyday Integrity

Organizational integrity doesn't just happen on its own. It happens because leaders decide to make it an essential part of their organizations. I used to be surprised by the ethical lapses that occurred in organizations run by seemingly honest and moral people. I have come to realize that having integrity and leading with integrity are very different. Personal integrity is the foundation upon which leadership integrity is built.

One of the best examples of leading with integrity that I have experienced took place during my work on Virginia governor George Allen's transition team. Many who work in politics are eager and passionate. Often political scandals stem from these overzealous followers who believe that the ends will justify the means. Many politicos believe it is acceptable to bend the rules for the sake of their cause. Governor Allen and his chief of staff, Jay Timmons, chose to confront this head on.

Jay was the quintessential chief of staff. He quietly worked, without fanfare or public recognition, to ensure that the governor's priorities were met and that everyone in the administration was serving Virginia honestly and effectively. During the hectic two months between the election and the inauguration, Jay led the effort to establish the leadership team for Virginia for the next four years. Simply finding and vetting candidates to fill the many roles was a full-time job. With just weeks to go before the inauguration, Jay called a meeting of the entire transition team personnel and gubernatorial appointees. The purpose of the meeting was to establish the standard of conduct for the administration.

Jay ended the meeting with a declaration that set the tone for the next four years. He reminded us that we were about to undertake something very special. We were going to make history. Then he said something that no one would forget. He made it perfectly clear that we were going to do this honestly, ethically, and within the confines of the law. Everyone in the room understood that if any of us violated the trust of the people of Virginia, we would be held accountable. It was not a threat. Jay just wanted to make sure his entire leadership team understood the governor's expectations. It should come as no surprise that Governor Allen's term was both highly productive and virtually scandal-free.

RECOMMENDED RESOURCES

Resources about Michael Collins:

Michael Collins: The Man Who Made Ireland by Tim Pat Coogan
Michael Collins: The Man Who Won the War by T. Ryle Dwyer
The Big Fellow: Michael Collins and the Irish Revolution by Frank O'Connor

Resources about Integrity:

Defining Moments: When Managers Must Choose Between Right and Right by Joseph L. Badaracco Jr.

Leadership and the Quest for Integrity by Joseph L. Badaracco Jr. and Richard R. Ellsworth

The Ethical Challenge: How to Lead with Unyielding Integrity by Noel M. Tichy and Andrew McGill

Winston Churchill's Self-Efficacy: The Confidence to Gain from Triumph and Disaster

If you can meet with Triumph and Disaster
And treat those two imposters just the same

CHURCHILL'S SELF-EFFICACY

Everyone experiences career highs and lows, but Winston Churchill's swings were epic. Churchill, however, never lost his supreme confidence in his own abilities. Neither extraordinary triumphs nor catastrophic disasters seemed to change his self-assessment that he was destined for greatness. Consider the following series of events. In 1911, Churchill was named first lord of the admiralty. Four years later, he resigned in disgrace. In 1924, Churchill was appointed chancellor of the exchequer; he was blamed for economic collapse and lost his post in 1929. From 1929 until 1939, Churchill was cast into political obscurity. In 1940, he became prime minister and led Great Britain to victory in the Second World War; he was ousted in the election of 1945, the same year the war ended. He was returned to office in 1951.

Given his volatile career, what gave Churchill his exceptional confidence in his own abilities? Certainly, his birth and family lineage played a part. He was born into one of Great Britain's most prestigious families. He grew up experiencing nothing but privilege. His father was a powerful politician, and his mother was a glamorous actress and socialite. However, his early years also had a dark side. In fact, Churchill's childhood, adolescence, and education were filled with events that should have ensured that he grew up with no confidence in himself or his abilities. His parents virtually ignored him. The only exception to this was his father's expressions of doubt about young Winston's prospects. Winston was a poor student. He had a severe speech impediment. But none of this seemed to bother him.

Historians and biographers have thoroughly celebrated Churchill's successes and triumphs, which are even more impressive when compared to his failures. Churchill failed early and often as a child, a pattern that continued throughout his life. The failures often seemed insurmountable. The greatest prewar challenge he faced came with the defeat of the Conservative Party in 1929. With his party out of power, Churchill entered what became known as his "wilderness years."

The wilderness years were the low point of Churchill's career. During this period of political isolation, he was frequently ignored and rebuffed by the government, his party, the media, and the British people. His ideas were out of sync with contemporary thought. But it was during this period that he best demonstrated his extraordinary self-efficacy.

Churchill may have been ignored politically during his wilderness years, but he continued to use his position in parliament to express his opinions and concerns. He spent much of this time warning anyone who would listen about the dangers that Hitler and Nazi Germany posed to European peace. He was vocally critical of Great Britain's prewar military and foreign policy, directing his criticism at both friends and foes. He strongly condemned his own party's approach to dealing with Hitler. He passionately advocated for Britain to increase its defense spending and military readiness. Churchill knew that the British appeasement of Hitler would fail. He savagely attacked the British government, stating, "You were given the choice between war and dishonor. You chose dishonor, and you will have war." He did not seem to worry that his ideas were unpopular or out of step with the mainstream. Nor did he become despondent when the government continuously ignored his warning and criticisms. He knew he was right.

Churchill also used the wilderness years to write. He knew he was destined for literary greatness—in addition to political greatness—and some of his best writing came from this period of his life. His writing kept him financially solvent. It also gave him an outlet for his ideas. Churchill used his writing, speeches, and busy social schedule to educate those who would listen. He maintained a small but loyal following, which became the base of support that returned him to power in 1940.

Churchill's confidence often became arrogance and superiority. He best exposed this in an exchange he had with a member of his personal staff. Following an argument with the man, Churchill said, "You were very rude to me, you know." The man replied, "But you were rude, too." Churchill replied, "Yes, but I am a great man." While this does not reflect the level of civility we might desire from a leader, the exchange revealed that even at his nadir, Churchill never doubted his greatness.

WINSTON CHURCHILL TIMELINE: THE HIGHS AND LOWS OF A SUPREMELY CONFIDENT LEADER

- ➤ **1874:** Born at Blenheim Palace, Oxfordshire, England
- ➤ **1899:** Ran for and lost his first parliamentary election; captured in Boer War but escaped from prisoner-of-war camp and became a national celebrity
- ➤ **1900:** Elected to parliament for the first time
- ➤ **1910:** Appointed home secretary
- ➤ **1911:** Appointed first lord of the admiralty
- ➤ **1914:** First World War began
- ➤ **1915:** Resigned as first lord of the admiralty following the disastrous Battle of Gallipoli; served in France as a British Army major
- ➤ **1916:** Promoted to lieutenant colonel
- ➤ **1917:** Returned to England to serve as minister of munitions
- ➤ **1919:** Appointed secretary of state for war and air
- ➤ **1920:** Appointed colonial secretary
- ➤ **1924:** Appointed chancellor of the exchequer
- ➤ **1929:** Resigned as chancellor of the exchequer following British financial crisis

➤ **1929–1939:** Became a political pariah during his wilderness years

➤ **1939:** Appointed first lord of the admiralty for the second time

➤ **1940:** Appointed prime minister of Great Britain; also served as defense minister

➤ **1945:** Allies won Second World War; Churchill defeated in general election

➤ **1951:** Appointed prime minister

➤ **1955:** Resigned as prime minister

➤ **1964:** Left parliament

➤ **1965:** Died at his home in London at the age of ninety

THE NATURE OF SELF-EFFICACY

Sam Esposito, a good friend of mine and a martial arts instructor, regularly tells students who are preparing for a particularly difficult challenge that the task is both the easiest and the hardest thing in the world. The children in his class always look at him quizzically and ask, "How can it be both?" He replies with a simple answer: "It all depends on what you believe." If the students believe the task will be easy, it will be. This is the essence of self-efficacy. Dr. Albert Bandura, the psychologist who first described and studied self-efficacy, defines it as "the belief in one's capabilities to organize and execute the courses of action to manage prospective situations." This is a concept familiar to many educators, athletes, coaches, and psychologists, but it is frequently overlooked as a leadership attribute.

Self-efficacy in leaders is critical because leadership requires that we believe we can have an effect on the world around us. Many psychologists believe that our self-efficacy affects most, if not all, of our social interactions. As leaders, it is essential that we learn how to build our self-efficacy while fostering its development in those we lead.

Highly self-efficacious people see triumph as the expected outcome. They will celebrate successes, but they quickly move on to the next challenge. Conversely, they see setbacks or failures as an opportunity to grow and learn, not as an indictment of their inherent capability. Self-efficacy can be confused with self-esteem, but psychologists distinguish between the two by examining the nature of one's confidence. They have learned that self-esteem often fails us. Setbacks or unexpected challenges can erode self-esteem. That is because self-esteem focuses on general self-worth. Self-efficacy is a fundamental belief in one's ability to achieve a desired result. It is not limited to what we know we have the specific skills to do. Self-efficacy reflects one's belief in the capacity to push beyond what has been learned and done. Another distinction between self-esteem and self-efficacy is the source of the confidence. Self-esteem often requires external factors, while self-efficacy seems to be more internally driven.

Like most strongly self-efficacious people, Churchill felt a sense of destiny. This sense of destiny helps the self-efficacious person achieve extraordinary results and overcome obstacles. People with high self-efficacy believe they can succeed, so they set high goals and are often rewarded for their accomplishments. Conversely, their risk taking can lead to failure. But self-efficacious people are more likely to learn from failure. They do not see failure as a permanent condition; rather, they see it as a temporary setback to overcome.

Two of the most important leadership roles we play are that of objective assessor and confidence builder. First, we must help others ground their self-assessments. This will keep people from either overestimating or underestimating their abilities. People with high self-efficacy may overestimate their ability to achieve their objectives, while those with low self-efficacy are less likely to push themselves.

Leaders often see things in others that they cannot or will not see in themselves. When we provide grounded assessments of their capabilities, we are helping build their self-efficacy. This means helping others expose and test their skills, abilities, and talents. This awareness will encourage them to tackle challenging tasks and gain valuable experience.

Self-efficacy is an important factor for individual success. It is also a strong predictor of leadership potential and success. Self-efficacious people often demonstrate traits exhibited by leaders. Their belief in themselves will inspire others to follow them. Their confidence will enable them to take risks and be aggressive. They will also seek and develop superior talent. There is an adage that says, "A players hire A-plus players, and B players hire C players." Self-efficacy breeds more self-efficacy. This pattern creates a powerful cycle of achievement, learning, and greater confidence.

CHURCHILL'S LESSONS

Winston Churchill's self-efficacy changed the world. He believed in his abilities. He never dwelled on the individual triumphs and disasters that filled his life. He learned from them, and he moved on. That is what prepared him to lead Great Britain to victory in the Second World War. What lessons does Churchill teach us? How can we build our own self-efficacy and that of those we lead? How can we use self-efficacy to lead more effectively?

1. *Churchill showed the importance of the leader as teacher.* He invested his energy during the wilderness years in writing and educating his cadre of followers and supporters. Often his topic was the threat of Germany and England's failure to prepare to meet that threat. These lessons epitomize his role as a leader-teacher. He was building the corps of leaders who would eventually serve him when he became prime minister.

   Situational leadership recognizes that those we lead will be in various stages of competence for the tasks before them. As leaders, we are responsible for assessing competence and providing appropriate support to facilitate growth and success. Educators understand the value of testing. So do great leaders. Testing enables leaders to assess individuals' competence while challenging them. Success will build each individual's confidence; failure will provide that person with an opportunity to learn.

   Churchill understood this power. He was constantly challenging and testing those around him. During the worst days of the Second World War, Churchill knew the British people were being tested. He considered the bombings, the threat of invasion, and the fact that England stood alone against

Germany to be tests that England must pass. And moreover, he helped the British people see that they had the ability to do so.

2. *Churchill was a role model and behaved accordingly.* He was aware that he was always in the public eye, even when he was a political outsider. He also recognized that he was leading by example. He knew that his response to any given situation would set the mood for those he led. For example, his criticism of appeasement and his antipathy for Hitler caused controversies during the wilderness years. When he was accused of irresponsibly destabilizing relations with Germany, Churchill quipped, "Perhaps it is better to be irresponsible and right than responsible and wrong." After the Allied victory at El Alamein, he reminded the British people that although this triumph was great, it was but one minor step on a long road to final victory. He said, "This is not the end. It is not even the beginning of the end. But it is, perhaps, the end of the beginning."

 Those around us will look at how we respond to our triumphs and disasters. They will take their cues from our reactions. Leaders need to meet both triumph and disaster appropriately. When things go wrong, we cannot panic, nor can we pretend nothing is wrong. When things go well, we must be our team's biggest cheerleader, celebrating their triumphs, but we can't let these successes go to our heads. Either way we must help maintain perspective and context. In disaster, focus on what we can learn. In triumph, recognize those who made it happen and see how we can repeat it.

3. *Churchill showed the value of both praise and criticism.* One of the most important factors in building our self-efficacy is learning to use feedback. Even when it is constructive or delivered in the form of praise, it can be difficult to hear. Churchill showed the value of learning which feedback to listen to and which to ignore.

Lesson 3a: He believed what people were saying about him.
During Churchill's career, many people saw and commented on his potential. In 1900, Mark Twain introduced Churchill as "the future prime minister of Great Britain." This was the same year Churchill was first elected to parliament. He was just twenty-six years old. On another occasion, a ship captain made a similar prediction. Those who respected and admired him were numerous. Churchill believed in his capabilities already, and this external reinforcement of his potential was strong validation that strengthened his confidence. But Churchill was discerning about whose praise he accepted. We can also choose to be selective and accept only well-grounded feedback. We should ask ourselves the question, "For the sake of what is this praise or criticism offered?"

Lesson 3b: He did not believe what people were saying about him.
In Churchill's case, this even meant ignoring his parents. Randolph Churchill, Winston's father, was highly critical of his son, and his criticism bordered on abuse. Rather than allowing his father's criticism to demoralize him, Winston turned his criticisms into a positive motivator. Churchill attributed much of his later success to this manipulation of the facts. Throughout his career, many of Churchill's colleagues, superiors, subordinates, and acquaintances held him in low regard. He never let their negative opinions affect his high opinion of himself. That does not mean he wasn't circumspect or that he failed to learn from critical feedback. He was just highly discriminating about whose feedback he accepted.

Whether the feedback was positive or negative, Churchill understood how to use it. He heeded the feedback that helped him grow or achieve his goals, and he ignored the rest. How can we better filter the feedback we are offered? How grounded are the assessments the feedback is based on? Chances are that there will be kernels of truth in all of the feedback we receive.

4. *Churchill constantly prepared to achieve the results he knew he was capable of.* When King George VI asked Churchill to become prime minister in 1940, he later recalled, "I felt as if I were walking with destiny, and that all my past life had been in preparation for this hour and this trial." He never doubted that it was his fate to lead the British people, so he spent a great deal of time and energy preparing for this eventuality. Churchill held every major cabinet post with the exception of foreign secretary. He knew he would be effective as prime minister because he was well prepared. Part of the reason we are in leadership roles is our confidence in our ability to achieve desired results. It is equally important that we acquire and develop the skills to exploit every opportunity. Great leaders always seek new opportunities. They try new things for the sake of learning and growth, thus reinforcing their confidence. Although Churchill was a mediocre student, he understood the value of learning and preparation. He read constantly, and he used his free time as a soldier to advance his education. Throughout his life, Churchill never stopped learning.

Churchill's greatest gift was his ability to see his own extraordinary capabilities. He saw excellence even where others saw nothing. Regardless of his triumphs or disasters, he spent his life attaining the greatness he believed was his destiny. Churchill's belief in his abilities—his self-efficacy—is evident in many of his most famous quotations. Consider the confidence of the person who said these words: "Let us therefore brace ourselves to our duties, and so bear ourselves that, if the British Empire and its Commonwealth last for a thousand years, men will still say, 'This was their finest hour.'" Churchill was rallying the British people to fight. He said these words during a radio address in which he advised his people that France had surrendered to Germany. To many, things seemed hopeless. Great Britain was alone. They faced an enemy who seemed unstoppable. Yet, Churchill believed Great Britain had the ability to win. And he believed in his ability to lead them to victory.

Churchill's faith in himself was not simply blind optimism. He was no Pollyanna. He faced moments of self-doubt and self-pity, but he always recovered quickly. Churchill teaches that if we believe we are capable of something, we probably are. Self-efficacy is a great predictor of success; therefore, building our own self-efficacy and that of those we lead will likely pay huge dividends.

Everyday Self-Efficacy

My wife, Laurie, commented recently that she can spend hours contemplating and deliberating over minor or inconsequential decisions. But when it comes to the big, important decisions in life, she moves boldly and decisively. She quickly and clearly sees what is needed, and she acts without hesitation. She also rarely second-guesses those decisions. To some, this behavior might seem backward. Some might even accuse her of recklessness. I see it as a reflection of her strong sense of self-efficacy.

Laurie is the product of a large, loving extended family that raised her to believe that she was truly exceptional. Her parents and her aunts never stopped telling her that she could accomplish anything she put her mind to. They also raised her with a strong faith in God. This upbringing built her self-esteem, but it also planted the seeds of self-efficacy.

Laurie also has superior intelligence, a hunger for knowledge, and remarkable determination and dedication. Combined with her upbringing, these characteristics fed and developed her self-efficacy. They created a woman who is internally driven and knows what she is capable of accomplishing. Laurie's confidence gives her the ability to see clearly what matters and to act on this clarity. In our sixteen years of marriage, Laurie has shown an uncanny ability to see the right answer quickly and to commit herself and our family to that answer.

RECOMMENDED RESOURCES

Resources about Winston Churchill:

Never Give In!: The Best of Winston Churchill's Speeches by Winston
    Churchill
Churchill: A Life by Martin Gilbert

The Last Lion: Winston Spencer Churchill: Alone, 1932–1940 by
William Manchester
*Forty Ways to Look at Winston Churchill: A Brief Account of a Long
Life* by Gretchen Rubin

Resources about Self-Efficacy:

Self-Efficacy in Changing Societies by Albert Bandura
Self-Efficacy: The Exercise of Control by Albert Bandura
Lucky or Smart?: Fifty Pages for the First-Time Entrepreneur by Bo
Peabody
Oh, the Places You'll Go by Dr. Seuss

Part 1 Summary: Self-Awareness and Leadership

The previous four chapters discussed and explored the role of self-awareness in effective leadership. Coming out of this section, you should better understand the first of the "If" Sixteen Leadership Framework questions: *Who am I, and what do I believe?* While simply reading this chapter will not make answering it any easier, you should have begun to see the power that self-awareness provides.

At the beginning of part 1, I encouraged you to contemplate what truly matters to you. What have you discovered about yourself? Have you exposed values of which you were previously unaware? Have you found opportunities to become more authentic? In the conclusion of this book, you will find exercises that should help you on your self-awareness journey.

Now consider the first four leadership attributes: character, authenticity, integrity, and self-efficacy. What have you learned about the distinctions among them? How will their interconnectedness affect how you choose to lead?

PART 1 LESSONS

Character

1. Character matters. Leadership means investing the time and energy to know ourselves.
2. Character means grounding our beliefs in principles and morality.
3. Character requires us to align our actions and decisions with our beliefs and values.
4. True character is tested. We must recognize and address misalignments between our actions and our values.
5. Leading with character means more than having character. It requires us to be open and public about our beliefs and values.

Authenticity

1. We build authenticity on a solid foundation—our character.
2. Authenticity means knowing who we are at any given moment.

3. Authenticity requires a great deal of commitment.
4. Leading and living authentically are essential to building meaningful relationships.
5. Authentic leadership means knowing who we are not.

Integrity

1. Integrity means seeking the truth and changing our positions when we gain better perspective.
2. Integrity requires leaders to accept the consequences of speaking and defending the truth.
3. Integrity may mean that others twist our words and manipulate the truth.
4. Leading with integrity means having the ability to anticipate what will prevent others from accepting the truth.
5. Integrity means having the patience to repeat the truth so others might understand it.

Self-Efficacy

1. Leading with self-efficacy means learning continuously and teaching those we lead.
2. Self-efficacious leaders model positive responses to triumphs and disasters.
3. Self-efficacy requires embracing the value of both praise and criticism.
4. People with high levels of self-efficacy constantly prepare to achieve the results they know they are capable of.

Knowing What You Want

Often one of the first questions we ask children when we first meet them is, "What are you going to be when you grow up?" Even if we don't ask the question, they are quick to tell us. Our obsession with what we want starts when we are kids and continues for the rest of our lives. Throughout our lives we dwell on what we want to achieve and what we want to be remembered for.

We live in a very results-oriented society. We reward achievement above all else, but how do we determine what we want to achieve? Our ability to know what we want is often constrained by the limits of our self-awareness. Many people prefer to jump right over *Who am I?* and move on to *What do I want?* But by first increasing our self-awareness, we open up our ability to see the problems that need solving and the opportunities that exist to effect change. Individual successes or failures take on new meaning. They stop being simply discreet tasks or accomplishments. When we determine our wants, goals, objectives, and missions in terms of a well-defined set of principles, patterns start to form and our priorities become clearer: our self-awareness allows us to put and keep them in context.

This section will help turn your self-awareness into a picture of the future that you can aspire to achieve. The clearer your picture, the easier it will be for you to share it with others. Increased self-awareness will help you answer the second of the "If" Sixteen Questions: *What do I want?* Self-knowledge enables us to see our lives as more than collections of actions, decisions, and relationships. When we know what matters to us we can begin to effect meaningful and lasting change. Self-awareness leads to greater clarity about what we want. By knowing what we want, we can create a plan to get there.

UNDERSTANDING THE NEXT FOUR ATTRIBUTES

This section examines the "If" Sixteen Leadership Attributes most closely related to recognizing, understanding, articulating, and acting on what we want. The next four attributes—ambition, vision, boldness, and resilience—are each unique and essential, yet they are all interdependent. They share a great deal in common, yet their distinctions matter. This is not simply semantics. The precise language I use will help you focus your attention and development, so you can build on your strengths while addressing your weaknesses. By understanding their similarities and differences, we can recognize the nuances in our behaviors that reveal these strengths and weaknesses. The first two attributes in this section—ambition and vision—are the most similar. Like character, authenticity, and integrity in the previous section, some people see a great deal of overlap between ambition and vision; however, Kipling's words helped me recognize the important difference between them.

Ambition

In the last two lines of "If," Kipling writes, "Yours is the Earth and everything that's in it, and—which is more—you'll be a Man, my son!" He is telling his readers that the key to achieving what they want is learning, understanding, and using the previous fifteen attributes that "If—" describes. He reminds us that the ultimate point of life is how we use our gifts and talents to leave our marks on the world. Our ambition defines how big each of us wants that mark to be. Kipling's words address ambition in the broadest sense. He is describing both our societal ambitions (how we want to change and improve the world around us) and our personal ambition (how we want to better ourselves). *Ambition* is defined as "an ardent desire for rank, fame, or power; and a desire to achieve a particular end." Chapter 5 examines ambition more fully using this definition, with a focus on understanding the importance of both societal and personal ambition.

Ambition is simply the desire to achieve something. It may be grand or modest, but no matter how well we understand and articulate it, our ambition is worthless on its own. Ambition does not define a path or offer a solution that motivates or compels action. That, instead, is vision, and therein is the distinction. Ambition is important because it sets the destination. Vision begins to define how we will achieve it. Simply, ambition is about our thoughts and our awareness of what we want; it is not about the actions. Ambition is related to achieving what we want in the same way that character relates to knowing who we are. Both are of limited value without the attributes that support them.

Chapter 5 uses Abraham Lincoln's life to illustrate ambition. As with so many of the other leaders in this book, Lincoln exemplified most of the "If" Sixteen Leadership Attributes, yet his ambition was a constant positive influence in his life and leadership. He possessed and demonstrated extraordinary societal and personal ambition. These ambitions complemented one another. Lincoln's dream of escaping the poverty that was such an integral part of his early life was purely personal. However, the fruits of this personal ambition—his wealth, status, and power—were essential to achieving his societal goals. Similarly, his reputation as an effective and successful political leader contributed to his personal success.

Vision

Vision is what takes our ambition out of the realm of desire and into the real world. Vision gives us the ability to describe the future we imagine. Without ambition, it is impossible to have vision. In their book *The Leadership Challenge*, James Kouzes and Barry Posner write, "Vision reveals the beckoning summit that provides others with the capacity to chart their course toward the future." Standard definitions limit vision to simply seeing and conceiving, but this understanding is no more action oriented than ambition. The real power that vision provides is its ability to motivate and impel action. Kouzes and Posner's description of vision captures both the ability to see what is needed and to provoke action.

When Kipling writes, "If you can dream and not make dreams your master; if you can think and not make thoughts your aim," he is advising his readers to dream and think big—to be *ambitious*. However, he is also reminding us that a vision must be much more than big dreams and thoughts. Our vision is only valuable when it is exposed and shared. Further, its ultimate value comes when it catalyzes action. That is the basis for visionary leadership.

There was never any doubt about who should illustrate vision. Martin Luther King Jr. will be forever remembered for his dream. Kipling's words "If you can dream" have always evoked in me King's immortal words "I have a dream." King's vision elevated the civil rights problems of the South to a national crisis. His words and vision addressed problems that many thought intractable. Yes, he had ambition, but beyond that he articulated that ambition as a vision that changed America.

Boldness

Our ambition starts to become real when we articulate a vision that motivates and inspires action. Our vision brings our ambition to life. Similarly, boldness brings our vision to life. Boldness gives us the ability to see the specific things that will make our vision tangible, and it gives us the will to take the chances required to achieve our vision. Risk is at the heart of boldness. Kipling's words—"If you can make one heap of all your winnings and risk it on one turn of pitch-and-toss"—remind us that without boldness, without the will to take risks, we can never fulfill our vision. More than that, without boldness, it is hard to imagine accomplishing anything truly meaningful.

Webster's Encyclopedic Unabridged Dictionary provides two definitions of *boldness* that apply to leadership: "not hesitant or fearful in the face of actual or possible danger or rebuff" and "beyond the usual limits of conventional thought or action, imaginative." Combined with the definition of risk—exposure to the chance of injury or loss—the role of boldness in leadership becomes clearer.

The problem with these definitions is that they only address the downside. Every leader knows that risk and reward go hand in hand. We take risks for the potential rewards associated with them. The other problem with these definitions is their similarities to courage, an equally important, yet distinct, attribute discussed in part 3. For the purpose of this discussion, the terms *boldness* and *risk taking* refer to the ability to recognize opportunities, calculate the dangers, and take appropriate action. Largely, boldness is about the potential risk, whereas courage is about our response when a risk becomes a reality.

Thomas Jefferson is an ideal model for boldness. He was open and passionate about his vision for America. From writing the Declaration of Independence to sponsoring the Lewis and Clark expedition, Jefferson's life was a series of bold decisions and actions. One of his greatest risks was the Louisiana Purchase. This decision took courage, but it also demanded the ability to see opportunities that others missed and to quantify and accept enormous risks. Jefferson's boldness fundamentally changed America, and his actions provide valuable leadership lessons.

Resilience

Resilience is the last attribute associated with knowing what we want. Leaders recognize that the risks and dangers that accompany boldness often create obstacles that will stand in our way. Leadership means acknowledging this truth and dealing with the obstacles when we confront them. We will never have exactly the right people, tools, or resources to achieve our goals. Some obstacles may seem insurmountable, and others may truly be insurmountable. Other times things just go wrong. Resilient leaders accept these eventualities. They anticipate and plan for them. They respond to them when they occur. They also recognize that resilience is an essential part of bold leadership because it plays an important role in understanding, measuring, and analyzing risks.

Resilience, defined by *Webster's Encyclopedic Unabridged Dictionary* as "the ability to recover readily from illness, depression, adversity, or the like," plays a twofold role in knowing what we want. First, as resilient leaders, we tend to be proactive so we can anticipate and plan for impediments, thus helping us to overcome objections and enlist support. Second, once we have decided what we want, our resilience helps keep us from giving up when we confront obstacles.

Harriet Tubman personified the resilient leader. Every time she overcame one obstacle, she confronted a new one. Even when she had seen slavery abolished, she looked for and found new challenges and encountered a different set of impediments. Her resilience enabled her to keep pushing forward regardless of the setbacks and adversity she faced. Her resilience made her the leader she was.

THE POWER OF KNOWING WHAT YOU WANT

It is inconceivable that we would follow someone who didn't know what she wanted. This doesn't mean we will only follow a leader with perfect clarity or precision, but it does mean that we should expect a general sense of direction and purpose. Whether our timeframe is the next month, the next week, or even the next hour, leadership means knowing what we want to accomplish.

We may find ourselves in situations where we are working for someone who doesn't know what he wants. He may have the authority to make us do as he asks, but he is not truly leading. This seems self-evident, but far too often, when we are in leadership roles, we fail to invest sufficient time and energy in understanding and articulating what we want. Because of this failure, our ability to lead is limited. Our wants can shift. Our plans may be erratic. Our goals and objectives may seem disjointed. Our ability to lead is directly related to our understanding of what we want. The clearer the picture, the easier it is for us to convince others of the quality and soundness of our plans.

As you read the next four chapters consider the importance of each attribute. Think about how they complement and support one another. Also, contemplate the importance of knowing who you are and what you believe in understanding your wants and desires.

How does your self-awareness increase your awareness of the world around you, and how does this increased awareness help you see what needs to be done? Your awareness of the problems, challenges, and opportunities around you will help you understand and prioritize what you want.

CHAPTER 5

Abraham Lincoln's Ambition: The Will to Make the World and Yourself What You Want Them to Be

Yours is the Earth and everything that's in it,
And—which is more—you'll be a Man, my son!

LINCOLN'S AMBITION

Abraham Lincoln had an unromantic recollection of his childhood. He once said, "It can all be condensed into a simple sentence: the short and simple annals of the poor. That's my life, and that's all you or anyone else can make of it." Fortunately, his humble beginnings generated in him a powerful ambition. This ambition in a lesser man could have become a selfish or even a dangerous force. In Abraham Lincoln, it generated greatness.

Lincoln's ambition fueled his success, and it changed America. Many historians would argue that it changed the world. It allowed him to achieve the power and position needed to preserve the Union and end slavery. No one, not even Lincoln himself, could have anticipated his success or influence.

What differentiated Lincoln's ambition from the ambition of lesser leaders? Lincoln understood the importance of balancing two powerful and potentially competing forces: personal ambition, the desire for personal advancement; and societal ambition, the desire to advance a cause. He was always motivated to better himself. Yet for most of his life, his personal desire for advancement and achievement yielded to his desire to improve the world around him.

Lincoln's personal ambition is understandable, given his childhood of privation. He was born on February 12, 1809, to Thomas Lincoln and Nancy Hanks, uneducated subsistence farmers. He grew up in a series of one-room log cabins in Kentucky and Indiana. During his childhood and early adulthood, Lincoln longed to escape poverty. As a youth, he swore he would never follow in his father's footsteps.

Lincoln's first endeavor to fulfill his ambition was his education. He was largely self-taught. Political pamphlets describing Lincoln stated, "The aggregate of all his schooling did not amount to one year." He left his family home with what he described as the basics of "readin', writin', and cipherin'." His real education started in 1830, at the age of twenty-one, when he arrived in New Salem, Illinois. Lincoln's first educational pursuit was grammar. He considered his greatest obstacle to fulfilling his ambition to be his inability to communicate clearly, effectively, and properly. Lincoln was a prolific reader, but he was very selective about what he read. He focused on subjects that would best serve his vocational interests: surveying, commerce, and the law.

Lincoln willingly undertook a variety of jobs to make his living and advance his goals. He lived much of his early adult life on the edge of insolvency but was always able to find work to stay afloat. As with his education, Lincoln worked hard at every job. These included working on a riverboat, managing a store, serving as a postmaster, commanding soldiers, surveying, and practicing law. He discovered early in life that the law and politics were his ultimate destiny.

Lincoln gained experience in his early jobs that would prove invaluable to him as a lawyer and politician. His work as a storekeeper and surveyor introduced him to his future clients and constituents. His work as postmaster provided him an endless supply of newspapers and other material to expand his education. His short stint as a soldier proved exceptionally important. It gave him credibility within his community. It also gave him one of his earliest political victories. In those days, the militia elected their leaders, and Lincoln's company overwhelmingly elected him commander.

In 1832, at the age of twenty-three, Lincoln's ambition led him into politics. He lost his first election, but he gained important experience. He ran again in 1834, and he won a seat in the Illinois House of Representatives. His first term was primarily educational, and it laid a foundation for him to emerge as a leader in the Illinois legislature. At this time, he also began to define himself politically. During these early years, Lincoln established some of his most important

political relationships, both allies and enemies, including his relationship with his future nemesis, Stephen Douglas.

Lincoln had an active and successful career in the Illinois House
of Representatives, but after four terms, he grew bored. His ambition was not being satisfied. He left office in 1841 to focus on his
legal career. He had built a solid law practice while serving in the
legislature, but it blossomed over the next fifteen years. Lincoln became one of the most successful and wealthy attorneys in Illinois.

Lincoln never truly left politics, always yearning to have an impact on Illinois and national Whig politics. In 1846, he was elected
to his first and only term in the United States Congress. Lincoln
had mixed results at the national political level. The most important
outcome of his congressional term was that it began to introduce
Lincoln to the American electorate. He gained notoriety by taking
principled stands on several contentious issues. His vocal opposition to the Mexican-American War was particularly unpopular. His
political opponents used this issue against him for the remainder
of his career. On issues like slavery, Lincoln was more successful.
During his single term in Congress, he established himself as a
strong advocate for antislavery and Unionist issues.

After leaving Congress, Lincoln remained a prominent political figure. Despite his relative youth, Lincoln assumed the role of
elder statesman. He spent his political energy trying to revive the
dying Whig party and championing its causes. The pivotal event
that aroused Lincoln's ambitions and passion was the passage of
the Kansas-Nebraska Act of 1854. Lincoln had long opposed the expansion of slavery, and this act undercut the compromises that had
restricted slavery's growth.

In response to the Kansas-Nebraska Act, Lincoln entered the
United States Senate race of 1856. He didn't win the senate race,
but he emerged stronger politically. During the campaign, he recognized that the antislavery candidates were dividing their support.
He withdrew from the race and threw his support behind a fellow
antislavery candidate, Lyman Trumbull. This selfless act ensured
that Lincoln's cause was successful, despite his personal failure. This
action also built his standing within the antislavery movement and

began to reveal that his societal ambitions trumped his personal ambitions.

In the mid-1850s, Lincoln became a founding member of the Illinois Republican Party, the party most aligned with ending slavery. Republicans considered him a potential vice presidential candidate in 1856. In 1858, Lincoln made another bid for the US Senate in an attempt to unseat Senator Stephen A. Douglas. Again, Lincoln lost, and again, he emerged from the loss stronger politically.

The campaign made him a national celebrity, largely because of the now famous Lincoln-Douglas Debates. Douglas was the most powerful member of the Senate. He was also the architect of the Kansas-Nebraska Act, one of the most divisive laws of the nineteenth century. The debates showed that Lincoln was a political force. They proved that he was the equal of any politician. During the campaign, Lincoln was composed and well spoken regardless of the intensity or hostility of the debates.

Had Lincoln defeated Douglas, he probably would not have been elected president in 1860. Lincoln's unlikely election as president came from years of dogged determination. Countless historians have told the story of Lincoln's greatness as president. His leadership saved the Union, ended slavery, and forever changed the role of the federal government. His ambition drove him. He was constantly striving to better himself and the world around him. He was also lucky. He was the right person at the right time and place to accomplish extraordinary feats. Had he been even slightly less ambitious, he likely would have achieved personal and professional success. Fortunately, Lincoln's overarching ambition propelled him to achieve the unimaginable.

ABRAHAM LINCOLN TIMELINE: THE SEEDS OF AMBITION

➤ **1809:** Born February 12 in Nolin Creek, Kentucky

➤ **1830:** Moved to Illinois with his family; delivered his first political speech

➤ **1831:** Left home to settle in New Salem, Illinois, to work as a clerk

➤ **1832:** Ran for and lost his first political office (in the Illinois legislature); enlisted to fight in the Black Hawk War; opened a store in New Salem

➤ **1833:** Went into debt, with his partner, when his store failed; appointed postmaster of New Salem; appointed deputy county surveyor

➤ **1834:** Elected to the Illinois legislature; began studying law

➤ **1836:** Reelected to the Illinois legislature; received license to practice law

➤ **1846:** Elected to the US House of Representatives

➤ **1849:** Left politics to practice law in Springfield, Illinois

➤ **1855:** Returned to politics but lost his US Senate race by withdrawing to support an antislavery ally

➤ **1856:** Assisted in the formation of the new Republican Party of Illinois

➤ **1859:** Lost second run for US Senate to Stephen A. Douglas; gained national recognition for the Lincoln-Douglas Debates

➤ **1860:** Nominated as Republican presidential candidate over better-known and more experienced competitors; elected sixteenth US president; seven states seceded in response

➤ **1861:** Inaugurated as president; an attack on Fort Sumter marks the start of the Civil War

➤ **1861–1865:** American Civil War

➤ **1863:** Issued the Emancipation Proclamation; issued Proclamation of Amnesty and Reconstruction

➤ **1864:** Reelected president

➤ **1865:** Delivered second inaugural address, encouraging reconciliation and restoration of the Union; Civil War ended; assassinated at Ford's Theater in Washington, DC

THE NATURE OF AMBITION

We have a love-hate relationship with ambition. Our conversations and small talk reveal how important it is to us. Regardless of the setting, ambition permeates our conversations. We ask small children, "What are you going to be when you grow up?" We ask students, "What do you plan to study in college?" We ask acquaintances, "What do you do for a living?" We ask those at the end of their careers, "What will you do in retirement?" These questions reveal our obsession with achievement and ambition.

Yet ambition has become almost a dirty word these days. While researching this book, I found that many of those I interviewed believed most leaders today overemphasize ambition. Many felt that this was an attribute to be discouraged. I respectfully ignored this advice and included it as an essential leadership element. In fact, I would rank ambition among the most important attributes for effective leadership. Without ambition, leaders would likely squander the benefits of their other attributes.

Like many of the other attributes described in this book, ambition is neither good nor bad in itself. An individual's nature determines its benefit or harm. Our nature influences our motivations, which in turn drive our actions. We must ask ourselves, "For the sake of what am I ambitious?" The answer to that question goes a long way in determining ambition's goodness or badness. If we aspire to greatness for the sake of ego, wealth, or personal gain, our ambition is unlikely to be a long-term positive force. If we seek first to improve the world around us, we increase our potential for sustained constructive outcomes.

What is ambition? Ambition is defined as "an ardent desire for rank, fame, or power; and a desire to achieve a particular end." This definition, when applied to an individual or a self-serving cause, is an unappealing attribute in a leader; generally, the desire for rank, fame, or power is self-serving. The phrase "a desire to achieve a particular end," however, begins to reveal the potential for something greater. This introduces an important distinction—personal ambition versus societal ambition.

Kipling's words speak to both types of ambition. He writes, "Yours is the Earth and everything that's in it, and—which is more—you'll be a man my son!" The order of his words matters. He is first speaking about our societal ambitions: "Yours is the Earth." This is not about control or power. It is about stewardship and accountability. His words challenge us to act on those societal ambitions that spring from our values and beliefs. While the word "earth" comes first, he is not telling us to ignore or dismiss our personal ambition. Rather, his words remind us that true personal achievement comes from doing what matters most.

Societal ambition does not preclude personal gain and accomplishment. Leaders with strong societal ambition are likely to have strong personal ambition as well. Lincoln's success shows that societal ambition can be personally rewarding. He transformed himself from a penniless social misfit to president of the United States in less than thirty years; and along the way, he became one of the wealthiest men in Illinois.

But societal ambition does not guarantee that the ambition is beneficial or noble. Many would argue that despots like Hitler, Stalin, and Pol Pot possessed strong societal ambition. Their goals focused on fundamentally changing the world in which they lived; however, those changes were rooted in hatred and immorality. Societal ambition is a product of our values and beliefs; therefore, the nature of our results is likely to depend on the nature of our character. Many of Lincoln's critics believed that his ambition was driven by a flawed set of values. History has proven the contrary.

The combination of personal and societal ambition enables leaders to achieve extraordinary results. What compels people to follow leaders? In large measure, it comes down to a leader's ability to demonstrate that their societal ambition outweighs their personal ambition. We have all seen leaders who espouse lofty goals to make fundamental improvements to our world. We become disillusioned and jaded when their personal ambition causes them to cut corners or abandon their principles. We lose confidence in leaders whose actions exhibit a disregard for the needs of others. True greatness comes from achieving one's personal and professional goals while working toward meeting the needs of others and accomplishing something greater than one's self.

Ambitious leaders typically have a fundamentally positive attitude about the future. Lincoln was optimistic about himself and his prospects. He desired rank, power, and wealth—and he believed in his ability to achieve those things. He was also optimistic about his country and its unrealized potential. He sought the preservation of the Union, the end of slavery, and the extension of universal human rights and freedom. Lincoln's life and accomplishments show the power of both personal and societal ambition. His actions—especially later in life—reveal that his societal ambitions were more important to him than his personal ambitions. This distinction helps distinguish Lincoln from other less effective leaders.

LINCOLN'S LESSONS

Leaders are typically ambitious. It is hard to imagine anyone following someone who isn't. It is equally hard to imagine someone whose ambitions are purely personal maintaining a sustained following. Lincoln is the ideal leader to illustrate the importance and power of ambition. His ability to integrate his personal and societal ambitions made him one of the greatest presidents in American history. He knew what he wanted for himself, and he knew equally well what he wanted for his country. Lincoln's balance of personal and societal ambition drove him to achieve personal success and historical greatness. How can we apply the lessons of Abraham Lincoln's ambition to our own experiences as leaders?

1. ***Abraham Lincoln taught the importance of discovering and understanding what we want.*** Lincoln knew what he wanted—and what he didn't want. Early in life, his foremost ambition was escaping poverty. He knew that the best way to do that was to earn his living by using his mind. When he left home at the age of twenty-one, he swore he would never pursue his father's career as a farmer and carpenter. Later in life, as his political career took off, his ambitions broadened. Over time, Lincoln became committed to ending slavery and preserving the Union. He knew what he wanted for himself and for

society. Similarly, we must know what we want. Like Lincoln, we may experiment to find what we want. We may set goals and then change them as we come to fully understand our ambition. Over time, we too may learn what we want to achieve and how we want to change the world around us.

2. ***Lincoln demonstrated the power of connecting personal ambition with societal ambition.*** Lincoln's personal desires for financial success and social advancement also served his overarching societal ambitions. His professional success allowed him to effectively promote his causes. Our own ambition will have some purely personal elements; no one can fault us for striving to better ourselves. However, our ability to lead will depend on our ability to inspire and motivate others. People will want to follow us if they see that we are working to achieve something meaningful. This brings us back to knowing who we are and what we believe. By linking our personal and societal goals, we can more effectively enlist others in our cause.

3. ***Lincoln exploited his talents and acquired the skills he needed to achieve his ambitions.*** Abraham Lincoln was highly intelligent; he was a master storyteller; and he possessed a methodical and logical mind. These and other skills helped him become a successful lawyer and politician. At the same time, Lincoln worked tirelessly to acquire the skills he lacked. He read constantly. Lincoln sought and accepted help when he needed it. He pushed himself physically, intellectually, and emotionally. His greatness came from applying his talents and newly acquired skills to his understanding and addressing the challenges he encountered.

In seeking to achieve our ambitions, we must ask ourselves what skills are required to achieve our goals. How do we hone the skills we have? What can we do to develop those we lack? Should we choose to enlist the help of others? Our success in achieving our goals is dependent on our ability to use what we have and obtain what we lack. This requires a high degree of awareness and a willingness to choose the courses of action we should take.

4. *Lincoln surpassed others who appeared to be more qualified.* On several occasions, Lincoln undertook roles even when he was not the ideal candidate. There were many occasions when Lincoln acted when others were more qualified, both on paper and in reality. Lincoln even took on jobs for which he was downright unqualified. Like many great leaders, Lincoln would not allow inexperience to stand in the way of achieving his ambitions. Whether it was taking a load of goods down the Mississippi River without any knowledge of the river, or drafting legal documents before he had studied the law, Lincoln never shied from a new challenge. The best example of this was his nomination and election as president in 1860. Lincoln acknowledged during the early days of the campaign that there were others in his party who were more qualified. William Seward, Salmon Chase, and Edward Bates all had résumés far stronger than Lincoln's. But Lincoln recognized that their qualifications alone were not sufficient to win. Lincoln's personal ambitions and his ambitions for his party and its causes propelled him ahead of those more qualified candidates.

There may be times when we fear that we are not the most qualified or best-prepared candidates for various jobs. Our combination of skills and ambition, however, may make us the best candidates. We may recognize this ourselves, or others may see it. Our advancement may place us in awkward situations. Like Lincoln, we may find ourselves leading people who are jealous or disdainful. We may even find ourselves leading a former boss or mentor.

5. *Lincoln enlisted both friends and foes to help him achieve his ambitions.* Doris Kearns Goodwin's book, *Team of Rivals*, exposes this extraordinary talent. Lincoln surrounded himself with the best and brightest, including his rivals. Of his top six cabinet posts, three appointments went to his principle

adversaries for the Republican nomination: Seward, Chase, and Bates. The remaining appointments went to three prominent Democrats. All six men had far more experience than Lincoln, and they all shared deep misgivings about Lincoln and his prospects. Lincoln's success in molding his rivals into a powerful and effective team is remarkable. Lincoln subordinated his personal feelings and uncertainties to advance his societal ambitions.

At times, our ambitions may demand that we do difficult or even unpleasant things. Success will demand that we recruit the best people to help us. It is easy to enlist our friends. But how can we be like Lincoln and enlist our foes or rivals? What is standing in our way? Our ability to build bridges and restore relationships may be the difference between success and failure. The challenge is not just about overcoming our own misgivings. We must make our rivals *want* to join us. Lincoln's success came from his empathy and ability to appreciate the position of his former rivals. This let him connect with them and attract them to follow him.

Many historians consider Abraham Lincoln to be the greatest American president. His ambition propelled his success. His personal goals fueled his professional, social, and economic advancement. More importantly, his societal aims drove him to change the world in which he found himself. Throughout his life, Lincoln's ambition evolved and grew. Ultimately, he rooted his ambition in his beliefs and principles, and the outcome of this belief was fundamental change. He preserved the Union and ended slavery. He redefined the role of the federal government. Lincoln's ambition fostered a greatness that even he never imagined.

What is the true nature of our ambitions? Great leaders understand that they must be driven by something greater than their own success. In itself, ambition is neither good nor bad. It can drive us to attain exceptional results, including positive and lasting change. The key is to understand our ambitions and to balance our personal and our societal goals.

Everyday Ambition

Often, people will see things in us that we cannot or will not see in ourselves. Frequently, this is simply a matter of perspective, but it can also be a function of authority and credibility. The perspective and opinion of someone we trust and respect can help us see what we are capable of achieving. This awareness can help us define and articulate our ambition.

My daughter, Mary Kate, loves horses. She has been riding since she was eight years old. About the time she turned thirteen, she transformed herself from a rider into an equestrian. That was when she started believing that she was truly gifted. Before that, she knew she had solid skills and abilities, but she never gave any thought to competing. Whenever I asked her if she wanted to participate in horse shows, she would dismiss the suggestion or change the subject altogether.

The year before her transformation from rider to equestrian, Mary Kate became friends with the owner of the horses she rode regularly. The horses' owner and the barn manager began to comment on Mary Kate's talent. Mary Kate started riding with them three to four times each week, and their encouragement and praise finally began to sink in. Mary Kate started believing that she had the talent to compete. The next spring, she entered her first show and performed exceptionally well. This success further built her confidence and fueled her ambition.

Regardless of how well Mary Kate performs, she now knows that her success started with her decision to achieve something. Her ambition continues to evolve. She believes in herself and her abilities. She is driven to grow and learn, and she has started to push herself to excel. Recently she said, "I am excited about my riding, and I believe it will lead to something special."

Mary Kate's ambition started with an external catalyst. Someone she trusted and respected planted a seed. Her early success helped the seed sprout and grow. Her self-awareness and commitment will nurture and feed it as she refines her ambition and makes it "something special."

RECOMMENDED RESOURCES

Resources about Abraham Lincoln:

Lincoln by David Herbert Donald

Team of Rivals: The Political Genius of Abraham Lincoln by Doris
  Kearns Goodwin
*What Lincoln Believed: The Values and Convictions of America's
  Greatest President* by Michael Lind

Resources about Ambition:

*What Should I Do with My Life?: The True Story of People Who
  Answered the Ultimate Question* by Po Bronson
*The 7 Habits of Highly Effective People: Powerful Lessons in Personal
  Change* by Stephen Covey
Leadership Is an Art by Max De Pree

CHAPTER 6

Martin Luther King's Vision: The Power of Having and Sharing a Dream

If you can dream—and not make dreams your master;
If you can think—and not make thoughts your aim

KING'S VISION

Dr. Martin Luther King's "I Have a Dream" speech was much more than one of the greatest oratorical moments of our time. It was an articulation of his vision for the United States of America. It was his dream of what America could be. For many, the speech was an introduction to Dr. King's dream. For those most closely associated with King and the civil rights movement, this speech was not new. Many had heard all or parts of it before. "I Have a Dream" was important because it was the national debut of King's precious dream. King's dream transformed the civil rights struggles of the preceding decades into the civil rights *movement*. Before, there had been isolated examples of heroic efforts to fight discrimination, prejudice, disenfranchisement, exploitation, and racial violence. King's vision focused and unified the struggle.

King's vision was the achievement of civil rights and equality for all Americans through nonviolence. In the introduction to a collection of King's words titled *I Have a Dream: Writing and Speeches That Changed the World*, James M. Washington writes of King, "He stood for a world free of bigotry and brimming with faith, hope, love, and justice. He dared to dream of a better day in the midst of the nightmare that surrounded him. He dared to believe and sacrificed his life for a future that some believe we are beginning to occupy." King had embraced and articulated his vision years before the "I Have a Dream" speech, and it remained consistent throughout his struggle. Underlying his dream were a variety of goals, objectives, strategies, and initiatives to enable the realization of his vision. While these evolved and changed over time, his vision remained the same.

To fully appreciate and understand King's vision, one must understand the influences that informed and influenced it. Martin Luther King Jr. was born on January 15, 1929. He was the son, grandson, and great-grandson of clergy, and he chose to follow the family tradition. While his middle-class economic status shielded him from some of the worst conditions of segregated America, King felt the effects of discrimination and segregation. Growing up black in America in the 1930s and 1940s—especially in the South—virtually guaranteed a life of hardship, regardless of one's socioeconomic status. Jim Crow laws and social norms made all African Americans second-class citizens.

Dr. King's education was extraordinary for an African American of his day. He earned three degrees, including a PhD, and King's education laid the foundation for his civil rights work. As a student, he read and studied widely. His influences included his family, various Christian scholars and teachings, Gandhi, Thoreau, and Howard Thurman, a theologian and civil rights leader. King spent much of his education and early career reconciling and aligning his spiritual and secular beliefs and influences. Many of these influences can be heard in his words. King's commitment to nonviolence came directly from Christianity, Gandhi, and Thoreau, while his commitment to economic equality, civil rights, and social justice stemmed from his many academic and secular influences.

In 1955, just prior to completing his education, King accepted the position of pastor at the Dexter Avenue Baptist Church in Montgomery, Alabama. His timing was perfect. He arrived to a community in desperate need of his leadership. His education, his position in the community, and his passion made him an ideal candidate to lead the Montgomery Improvement Association, which organized and supported the bus boycott stemming from Rosa Parks's case the previous year. This marked the formal beginning of Dr. King's leadership in the civil rights movement.

King's efforts helped lead to the successful desegregation of the Montgomery Bus Company. This victory led to more and bigger opportunities as he emerged as a civil rights leader. He addressed the national convention of the National Association for the Advancement of Colored People (NAACP) in 1955. He formed and was elected president of the Southern Christian Leadership Conference in 1957. He was instrumental in the formation of the Student Nonviolent Coordinating Committee in 1960.

King began to speak and publish widely. His vision crystallized during these early leadership years. Much of the content and the most familiar quotations from his "I Have a Dream" speech can be found in his writings between 1955 and 1961. King revealed his personal commitment during these early years. He was arrested on numerous occasions. His life, his family, and his friends were threatened. His home was bombed. The media and his fellow clergy criticized and defamed him. He almost died when a would-be assassin stabbed him. In spite of these trials—or perhaps because of them—King's vision took root and flourished.

The importance of the "I Have a Dream" speech was its ability to motivate a large and diverse group. Prior to the speech, many Americans viewed the civil rights movement as a southern issue. They saw civil rights leaders as radicals and troublemakers. Following King's speech, Americans began to see discrimination and segregation as national evils, not just a southern or a black problem. Dr. King continued to reiterate this vision until his assassination in 1968, and most of his followers remained true to his vision as they continued his struggle after his death.

The power of King's vision was proven by the successes he and the civil rights movement achieved. His vision motivated and compelled fundamental change, including the integration of the Montgomery Bus Company in 1956, the Civil Rights Act of 1957, the integration of the universities of Mississippi and Alabama, the dismantling of Birmingham's discrimination laws, the Civil Rights Act of 1964, the Voting Rights Act of 1965, and the elimination of Jim Crow laws all through the South. And these are just some of the legal changes King's dream set in motion. There have been equally important societal and economic gains that are less easily measured. King's vision laid the foundation for a generation of change, and it changed America.

MARTIN LUTHER KING JR. TIMELINE: THE PATH TO A DREAM

- ➤ **1929:** Born in Atlanta, Georgia
- ➤ **1948:** Graduated from Morehouse College and entered Crozer Theological Seminary; ordained as a minister
- ➤ **1953:** Married Coretta Scott; moved to Montgomery, Alabama; appointed pastor of the Dexter Avenue Baptist Church
- ➤ **1955:** Received a PhD from Boston University; joined Montgomery bus boycott; elected president of the Montgomery Improvement Association
- ➤ **1957:** Formed the Southern Christian Leadership Conference; spoke to a crowd of 15,000 in Washington, DC; first used "My Country 'Tis of Thee" lyrics in a speech
- ➤ **1958:** Witnessed passage of the first Civil Rights Act; published first book, *Stride Toward Freedom*; stabbed and nearly killed; met with President Dwight D. Eisenhower
- ➤ **1959:** Visited India to study Gandhi's philosophy of nonviolence
- ➤ **1960:** Arrested during a sit-in and sentenced to four months in jail; helped found the Student Nonviolent Coordinating Committee
- ➤ **1961:** Federal government banned segregation for interstate travel
- ➤ **1962:** Arrested and jailed in Albany, Georgia
- ➤ **1963:** Arrested in Birmingham, Alabama; wrote "Letter from Birmingham Jail"; led the March on Washington and delivered his "I Have a Dream" speech to 250,000 attendees
- ➤ **1964:** Named *Time* magazine's Man of the Year; passage of the Civil Rights Act of 1964; awarded the Nobel Peace Prize
- ➤ **1965:** Arrested in Selma, Alabama; passage of Voting Rights Act
- ➤ **1968:** Assassinated in Memphis, Tennessee

THE ESSENCE OF VISION

Dreaming and thinking big are essential to leadership; they are the keys to creating a compelling vision for others to follow. All of the leaders in this book, in fact all *true* leaders, have the ability to articulate their visions for the future. Vision is the ability to see things as they could be, not as they are. Kipling clearly understood the importance of vision—his words encouraged us to dream and think—but he also understood that a true vision compels action. It must drive change. Poets and philosophers can enjoy the luxury of dreaming and thinking for their own sake. Leaders cannot.

There are innumerable descriptions of what it means to lead, but every leadership theory has vision at its core. It does not matter what we call it: vision, dream, aspiration, cause, or mission. What matters is that it has certain essential elements. A vision expresses a desire to do something meaningful. It describes a future that is different from—and presumably better than—the present. It gives a leader's followers a general idea of the direction he or she will take, and a vision demonstrates a leader's personal commitment.

Consider vision in the context of a journey. Our vision says where we want to be, why we want to be there, how we can best get there, and what is required to reach our destination. When Meriwether Lewis and William Clark started their voyage of discovery, they knew that they were seeking a route to the Pacific across North America. They understood that this would open the West to Americans and strengthen the nation's position and standing on the continent. They knew, presumed, or hypothesized certain key facts about how they would get there—the general route they would take, the modes of transportation they would likely use, and the resources they would need. Finally, they became the personal embodiment of their vision: they committed themselves completely.

What prompts us to take our vision beyond the realm of thought and into the real world? Most people have visions, but for many, their visions never leave their heads. We think, "Wouldn't the world be better if . . . ?" This is where the vision ends; it is never stated, and it compels no one to act.

Compelling visions generate energy, excitement, and passion.

They are communicated clearly and consistently. They are repeated often, and they are spoken with excitement. They cause others to embrace them as their own. They drive us to take action and to invest ourselves in making them real. A compelling vision motivates ordinary people to do extraordinary things. Truly compelling visions inspire entire organizations or even societies to align behind them and act.

KING'S LESSONS

Each of us is motivated and inspired by our own dreams. Dr. Martin Luther King Jr.'s dream went beyond being his personal dream and became the vision for the civil rights movement. This vision changed America and influenced leaders around the world. King's vision—his dream—helped others to broaden and expand their own dreams and even make their own dreams real. The "I Have a Dream" speech was a powerful articulation of a compelling vision. Leaders like King have the ability to dream and to articulate their vision in a way that draws us in. What can we learn from King?

1. ***King demonstrated the power of a compelling vision.*** He knew people needed a vision to follow to help sustain them during the struggle for civil rights. King's vision transformed a regional issue into a national cause. We all want to be a part of something important, and a compelling vision gives us something to which we can aspire. One of the most common complaints among employees is that they don't know what their organizations stand for. People need to know that what they are doing matters, and they must understand how their work fits into the bigger picture. This means that leaders at all levels should strive to articulate compelling visions. It is easy for a middle manager or other leader to believe that vision isn't part of the job. Many leaders sit back and wait for their CEO or others to provide the vision. But what if they don't? Or what if the vision they put forth doesn't speak to employees at all levels? Leaders within larger organizations have the challenge of putting the enterprise's vision into context.

Teams need something to connect them to the larger organization. A leader's vision provides that connection.

2. **King showed the importance of basing one's vision on values, beliefs, and principles.** King's life, his education, and his career were rooted in a belief system based on equality and justice. The power of King's vision came from the strength of his beliefs and convictions. Our vision should also reflect who we are and what we believe. Our passion for our vision will attract those we wish to lead. When we believe in our vision, people know it. And the virtue and merit of our beliefs will help determine the virtue and merit of our vision. Hitler, Pol Pot, and Stalin all had visions that were tied to their principles but lacked virtue. As with character, our vision must be rooted in morality. King's vision certainly was.

3. **King's vision spoke to both his core supporters and extended stakeholders.** King's vision first addressed his core constituents' needs. His message to them was simple: equality and the end of segregation are achievable, and nonviolence is the only option. Prior to this, many African Americans had lost hope. The discrimination, prejudice, segregation, and hatred they faced had beaten them into resignation. Others felt that the only response to violent discrimination was violent resistance. King knew that he must give hope to the hopeless while calming the more radical factions. At the same time, King knew he needed to allay the fears of groups like moderate whites and middle-class African Americans—his extended stakeholders.

    Our own vision should speak to the specific needs of both our core supporters and our extended stakeholders. To our base it must say, "Our leaders understand this problem, and here is a way to solve it." To the broader stakeholder group it must say, "This problem is bad for all of us, and this solution will fix it without causing us harm." Compelling visions speak first to the heart and then to the mind. They can motivate us to deliver extraordinary results. King's vision motivated his core to tolerate horrific violence and imprison-ment, while at the same time motivating his extended stake-holders to change laws and culture to end segregation and discrimination.

4. *King's vision revealed the power of being audacious while remain-ing credible.* Dr. King knew that his vision needed to be big and meaningful. He also recognized that it had to be believ-able. Achieving equality and the end of segregation through nonviolence was an audacious idea. But King painted a pic-ture that was both bold and achievable. King was able to build credibility by highlighting the successes of other nonviolent efforts like Gandhi's success, the *Brown v. Board of Education* decision, and the Montgomery bus boycott.

We must strive to find the right balance between big and believable when articulating a vision. We build credibility by proving our capacity to achieve what we propose, our appre-ciation of how big our vision is, and our awareness of what we will need to achieve it. We can assemble a team with the necessary skills, and we can use our past successes to build credibility. Finally, we can cultivate powerful allies and spon-sors to champion our shared cause. During the civil rights movement, King employed such allies. President Johnson and Robert Kennedy became supporters of King's dream. The credibility of our vision is just like our personal credibility—we must earn it.

5. *King showed the impact of a simple message repeated with convic-tion.* His words stuck. King's messages were amazingly clear. He stated the problem: inequality. He defined a solution: civil rights and the end of segregation and discrimination through nonviolence. He did not list all of the laws and regulations that had to change. He did not identify all barriers and ob-stacles that had to be removed. He kept successes in perspec-tive to reduce the risk of derailing the vision. His approach enabled King to keep his followers focused. It also prevented anyone from confusing individual actions with the broader

vision. He reused the same stories and sayings throughout his career. King first used the powerful lyrics from "My Country 'Tis of Thee" in 1957: "Let freedom ring from the prodigious hilltops of New Hampshire," he began. He spoke and wrote those words often. He may have tired of his own words, but as a preacher, King knew the power of repetition. We need to understand the same thing about our vision. We may begin to think we are sounding like a broken record. We must remember that people will need to hear our vision many times before it sinks in. Finally, we need to remember that simplicity keeps our message clear and memorable. Keep it simple, and keep repeating it.

King's dream mattered because it enabled him to motivate and inspire others to act. His thoughts were never his aim. Rather, they were tools that helped him destroy a corrupt and evil system. Like King, true leaders understand the importance of dreaming and thinking big. They heed Kipling's advice to dream and not make dreams your master and think and not make thoughts your aim.

As followers, we expect our leaders to deliver results. And as leaders, whether we are CEOs leading thousands to change industries or parents raising families, our dreams are what attract others to follow. When we speak with passion about what we believe and act on those beliefs, we touch the hearts of those we lead.

Everyday Vision

Fay Lohr is the CEO of FeedMore, Inc. Fay has a vision for ending hunger in Central Virginia, and FeedMore is the product of Fay's passion, born of that vision. Even the organization's name, FeedMore, speaks to Fay's vision. She has been working in human services for her entire career. She has done it all, from working in the trenches providing services to the needy, to leading fundamental change in the field of human services. I witnessed firsthand Fay's leadership when she led the implementation of Virginia's groundbreaking welfare reform program.

Fay became the CEO of the Central Virginia Food Bank in 2000. She took control of an organization in disarray and on the verge of insolvency and spent the next several years cleaning house. Under Fay's leadership, the Central Virginia Food Bank became one of the premier food banks in the country.

Fay focused on the greatest obstacles to her vision: inefficiency and ineffectiveness. She often expressed her frustration about the lack of discipline within many nonprofit organizations. She saw unacceptable overlap between charities working to solve identical problems. She lamented the fact that groups were fighting for the same limited funds and support. In 2005, Fay identified the perfect opportunity to address one such overlap. She proposed the merger of the food bank and Meals on Wheels in Central Virginia. Both organizations were planning significant investments in infrastructure, and much of that investment was duplicative. This was an ideal opening for collaboration, one with the potential to further Fay's vision of ending hunger.

Fay's idea met immediate and stiff resistance. Members of the boards of both organizations expressed concerns about the merger. They feared it would distract them from their missions. Fay was undaunted. She began to paint a picture for the organizations and their supporters of what they could accomplish together. She articulated a vision for a new organization that was greater than the sum of its parts. It took her nearly three years, but on July 1, 2008, FeedMore was born. Today FeedMore is doing more than anyone ever anticipated. Under Fay's leadership, FeedMore is moving toward its mission: to work to efficiently and effectively fight hunger and enhance lives in the local community.

RECOMMENDED RESOURCES

Resources about Dr. Martin Luther King Jr.:

Parting the Waters: America in the King Years, 1954–1963 by Taylor Branch

I Have a Dream: Writings and Speeches That Changed The World, by Martin Luther King, Jr., edited by James M. Washington

The Autobiography of Martin Luther King, Jr. by Martin Luther King Jr. and Clayborne Carson

Martin Luther King, Jr., on Leadership: Inspiration and Wisdom for Challenging Times by Donald T. Phillips

Resources about Vision:

Transforming Leadership by James MacGregor Burns

Harvard Business Review on Change by Harvard Business School
    Press

Made to Stick: Why Some Ideas Survive and Others Die by Chip Heath
    and Dan Heath

The Leadership Challenge by James Kouzes and Barry Posner

*Leading Out Loud: Inspiring Change Through Authentic
    Communications* by Terry Pearce

CHAPTER 7

Thomas Jefferson's Boldness: The Reward of Risking It All

If you can make one heap of all your winnings
And risk it on one turn of pitch-and-toss

JEFFERSON'S BOLDNESS

Imagine traveling west across the United States, only to find that the country ends at the Mississippi River. America's character, geography, and history would have been radically different had President Thomas Jefferson been less bold regarding the Louisiana Purchase. The story of the purchase defines strategic boldness. It started relatively small, but it became one of the greatest presidential decisions in US history.

The city of New Orleans was at the heart of the Louisiana Purchase. It was the tail that wagged the dog that was the Louisiana Territory. Jefferson and his administration entered the negotiations with France to acquire New Orleans and a small strip of territory along the western shore of the Mississippi. Instead, they more than doubled America's size, taking up territory that included the Great Plains and stretched as far west as Montana and Wyoming.

New Orleans sits at the mouth of the Mississippi River, and during Jefferson's time it controlled the fortunes of everything upriver. In 1800, when Thomas Jefferson was elected president, the United States was troubled about the ownership of New Orleans. The Mississippi River was one of America's two coasts. Americans had been settling the country east of the Mississippi for decades, and the settlers in this area had grown dependent on the Mississippi. This "western" American economy was contingent upon a free and open New Orleans.

In 1762, ownership of New Orleans had passed from France to Spain. In 1800, Spain secretly returned it to France under the terms of the Treaty of San Ildefonso. Americans had enjoyed the right to use New Orleans as a transshipment point for their goods, and the uncertainty regarding which European power controlled the city jeopardized that right. New Orleans in hostile hands would strangle America's economic growth. Jefferson knew he must resolve this uncertainty; his presidency and the country's future depended on the outcome. Having narrowly won the election of 1800, Jefferson realized this challenge would be a major test of his leadership and foreign policy.

At the time, America was weak compared to England and France, and the country had strained relations with both. In addition, Spain, although a waning power, was still a formidable adversary. All four countries had an interest in New Orleans. Thomas Jefferson and his secretary of state, James Madison, understood that America's only strength with regard to New Orleans was proximity. If hostilities were to erupt over New Orleans, America's only hope would be its ability to quickly move large numbers of soldiers and supplies to the fight. The length of European supply lines would jeopardize their own military superiority.

For much of 1801 and 1802, America and France had a series of discussions about New Orleans and other American concerns. These discussions failed to resolve the issues. Neither country was clear about what its true intentions were. The French government vacillated between wanting to establish a major French colony in the Louisiana Territory and the desire to sell the territory to help fund its wars with Great Britain. America desired to maintain its shipping rights. Unfortunately, neither Jefferson nor Madison could formulate a strategy that would best achieve this goal. Their positions ranged from waging war with France to purchasing New Orleans. They even contemplated an alliance with Great Britain that would allow the British to take control of the city.

During this period and into 1803, the American ambassador to France was Robert Livingston. Jefferson and Livingston had known each other since the Second Continental Congress in 1776. They had served on the committee that drafted the Declaration of Independence, and they were also members of the same political party. Unfortunately, despite all this, they did not trust one another. Madison shared Jefferson's mistrust of Livingston, and their relationship was often rocky. Jefferson and Madison retained Livingston in this key position out of fear that his removal would make America seem weak and indecisive. Ironically, the decision to retain Livingston did just that. Jefferson's failure to give Livingston clear direction or demonstrations of support actually undermined America's diplomatic position with France, as American interests were often poorly communicated to the French government.

By late 1802, Jefferson had decided that the best course of action was to purchase New Orleans from France. Not trusting Livingston to effectively negotiate this deal, Jefferson sent James Monroe, one of his most trusted political advisers, to France. Jefferson did not send Monroe to replace Livingston; Monroe's sole responsibility was to lead the negotiations to acquire New Orleans. Monroe was authorized to spend up to $10 million. At about the same time, Napoleon decided to sell the entire Louisiana Territory to the Americans. He hoped to raise between $15 million and $20 million to finance his military expenditures. Napoleon's price and the scope of the negotiations far exceeded Monroe's authority. Fortunately, Monroe recognized the outstanding opportunity and was prepared to act. Prior to dispatching Monroe to France, Jefferson and Madison had shared with him the details of their discussions and debates about Louisiana. He also knew Jefferson well enough to know that he would support Monroe's decision to exceed his authority and budget. This knowledge emboldened Monroe to act on this opportunity.

Some observers could argue that the Louisiana Purchase was a demonstration of Monroe's and Livingston's boldness, not Jefferson's. Certainly, they played important roles, but Jefferson was ultimately accountable and bore the risk of this boldness. It was his leadership that created the opportunity.

In many ways, the challenges of negotiating the treaty with France were minor compared to the obstacles that Jefferson and Monroe faced at home. First, while Jefferson had the constitutional authority to negotiate treaties, only the Senate was empowered to ratify them, and Jefferson was unsure whether he would obtain the necessary votes. He also lacked the funds to execute the deal. Assuming that the Senate ratified the treaty, Congress would still need to appropriate the funds to pay for it. Jefferson faced stiff opposition from the Federalists, and even some members of his own party expressed strong reservations. Congress remained justifiably concerned. The treaty's $15 million price tag was nearly double the entire 1803 federal budget.

Jefferson also had philosophical hurdles to overcome. He felt that France's claim to Louisiana was illegitimate, but by entering into negotiations for its purchase, he was legitimizing the French claim. He also feared that his actions would strengthen the federal government and the presidency. He fundamentally believed that both institutions had already become too strong.

In spite of the risks and concerns, Jefferson and his subordinates pressed on, and on April 30, 1803, Monroe and Livingston signed the treaty. Jefferson received it in Washington on July 3. As Jefferson had anticipated, opposition was strong and immediate. Many Federalists were outraged, and a group of northern states threatened secession over the treaty. Jefferson rallied support, and ultimately, Congress appropriated the funds. The Senate ratified the treaty on October 20 by an overwhelming majority. Meanwhile, many critics believed that the United States had overpaid for the territory, and others feared that the treaty would lead to war.

Supporters of the treaty recognized its monumental importance. Robert Livingston articulated this best following the signing of the treaty, declaring, "We have lived long, but this is the noblest work of our whole lives. . . . From this day the United States take their [sic] place among the powers of the first rank."

Jefferson's risk taking resulted in a major victory for America, but what if he had failed? Failure to ratify the treaty or fund the purchase would have been disastrous. It would have weakened already strained relations with France, which could have led to war. It would have likely cost Jefferson the next presidential election, and it could have rendered him politically impotent. Failure could have created a constitutional challenge that would have weakened America. The secessionist movement might have led to the dissolution of America. All these scenarios and many more were uncertainties that Jefferson had to contend with. He could have sought an easier and safer course in resolving the New Orleans problem. Had he done so, America's history would have been radically different.

Instead, Jefferson fully exploited the opportunity he faced. He confronted the many obstacles that were in his path. He overcame his own misgivings. He relied on a combination of his instincts and skills to "risk it on one turn"—and he won.

THOMAS JEFFERSON TIMELINE: THE BOLDNESS OF THE LOUISIANA PURCHASE

- ➤ **1762:** France ceded New Orleans and Louisiana west of the Mississippi to Spain
- ➤ **1783:** The Treaty of Paris ended the American Revolution and gave the United States free access to the Mississippi River
- ➤ **1784:** Spain closed the lower Mississippi and New Orleans
- ➤ **1795:** Spain reopened the Mississippi and New Orleans to Americans
- ➤ **1800:** Spain secretly agreed to return Louisiana to France; Jefferson was elected president
- ➤ **1801:** Jefferson, concerned about the status of the Mississippi River and New Orleans, ordered Livingston to France to assess the situation and authorized him to purchase New Orleans
- ➤ **1802:** Spain ceded Louisiana back to France; New Orleans was closed to American shipping
- ➤ **1803:**
  - ➤ **January:** Jefferson sent James Monroe to France to take over the negotiations to resolve the New Orleans crisis; Jefferson authorized Monroe to spend up to $10 million to acquire New Orleans
  - ➤ **April:** The French government proposed to Livingston the sale of the entire Louisiana Territory; Monroe arrived in Paris and joined negotiations; Monroe and Livingston signed the treaty
  - ➤ **July:** Monroe returned to Washington with the treaty; Jefferson announced the treaty
  - ➤ **October:** Senate ratified the treaty

➤ **December:** France transferred New Orleans to American control

THE ESSENCE OF BOLDNESS AND RISK TAKING

Consider Kipling's words: "If you can make one heap of all your winnings and risk it on one turn of pitch-and-toss." He was suggesting that there are times when we must be willing to take huge risks—to wager a great deal for the sake of a greater good. He was not saying one should risk everything. A judicious risk taker always keeps his stake so he can start again. Kipling's choice of the game pitch-and-toss (that is, pitching pennies) is also telling. While it is no longer popular, it was a common pastime for schoolchildren, requiring both skill and luck. Players toss a coin at a wall, aiming to have the coin land as close as possible to it. No matter how skilled one is, minor imperfections on the throwing surface can materially change the results. Had Kipling chosen a game like chess, where one's skill and intellect are the deciding factors, this line of the poem would have a completely different meaning. Kipling understood that leadership requires us to take chances. It requires each of us to be a bit of a gambler.

Risk taking is essential to individual and organizational growth, change, innovation, and excellence. An organization that stops taking risks will stop maturing and advancing. Any organization that stops advancing will die. At the same time, risk must be assessed judiciously. A leader must be able to assess a given risk's benefits compared to its potential penalties or costs. These, however, are rarely quantified easily, and the uncertainty and imprecision of risk taking can be daunting for many leaders.

We often think of boldness and the quantification of risk in today's terms. We take for granted the resources and tools that allow us to calculate probability. Jefferson and other leaders of his day lacked even some of the most basic instruments to measure the risks they faced. It would be more than 100 years before gaming techniques and other risk tools that are integral to modern risk assessment were invented. These tools and resources come with their own challenges. Today, leaders often overanalyze problems or rely too heavily on models. The right tools for measuring and understanding risk can be invaluable, but they cannot replace sound judgment.

What constitutes good risk taking, and how can leaders position themselves to take appropriate risks? Like so many other leadership attributes, risk tolerance is directly tied to one's personal beliefs and values as well as the beliefs and values of one's organization. Understanding these tolerances is critical to managing risks.

JEFFERSON'S LESSONS

Our boldness will determine the risks we are willing to take. Jefferson's life was full of bold and often risky acts. His authorship of the Declaration of Independence marked him as a prime target for the British during the American Revolution. Many of his strongest political stands put him at odds with former colleagues. Whether the Louisiana Purchase was his greatest act of boldness is debatable, but it did represent a huge gamble for Jefferson and the fledgling United States. Fortunately, this risk paid off.

How can we learn from Jefferson's understanding of risk and from his boldness? As leaders, how can we apply these lessons and hone our skills to improve the quality of our decision making? How can we increase the likelihood that the risks we take will ultimately be rewarded?

1. ***Jefferson saw opportunities that others missed.*** Jefferson and Madison invested themselves sufficiently to understand the details of the New Orleans problem that confronted them. They explored every conceivable option. They did not accept conventional wisdom or approach the issue as a tactical problem. This perspective allowed Jefferson and Madison to turn a problem into an opportunity. On its surface, the situation was an opportunity to make incremental improvements to the status quo. They could have responded by focusing solely on solving the immediate problem of shipping rights. Instead, they thought strategically and considered the long term implications. They understood that their problem required a

permanent solution; and a permanent solution required them to examine the problem completely and to weigh the myriad possibilities, even unconventional options: alliances, war, new treaties, financial incentives, and so on.

As leaders, we have many opportunities to act boldly. Our risks pale compared with those Jefferson took, but they are still important. It is easy to get stuck in the status quo or in incremental solutions. As leaders we must explore beyond the known options and see opportunities that others—especially our competitors—miss.

2. *Jefferson objectively assessed the relative strengths and weaknesses of his options.* Forging new alliances would have been an easy solution. America could have picked France or England to become its protector. Jefferson, however, understood that any such alliance would put America at a strategic disadvantage. War would have been bloody and costly. If America were to lose, it would jeopardize its independence. Ultimately, Jefferson reached the decision to buy the Louisiana Territory as a way to permanently eliminate the risk to America's interests on the Mississippi River. He recognized that the benefits of a negotiated purchase outweighed the risks.

Our ability to objectively vet options is essential to effective risk taking. It is easy to see one answer as the best, especially when it is our own. Great leaders have the ability to see the weaknesses in their own ideas while seeing the strengths in those of others. We must give some thought to what prevents us from objectively assessing the options to our greatest challenges.

We now have tools, which Jefferson lacked, that allow us to measure and understand risk. We take for granted our ability to calculate the likelihood of an outcome, yet Jefferson didn't even know that such calculations existed. In his book *Against the Gods*, Peter Bernstein explores the history of risk and people's ability to quantify it. His work provides important lessons about understanding and managing risk.

3. *Jefferson seized the opportunities presented to him.* Jefferson identified the options and fully vetted them, but he didn't stop there. He had the strength, wisdom, and boldness to act on his ideas. This lesson begins to delve into the realm of courage, which we will discuss fully in chapter 10. Risk taking requires action. Jefferson identified the best course of action, and he decisively executed it. It is easy for leaders to engage in analysis paralysis. True leadership means having the guts to make a decision. Making a choice and taking action—or deciding that the best choice is no further action—is where the risk becomes tangible.

4. *Jefferson leveraged others and empowered them to act.* When James Monroe arrived in Paris to begin negotiations, he learned that the French had made a shocking offer. France would sell the entire Louisiana Territory for $15 million. This was a fantastic opportunity. America would be paying less than three cents per acre. Monroe knew that he had to act quickly. Napoleon's mercurial nature meant that if Monroe delayed while awaiting authorization he might jeopardize the agreement. Monroe chose to act because he knew that he had Jefferson's confidence and that Jefferson would support his action. Their mutual trust was based on their long and tested relationship. All through the process, Jefferson's actions were informed by the wisdom and experience of both friend and foe alike.

     As leaders, we must learn to leverage others in this same way, and we must know when and how to effectively empower others to act. Do we have confidence in those we lead? If so, do they know that we trust them to act appropriately and to use their own judgment? How can we expect others to seize the opportunities they confront if they do not know that we will support their actions? How well do our followers know us and our priorities? The better they know us, the greater the likelihood that they will act as we would want them to when faced with ambiguity. Similarly, how comfortable are we, when not in defined leadership roles, in assuming authority that isn't clearly ours? While others may judge us for overstepping our authority or for using poor judgment, they may also judge us for our failure to act. Balancing the risks is difficult. It is also at the heart of leadership.

5. ***Jefferson took action in the face of ambiguity.*** In the absence of clear authority, Jefferson took control. Jefferson knew that he had no legal basis for his actions. Equally important, his action required him to test his own beliefs. Leaders understand that unanticipated events occur. We often face uncertainty regarding our authority or boundaries. In these situations, the easy answer is to defer action or take the path of least resistance. Jefferson understood that action meant claiming authority that was not explicitly his. This decision alone required boldness. Once he assumed authority, he used it decisively.

The Louisiana Purchase proved to be one of the greatest decisions in American history. It could have easily turned out differently. Rather than being a major step toward making America a great nation, the purchase could have been the event that destroyed it in its infancy. What is certain is that America's history would have been radically different had Jefferson or his subordinates moved less boldly and taken a safer path.

Everyday Boldness

Every day, we confront opportunities that force us to assess risks and make decisions that reveal our boldness—or lack thereof. The risks we face will likely never be as great as those that Jefferson faced. They may even seem insignificant or trivial. Some, however, will be memorable and will have lasting implications, especially for those we lead.

In January 1957, at the end of the first semester of his plebe year, my father failed out of the United States Naval Academy. Although my father was highly intelligent, he had been unprepared for the school's academic rigor. His high school curriculum had prepared him to be a bookkeeper or clerk, not a naval officer. My father had never intended to go to college. He was from a poor working-class neighborhood where finishing high school was a measure of academic distinction.

After high school, my father had enlisted in the navy, and in 1955, he received a fleet appointment to the Naval Academy after his officers identified him as having the potential to become an officer. But after that first semester, because he had failed two classes, he was going home in disgrace.

Fortunately, my father was on the Naval Academy crew team, and he had made an impression on his coach, Lieutenant Commander Davidson. My father was not the best athlete on the team, but he was dedicated. He worked hard, inspired and motivated his teammates, and provided strong leadership to the team. His coach saw his potential, so he took a risk for my father. Davidson convinced the commandant of midshipmen to allow my father to retake the exams he had failed. In so doing, Davidson risked his reputation and jeopardized his own position.

The commandant approved the reexaminations, and my father passed both. He avoided expulsion from the Naval Academy. He graduated with the class of 1960, and he served his country with distinction for thirty years. His life was changed by one man's ability to see something in my father that was worth fighting for. Davidson had seized the opportunity that was before him. He might not have known the long-term impact of his bold action—my father did.

RECOMMENDED RESOURCES

Resources about Thomas Jefferson:

Thomas Jefferson by R. B. Bernstein

Jefferson's Great Gamble: The Remarkable Story of Jefferson, Napoleon and the Men Behind the Louisiana Purchase by Charles A. Cerami

American Sphinx: The Character of Thomas Jefferson by Joseph J. Ellis

Resources about Boldness:

Against the Gods: The Remarkable Story of Risk by Peter Bernstein

The Innovator's Dilemma: When New Technologies Cause Great Firms to Fail by Clayton M. Christensen

Strategic Analysis and Action by Mary Crossan, Joseph Fry, J. Peter
    Killing, and Michael Rouse
*Leadership Agility: Five Levels of Mastery for Anticipating and
    Initiating Change* by Bill Joiner and Stephen Josephs

CHAPTER 8

Harriet Tubman's Resilience: The Ability to Bounce Back from Adversity

Or watch the things you gave your life to, broken,
And stoop and build 'em up with worn-out tools

TUBMAN'S RESILIENCE

The abolitionist movement required extraordinary resilience from its many great leaders as they fought to end slavery. Harriet Tubman stands out among these for her resilience in the face of daunting obstacles. She was born the daughter of slaves in the early 1820s, in Dorchester, Maryland. In spite of her illiteracy, poverty, and poor health, Tubman escaped slavery alone. But, rather than simply enjoying the rewards of her hard-won freedom, she became one of the most successful leaders of the Underground Railroad. She was in constant danger of capture. Her commitment to freedom and her desire to lead and help others enabled her to deal with the risks and bounce back from adversity. Over the course of eleven years, she made thirteen trips to free slaves. She earned the nickname Moses by leading seventy people to freedom.

Tubman's resilience did not start with her abolitionist efforts. Early on, she revealed her ability to bounce back stronger from every adversity that life threw at her, and as a slave, her adversities were constant. Slavery broke up her family. Three of her sisters were sold when she was a child, and she never saw them again. Her mother's work kept her from the family, so Tubman was expected to care for her siblings. Around age six, she was taken away from her family to work for a cruel and violent woman who often beat her. One of her greatest challenges occurred in her teens, when she was struck in the head by a two-pound weight. This near-fatal injury caused her severe health issues—epilepsy and debilitating headaches—for the remainder of her life. Even Tubman's first attempt at freedom resulted in failure when her brothers lost their resolve, gave up, and returned to slavery.

This sort of adversity is difficult to comprehend. Most people would have become despondent about the setbacks, unfairness, and hardships; but Tubman remained positive and determined. Her ill treatment only intensified her desire for freedom. Even her brothers' change of heart during her first attempt at securing her freedom became a positive force. It strengthened her resolve and forced her to become more self-reliant. Every setback made Tubman stronger, and this strength ultimately led her to freedom. She even treated as a gift the epilepsy that she suffered because of her childhood head injury. Tubman was deeply religious, and she saw her seizures as a way of communing with God.

In the fall of 1849, Harriet Tubman escaped alone to freedom, leaving behind her family, including her husband John Tubman. Following the Underground Railroad and using her familiarity with the woods and swamps, she made her way to Philadelphia, Pennsylvania, where she quickly found work to support herself. Tubman immediately began planning and saving for a return to Maryland to free her family. Before she could make her first trip back, however, Congress passed the Fugitive Slave Act, which required authorities in so-called free states to aid slave owners in capturing and returning runaway slaves. This immediately made Tubman a fugitive again. Rather than being discouraged by the Fugitive Slave Act, she became even more committed to her fight for freedom. She recognized that the new law proved that the situation for slaves was worsening. Tubman returned to Maryland late that same year on her first of thirteen trips to lead slaves to freedom. On this first trip, she helped four members of her family to freedom.

Each trip Tubman made put her in jeopardy, and she had many narrow escapes from "slave catchers" and her former owners. Even those she came to help sometimes unwittingly found ways to make her life more difficult. In 1851, Tubman returned to Maryland to help her husband escape. When she arrived, she found that he had remarried, and he refused to leave. Rather than losing heart, Tubman found another group of slaves and led them to freedom instead.

The Fugitive Slave Act made Tubman a fugitive in her new home in Pennsylvania, which in turn made her journeys considerably longer and more dangerous. Rather than traveling ninety miles from Dorchester to the Pennsylvania state line, she was forced to lead her charges nearly 500 miles to Saint Catharines, Ontario. The hardships and challenges of these trips strengthened Tubman's leadership within the abolitionist movement. The trips helped her grow her network and build a base of support. It was through these trips that she came to know Fredrick Douglass and Senator William Seward, both of whom became her strong supporters.

Tubman saw the Civil War as the greatest opportunity to end slavery in America, but even this opportunity created unexpected adversity. President Lincoln refused to emancipate slaves in the Southern states until January 1863. Prior to that, many runaway slaves were considered "contraband," seized property, by Union leaders. Even so, Tubman maintained her commitment to her cause. She served as a nurse and guide to the Union Army for much of the war. On one occasion, she became the first woman to lead a military assault during the Civil War. The raid was a military success, and better still, it resulted in the rescue of more than 700 slaves.

With the Union victory and passage of the Thirteenth Amendment in 1865, Tubman's work toward freeing slaves was done. She had given much of her life to this cause, and now she faced a new challenge: deciding where to devote her boundless energy. One cause that consumed her energy was personal. Tubman had worked and fought for the Union Army, but she was not given a pension. She battled the United States government for decades, finally receiving a pension in 1899, as the widow of Nelson Davis, her second husband. Her work and generosity had left her constantly on the edge of poverty, so Tubman spent much of her time and energy just staying afloat financially. Later in life, she became active in the cause of women's suffrage. As with her fight against slavery, Tubman overcame many obstacles fighting for women's rights. In the face of these obstacles, she continued to show her remarkable resilience.

HARRIET TUBMAN TIMELINE: A RESILIENT LIFE

- **Circa 1820:** Born in Dorchester County, Maryland
- **1820s:** Three siblings sold
- **1834:** Struck in the head with an iron weight and nearly killed
- **1844:** Married John Tubman
- **1849:** Unsuccessfully attempted to escape with her two brothers; her brothers returned and she successfully escaped alone to Philadelphia, Pennsylvania
- **1850:** Fugitive Slave Act was enacted; Tubman returned to Maryland to assist three family members to escape
- **1850–1861:** Made thirteen trips and led more than seventy slaves to freedom
- **1859:** Acquired a home in Auburn, New York
- **1861:** Volunteered to serve in the Union Army at the start of the Civil War as a cook, nurse, laundress, scout, and guide
- **1863:** Emancipation Proclamation issued; Tubman led Combahee River Raid, freeing more than 700 slaves
- **1865:** End of the Civil War; Tubman returned to Auburn, New York; her arm was broken on the train trip home when a racist conductor physically forced her to move
- **1869:** Married her second husband, Nelson Davis
- **1890s:** Became active in the suffragist movement
- **1913:** Died of pneumonia, in Auburn, New York

THE ESSENCE OF RESILIENCE

In his book *The Road Less Traveled,* M. Scott Peck writes, "Life is difficult. This is a great truth, one of the greatest truths. It is a great truth because once we truly see this truth, we can transcend it. Once we truly know that life is difficult—once we truly understand and accept it—then life is no longer difficult. Because once it is accepted, the fact that life is difficult no longer matters." Peck and Kipling are of like minds on this issue. Life presents us with challenges and obstacles, and we can choose how we respond. At the center of how we respond is resilience.

The fact is, sometimes bad things happen to good people. We all experience adversity in our lives. We are passed over for a promotion that we deserved. We don't get the bonus or raise we feel we have earned. We aren't hired for a position for which we are ideally qualified. These are realities. They are unpleasant, but we accept them and move ahead. That is the key to resilience: moving ahead.

In physics, resilience is the capability of a strained body to recover its size and shape after deformation caused especially by compressive stress. The parallels to human resilience are remarkable. Our ability to absorb and recover from the stress that we encounter is essential for our basic survival. We confront pressure in the form of change, obstacles, impediments, distractions, or personal setbacks every day. While it is impossible to measure empirically our ability to absorb the emotional energy associated with these pressures, we do know our limits, and those around us should know them as well. An important determinant of a leader's effectiveness is his or her capacity to absorb and recover from stress effectively.

As individuals, our resilience in the face of change will determine our ability to manage through that change. For leaders, the value of the opportunity is even greater. Leaders see the potential that change creates, and we can use this potential to generate enthusiasm and energy as a catalyst for the things we want to achieve. We can also use change to help teach and instill resilience in others. People look to leaders to see how they respond to change and the pain that often accompanies it. By showing our resilience, we help others accept and embrace change.

Leading with resilience requires many of the attributes discussed in this book, especially self-efficacy. Resilience builds on the confidence and optimism associated with high self-efficacy. This confidence helps one to anticipate and tolerate challenges and obstacles. It gives us the ability to see the possibilities that problems present. Kipling's reference to "worn-out tools" reminds us that we must believe we possess the capacity to take on the challenges we face, even when our tools are not perfectly suited for the challenges. We simply keep moving ahead with the tools we have and acquire those we need as we are able.

Resilience also requires us to see what others don't. Hockey great Wayne Gretzky is famous for saying, "Some people skate to the puck. I skate to where the puck is going to be." Many people don't see opportunity in a particular situation; they only see the puck slamming into the glass. They focus on the impact, and they miss the ricochet that sends the puck down the ice. They miss the opportunities because they are focused on the wrong things.

Consider the devastation that Europe faced following the Second World War. The concept of bouncing back from the destruction wrought by years of war overwhelmed most leaders, who were only focused on cleaning up the mess. There was very little thought about long-term stability or economic prosperity. But Secretary of State George Marshall and others saw an opportunity in the devastation. The Marshall Plan became one of the most important and effective American foreign policy initiatives ever, and its success enabled an unprecedented return to economic prosperity while slowing the spread of communism.

Resilience also requires a high degree of creativity and innovative thinking. Often the problems we face seem most daunting when addressed head on, so perspective can be critical. As leaders, we must look at problems from many angles and enlist the help of others with differing perspectives. Using creative problem solving, we can find solutions to the challenges we face.

Resilient leaders are proactive. Waiting for problems to pop up and then reacting to them is not their style. Resilient leaders prepare for change and anticipate obstacles. Leaders know that contingency planning is essential to success. They prepare by identifying likely risks, so they can plan accordingly. Since no one can possibly predict every potential issue that may arise, if we are to be resilient leaders, we must be responsive. We must quickly assess a situation, take appropriate action based upon the facts at hand, and maintain composure. We must then focus our energy on effectively responding while rallying others to do the same.

TUBMAN'S LESSONS

Harriet Tubman was a study in resilience and tenacity, and her leadership has made her an American icon. She never allowed hardship to interfere with her mission; rather, she used adversity to make her stronger. So what can we learn from this amazing leader?

1. ***Harriet Tubman maintained a positive outlook and always looked forward.*** Regardless of what happened, she remained focused on what she wanted. Consider Tubman's experiences during the years 1849 and 1850. She chose to escape slavery only to be disappointed by her brothers. Several months later, she successfully escaped to freedom in Philadelphia. Less than a year later, the Fugitive Slave Act put her freedom in jeopardy. Despite the danger, that December she returned to Maryland to help four relatives escape. No obstacle would prevent her from achieving her aims. She was determined. One of the primary factors contributing to this positive attitude was her strong faith and spirituality. She believed that it was her destiny to be free and to help free others.

   As leaders, we have to understand the power of a positive attitude, and we must work to maintain our own forward-looking perspectives. Obstacles will get in our way. Our best-laid plans will come apart. That is part of leadership. But our ability to keep everyone, including ourselves, looking forward is an essential leadership characteristic. At the heart of maintaining a positive attitude is believing in something bigger than ourselves. This belief may be grounded in religion or traditional spirituality, or it may simply be rooted in our secular goals. What matters is our commitment.

2. ***Harriet Tubman was a creative problem solver.*** It is one thing to be optimistic; it is quite another thing to constantly overcome every obstacle you face. On one of her trips to Maryland to free slaves, Tubman heard a group of men coming after her. Rather than hiding, she entered a nearby farmyard and started to work. Although they were looking for her, the men

passed her without incident. Tubman also used timing to her advantage. She always traveled in winter, because the longer nights provided better cover. In addition, she would always begin a journey to freedom on a Saturday evening because the newspapers were not published until Monday, giving her and her charges a better head start.

As leaders, we must have the ability to step back from our problems and find new solutions to every new challenge. This often means leveraging the talents of others. Tubman relied on herself, but she also had a strong support network, who willingly aided her when she faced adversity. Like Harriet Tubman, we must build and nurture our networks and support systems.

3. **Tubman planned ahead and remained focused on her end goal.** Part of Harriet Tubman's creative problem solving stemmed from her proactive nature and her forward-looking attitude, but it also relied on her ability to think and plan. She anticipated problems and built contingencies into her plans. This gave her the ability to respond effectively when things didn't go as planned. When she found that her husband had remarried and was unwilling to escape with her, she went with plan B. She might not have consciously planned for this contingency, but her actions illustrated her flexibility. As leaders we must do the same. Regardless of the obstacles or impediments, leaders keep their goals and objectives top of mind. By remaining focused on what we are trying to accomplish and not the things that stand in our way, we can remain resilient.

4. **Tubman never allowed the weakness or failings of others to dissuade her.** Throughout her life, others failed Harriet Tubman. Some failures weren't surprising, like when her owners broke up her family. Other disappointments were probably more difficult to understand or accept. When her brothers lost their nerve on her first attempt to escape, she was probably frustrated, even angry. When her husband remarried and refused to escape when she came for him, she may have

been outraged. When President Lincoln initially refused to free the slaves, she may have been indignant. But no matter the failure, Tubman always bounced back.

As leaders, we must also be prepared to bounce back. Our friends and colleagues are likely to let us down at some point. It happens. They may even do things to undermine our efforts. It is easy to become judgmental or to express our frustration about those who disappoint us. Exceptional leaders don't. They recognize that this is just another obstacle or barrier to overcome. Leaders get past disappointment and bounce back from adversity.

5. **Tubman taught that resilience means accepting and using the resources we have.** Tubman had all of the odds stacked against her. She lacked the most basic tools one would need to escape slavery. She did not have a map, supplies, tools, or shelter, nor did she have any support. During most of her trips, she usually had only the clothes on her back. She never waited until she had everything she thought she would need. Instead, she made do with what she had.

Similarly, we may find ourselves undertaking an effort without the perfect set of tools. It is easy to deliver superior results when we have available to us everything that a task requires. More often, we find ourselves facing challenging objectives with insufficient time, money, and resources. Leaders find ways to achieve results despite insufficient resources or "worn-out tools."

Kipling's words "Or watch the things you gave your life to, broken, and stoop and build 'em up with worn-out tools" address a person who has something and then loses it. What made Harriet Tubman so extraordinary was her ability to maintain this type of resilience, as she started with almost nothing. Many people believe that one cannot miss what one has never known, but Harriet Tubman's resilience sprang from a soul that craved what it had never known—freedom.

Everyday Resilience

On a winter night in 1927, a small Italian grocery store was robbed at gunpoint. The quick-thinking daughter of the owners grabbed the store's weapon and huddled in an aisle with her mother. As the robbers prowled the store, the daughter slid the weapon to her mother. One of the intruders saw the action and shot both mother and daughter. The mother was killed instantly. Newspaper accounts reported that the sixteen-year-old daughter's chances for recovery were slight.

The daughter survived her physical wounds, but she carried the guilt of her mother's death for the next eight decades. When asked by a family member to recount the event, she said, "Oh, don't ask me to talk about that. It was all my fault." That woman was my wife's great-aunt Anna.

I wish I could say that things got easier for Anna after the incident, but they didn't. Her father died eight years after her mother, and Anna was left to care for her four younger siblings. She married the love of her life, but he also died young. Unable to have children of her own, Anna adopted a baby girl. Eleven months later, the birth mother decided she wanted the baby back.

You might imagine that someone who had survived these tragedies would be bitter, angry, and defeated. Most of us would be. But Anna's unfaltering faith in God and her incredible resilience made her special. In fact, anyone meeting Anna on the street would have guessed that this beautiful and enlightened lady had led a life of privilege.

Anna kept going, no matter what challenge life dealt her. She didn't just survive—she thrived. She was a strong leader in the Catholic Church at the national and international levels. Anna was the matriarch of her large family. She played an active role in raising and educating her thirteen beloved nieces and nephews, with whom she traveled America and the world. Anna was a devotee of parliamentary procedure and became a professional registered parliamentarian. She amassed a small fortune by educating herself and investing in real estate and cattle.

At the age of ninety, Anna tripped while walking across a porch and toppled headfirst into a bush. As I watched this happen, I was sure she was seriously injured. Before anyone could respond, Anna just popped up and kept going. That's what Anna taught us. You pop up and keep going.

RECOMMENDED RESOURCES

Resources about Harriet Tubman:

Harriet Tubman: The Road to Freedom by Catherine Clinton
Bound for the Promised Land: Harriet Tubman: Portrait of an American Hero by Kate Clifford Larson
Harriet Tubman: Imagining a Life by Beverly Lowery

Resources about Resilience:

The Power of Resilience: Achieving Balance, Confidence, and Personal Strength in Your Life by Robert Brooks and Sam Goldstein
Overcoming Buffaloes at Work and in Life: What You Need to Increase Productivity, Overcome Setbacks and Stay Motivated Without Leaving Your Life Behind by Dr. Vincent Muli Wa Kituku
The Resilience Factor: 7 Keys to Finding Your Inner Strength and Overcoming Life's Hurdles by Karen Reivich and Andrew Shatte
Holding the Center: Sanctuary in a Time of Confusion by Richard Strozzi-Heckler

Part 2 Summary: Leadership and Understanding What You Want

What do I want? Now that you've read the previous four chapters, this question should have new meaning. Each of the four attributes examined in this section plays a critical role in answering it. Ambition, vision, boldness, and resilience are independently and collectively important. As you contemplate these attributes, consider how they are unique. Consider their interdependence and distinctions.

PART 2 LESSONS

Ambition

1. Ambition builds on the investment we make in learning who we are so we can then understand what we truly want.
2. Real power comes from connecting personal ambition with societal ambition.
3. Achieving our ambition depends on our ability to exploit the talents and skills we have and acquire those we lack.
4. Ambition sometimes means surpassing others who appear to be more qualified.
5. Leadership demands that we enlist both friends and foes to help us achieve our ambitions.

Vision

1. Leaders understand that having and sharing a compelling vision enables others to see what we see.
2. Our visions have power when they reflect our values, beliefs, and principles.
3. Our visions must speak to both our core supporters and our extended stakeholders.
4. Powerful visions balance audacity with credibility.
5. Clarity matters. Leaders understand the power of simple messages repeated with conviction.

Boldness

1. Boldness starts with seeing things others miss.
2. Boldness means assessing the relative strengths and weaknesses of our options.
3. Leaders seize the opportunities presented to them.
4. Leaders recognize that boldness depends on leveraging others and empowering them to act.
5. Leaders act despite the ambiguity they may confront.

Resilience

1. Leading with resilience means maintaining a positive outlook. Leaders keep looking forward.
2. Resilience requires us to be creative problem solvers.
3. Resilient leaders plan ahead and remain focused on their end goals.
4. Leaders acknowledge the weaknesses or failings of others without allowing those factors to discourage or dissuade them.
5. Resilience means accepting and using the resources we have.

Attracting and Motivating Others

One of the underlying premises of this book is that people choose whom they follow. If that is true, what makes one leader more attractive to follow than another? Certainly, charisma plays some part in drawing us to some leaders. We are naturally attracted to certain characteristics and traits. We want to be around people who are fun, interesting, positive, and entertaining. These assessments are often based on first impressions of others, which in turn are based on cursory assessments and limited information; as a result they can be superficial or misleading. While someone may entice or intrigue us with his or her charm, this attraction is not leadership. In fact, it is more like infatuation. It is not the basis for a sound relationship.

Leadership, at its core, is about the relationships between leaders and the individuals who follow them. Some leadership relationships may start with superficial attraction, but we build real leadership on a more substantial foundation. Leadership requires that we attract others and connect with them in meaningful ways. Without this connection, we will be limited in our ability to get others to embrace our issues and causes. Our success as leaders depends largely on how we make people feel at a deep and fundamental level. Do we instill trust, respect, enthusiasm, confidence, and energy? These types of feelings are the basis for a powerful and lasting attraction.

Organizations spend millions of dollars every year trying to understand and cultivate employee engagement, the degree of employees' emotional attachment to their jobs or organizations. Engagement is a primary driver of productivity and customer satisfaction. These organizational efforts often fail because they do not recognize an important reality. Most people are not attracted to organizations; rather, they are drawn to individual leaders within an organization. True engagement occurs at the individual level, one leader and one follower at a time. Most often, the strongest connections are between an employee and his direct supervisor. Organizations are most successful in building employee engagement when they teach and encourage leaders throughout the organization—from the CEO to the line supervisors—to build solid relationships.

Part 3 is the first section of the book that focuses on our relationships with those we lead. Largely, up until now, the book has dealt with leaders as individuals. The attributes in this section start to reveal how our actions and behaviors affect those around us. Our behaviors either draw people to us or repel them. Over time, our behaviors reveal the type of leader each of us is, and they play an important role in creating a leadership identity and reputation for each of us as well. Developing a strong and credible reputation for being an attractive leader requires repeated and consistent behavior over an extended period. Reputations are significant, because they are often the basis people use to determine whether they want to follow someone.

All of the "If" Sixteen Leadership Attributes are important to attracting others to us; but they are important for very different reasons, and they attract people in very different ways. The attributes discussed in the previous two sections allow others the opportunity to know us and to know what we want to achieve. This awareness gives people a sense of our worthiness as leaders and the merits of our causes. The next four attributes—inspiration, courage, selflessness, and stamina—begin to introduce others to our leadership styles. As we come to understand and develop these attributes, we can begin to demonstrate behaviors that will induce people to follow us. The problem is that these attributes and their associated

behaviors can be extremely challenging. They require constant attention and a great deal of hard work. They often require us to expose ourselves to difficulty and adversity. The advantage of making
the investment in developing these qualities is the opportunity to
build and foster deeper and richer relationships with those we lead.

Inspiration, courage, selflessness, and stamina, like the other "If"
Sixteen Attributes, are essential to effective leadership. These four
attributes are connected and related to all of the other "If" Sixteen
Leadership Attributes, but they are much more distinct from one
another. There are some similarities among them, but they tend to
have more in common with attributes discussed in other sections
of the book. For example, inspiration shares certain characteristics
with enthusiasm; courage shares traits with boldness; and stamina
and resilience have noticeable similarities.

While reading this section, concentrate on the behaviors associated with inspiration, courage, selflessness, and stamina. Consider
how those behaviors make you feel. Often you may find that these
behaviors are what attracted you to leaders you have admired or
respected.

Inspiration

What do we mean when we refer to someone as an inspirational
leader? How does this person make us feel? What specifically about
this person draws us in and makes us want to join him or her? We
often hear people talking about the energy they feel or the spark
that is ignited when they meet an inspiring leader. Even as I write
this, my personal memories of inspiring leaders get my blood pump-
ing. What is it about inspiring leaders that makes us feel this way?
One of the most common traits they share is an absolute commitment to their cause or goal. Their ability to inspire others is rooted
in their own inspiration. They rarely try to inspire; it just happens
naturally. It often seems that these leaders don't care what others
think. They are so confident in themselves and their causes that
they simply assume others will share their passion.

Kipling's words about inspiration capture this. When he writes,
"If neither foes nor loving friends can hurt you, if all men count with

you, but none too much," he is telling his readers that inspiration starts within us. Others may not understand the root of our inspiration, but that is unimportant. Only when we understand it and embrace it can we hope to get others to do the same.

When we inspire, we breathe life into an idea or activity. We motivate people and impel them to achieve things they may not have thought possible. Many of the behaviors associated with the "If" Sixteen Leadership Attributes can be inspirational. Some of these behaviors catalyze action. Other behaviors inspire us to keep going when things get difficult. For the purposes of this discussion, we will focus primarily on the former: inspiration that impels us to act. This type of inspiration lies at the heart of attracting others to join our cause, which is the key to inspirational leadership.

Inspiration has much in common with another "If" Sixteen Attribute, enthusiasm, which we will discuss in part 4. The primary distinction between them is that inspiration instigates change and enthusiasm sustains it. Anyone who has ever built a campfire understands this concept. Inspiration is like the spark that ignites the tinder and creates the initial flame. Enthusiasm is what keeps feeding the fire through the night.

Mother Teresa's life illustrates the power of inspirational leadership. While she demonstrated a variety of leadership attributes throughout her life, her inspiration to help the poorest of the poor changed the world. She often spoke of the moment she became aware of the need to address the poverty and suffering in Calcutta. She said she felt called to act. She described her inspiration as a "calling within a calling." Her inspiration and subsequent actions inspired millions around the world to support her efforts.

Courage

Kipling clearly understood the concept that leaders must confront danger. He demonstrates this understanding when he writes of "forc[ing] your heart and nerve and sinew to serve your turn long after they are gone." Courage often requires us to do things that we feared or thought impossible. It means placing ourselves in harm's way while resisting every impulse from our heart and nerve and sinew to run away or give up. As leaders we must be willing to expose ourselves to danger. For most of us, the dangers we face are rarely physical. More often, we face threats to our professional standing, our financial security, our reputation, or our social status. These dangers are just as real as any physical threat, and they can be just as daunting.

In the previous section, we examined the roles boldness and risk taking play in leadership. Courage and boldness can seem similar, even duplicative. The important difference between them is the immediacy and the reality of the situations we confront. Boldness involves the intellectual capacity to understand, quantify, and accept potential danger. The risks are real, but the threat is still theoretical, no matter how likely. We demonstrate courage when the risks become real threats and we are actually confronting the dangers. We have moved from the theoretical to the practical. Courage is the capacity to confront the risks when they become real. Courageous leadership involves guiding others through these dangers.

Courage also shares some of the same characteristics as composure. The distinction between the two is that courage involves confronting our fears and the fears of those around us; courage means holding your position despite the fear. Courage can lead to composure. Our fortitude in the face of danger can help stabilize the situation. Composure allows us to convert the fear or anxiety a danger creates into productive action.

I decided to choose John Paul Jones to illustrate courage in this book while on a visit to the United States Naval Academy with my father in 2008. While my father was showing me his alma mater, we visited Jones's crypt. I had read his two most famous quotes on numerous occasions: "I have not yet begun to fight," and "I wish to have no connection with any ship that does not sail fast; for I intend to go in harm's way." Both of these quotes had always resonated with me as a testament to Jones's courage. What struck me that day was the example that Jones had set for generations of naval officers. More compelling than these quotes or his story was the culture of courage that Jones fostered in the United States Navy. Throughout the Naval Academy Yard, there are countless small plaques and memorials honoring acts of heroism by naval officers whom Jones had inspired. His actions and his words drove him and his crew to greatness. Since that time, they have aroused the bravery of others, and they continue to encourage us to face down our fears.

Selflessness

Whether we call it selflessness, altruism, or servant leadership, people who put their causes and their associates ahead of themselves are changing the way we think about leadership. These leaders don't see the accomplishment of their personal objectives as a means for advancement and self-promotion. Rather, they see these achievements as contributions to something bigger than themselves. In businesses, they don't treat employees as objects or tools whose only purpose is to help them advance and move up the corporate ladder. These selfless leaders see their employees' happiness, achievement, and well-being as critical measures of their own achievement. Some of the most successful entrepreneurial companies, including Southwest Airlines and Starbucks, have made servant leadership cornerstones of their corporate cultures.

As we become more self-aware and more aware of the world around us, we may also begin to better understand our motivation to lead others. For many of us, the initial appeal to lead is the allure of being in charge and the power and status that come with it. That feeling typically fades. As we mature and grow, we begin to see leadership for what it is—a huge and demanding responsibility. We also realize that leadership is not an end unto itself; rather, it is an enabler that helps us achieve our goals and objectives. With this maturity, we may also begin to see that leadership is a great honor. This realization can be the genesis of selfless leadership.

Patterns of selfless behavior and leadership help build others' confidence and trust in us. People want to follow those who are committed to those they lead. We want leaders who will look out for our best interests. Selfless leaders demonstrate this when they gladly put their people and causes ahead of their personal gain. In turn, selfless leaders often have their pick of the best and brightest employees and supporters, which in turn enables them to achieve extraordinary results.

Nelson Mandela's life is a story of selfless leadership. Mandela also led with vision, stamina, boldness, courage, and so much more, but it was his willingness to put his own suffering and abuse behind him that defined his leadership. He acted for the good of his country and his cause, and this selflessness gave him the ability to lead South Africa out of apartheid. His readiness to reach out to his former enemies and work with them reduced the violence and suffering that many predicted would consume South Africa when he took power.

Stamina

Life is hard, and leadership can be downright exhausting. Leadership requires tremendous stamina because it is demanding physically, mentally, emotionally, and spiritually. As leaders, we must be aware of our own energy levels, as well as the energy levels of those we lead, because our behaviors affect both. Either we promote behaviors that increase energy and stamina, or we promote behaviors that diminish them.

Most of us have experienced the feeling of walking into an organization that is so full of energy that it is almost palpable. We have also seen groups where the energy level is so low that the employees barely make it through a typical day and seem ready to fall asleep at their desks. What causes these differences? How does leadership influence this? What role does energy-building leadership play in attracting others?

Leaders affect all four types of energy—physical, mental, emotional, and spiritual. We are often most aware of physical energy and stamina, because they are the most obvious. Unfortunately, we also usually focus on the symptoms of low energy rather than on the behaviors that encourage high energy. We address exhaustion and burnout rather than the behaviors that are their source—lack of exercise, poor diet, insufficient sleep, stress, overwork, monotony, and so on. These behaviors can drain us, but reversing them can restore energy and build stamina. When we ask those we lead to make difficult moral or ethical decisions, we contribute to their spiritual or psychological exhaustion. It is essential that leaders pay attention to all four types of energy because they are interconnected and equally important. Our ability to create high-energy workplaces will make us leaders who are more appealing and attractive to follow.

Great leaders in difficult situations recognize and respond to the energy level and stamina of those around them. They anticipate the effect that difficult circumstances may have on them and their teams. Jim and Louise Mulligan experienced this while he was a prisoner of war in Vietnam and she raised a family without him and fought for his release. Both of them experienced extreme exhaustion, and they both overcame it while leading others to do the same.

THE POWER OF ATTRACTING OTHERS

Creating an attractive workplace has very little to do with the type of work one does. It is much more dependent on the atmosphere that the leader creates. I once worked for a leader who created such an appealing work environment that I would have jumped at the chance to work for him again. He was one of the most demanding and challenging leaders I have ever worked with, yet his leadership style and the combination of the "If" Sixteen Leadership Attributes that he possessed made the work exciting, fun, and rewarding. His inspiration for the work we were doing inspired me and others. His courage to speak the truth and confront his fears encouraged me to do the same. His willingness to sacrifice his personal agenda for the sake of the organization's agenda led me to make similar sacrifices. His commitment to his own health and stamina created an energy-rich workplace. People wanted to follow him because he had established a pattern of behaviors that instilled confidence. This was not an act: he had proven over time that these attributes were an essential part of who he was.

Leadership depends on getting people to choose to follow our lead once we know who we are and what we want. The next four chapters highlight leadership attributes—inspiration, courage, selflessness, and stamina—that draw others to us. As you read on, keep in mind the third of the "If" Sixteen Leadership Framework questions: *How will I attract and motivate others to choose to follow me?* Consider how your use of these attributes can give others a sense of who you are and how you lead. Also keep in mind how your actions enable your followers to determine whether you are worthy of their trust and followership.

CHAPTER 9

Mother Teresa's Inspiration: The Ability to Connect and Motivate

If neither foes nor loving friends can hurt you,
If all men count with you, but none too much

MOTHER TERESA'S INSPIRATION

On September 10, 1946, aboard a train climbing the foothills of the Himalayas, an unremarkable Romanian nun began to transform herself into the leader the world would come to know as Mother Teresa. She would not earn the title "Mother" for several years, and she would struggle in obscurity for decades, but the inspiration she felt that day changed her life and changed the world.

On the train, Teresa felt a profound confluence of her personal need for meaning and the desperate needs of the poor. She described this event later in life, stating, "I was to leave the convent and help the poor while living among them. It was an order. To fail would have been to break the faith." What makes this event extraordinary is that her faith at that moment was not particularly strong. She seemed to believe in this calling, even though she questioned the faith that inspired it.

What turned this ordinary nun into an extraordinary leader? What happened to her on that train that changed her life and the lives of millions around the world? Teresa was inspired. She heard a higher calling. She was divinely moved. She felt the need to act. Mother Teresa spoke of her inspiration as her "calling within a calling." God had called her to be a nun, and then he called her to serve the poor.

Mother Teresa saw a problem that demanded action. The abject poverty of Calcutta, India, moved her to leave a life she knew and loved. For years, she had seen the poverty and done nothing. Now she felt compelled to help the poor and suffering. Her personal inspiration was the first step toward becoming an inspirational leader.

Mother Teresa was born Agnes Gonxha Bojaxhiu in Skopje, in present-day Macedonia, in 1910. Her family was poor and very religious. Her decision to become a nun surprised no one. In 1928, she joined the Sisters of Loreto, an Irish order that ran missionary schools in India. After Agnes completed two years of training, the Sisters of Loreto sent her to Calcutta, where she took the name Teresa. Sister Teresa taught for nearly fifteen years at St. Mary's School, which served mostly middle-class Indian girls. She loved the school, and she loved teaching. At the same time, she was moved by the suffering that filled the streets of Calcutta. Accordingly, in 1946 she decided to act. She requested permission from the Catholic Church to leave the Sisters of Loreto to establish a new religious order of nuns. Later in life, Mother Teresa revealed that leaving the convent and school was the greatest sacrifice of her life.

Two years later, in 1948, Sister Teresa received permission to leave the Sisters of Loreto. Initially, she worked alone helping Calcutta's poor and dying. Former students began to join her, however, and in 1950, she founded her first religious order, the Missionaries of Charity. Sister Teresa had no experience or money, and her only medical training was a three-month course in basic medical care. She lacked the skills and resources required to help the poor break the cycle of poverty. Her work took her into the poorest slums. She was not deterred.

Mother Teresa possessed and exhibited a characteristic common among entrepreneurs: inspiration. She was inspired to act, and that inspiration drove her to overcome her many obstacles. That same personal inspiration attracted others to join her cause.

Mother Teresa gradually raised money and support for her budding enterprise. She started small, working and living in a donated space. Her continued personal inspiration and her ability to inspire others enabled her to quickly grow and expand her enterprise. Money and supplies began to flow in. Her support grew. The Missionaries of Charity began to capture the world's attention. Between 1948 and her death in 1997, Mother Teresa established missions, schools, and clinics in more than 100 countries. Ultimately, she inspired popes, presidents, prime ministers, philanthropists, and business leaders. She founded five religious orders, attracting thousands to join them. Millions more followed her by providing financial, volunteer, and spiritual support to her cause.

Mother Teresa's initial work in India revealed her ability to connect and inspire people, regardless of religious or cultural barriers. Her later work took her to countries that supported her beliefs, as well as countries that opposed them. At the height of the Cold War, she was able to establish missions in most of the communist countries of Eastern Europe. In 1986, Mother Teresa convinced Fidel Castro, who had a long-standing conflict with the Catholic Church, to allow her to establish operations in Cuba. During her lifetime, she received numerous awards for her work. In 1979, she received the Nobel Peace Prize. In 1999, *Time* magazine recognized Mother Teresa as one of the "Time 100," designated the most important people of the century.

To understand Mother Teresa's ability to inspire others, we must understand her personal inspiration. As a teaching nun, Mother Teresa was successful and content. She had become the director of studies at the school where she taught. She was, by her own account, "the happiest nun in the world." Yet she was also increasingly disturbed by the poverty and suffering that she saw around her. At the same time, she was struggling with her own beliefs and faith. She had a need for greater meaning in her life.

Mother Teresa admitted that during the five decades of her "calling within a calling," her beliefs were tested, and her faith was often weak. Even so, she continued to be inspired by her mission to serve, which in turn inspired others.

Mother Teresa's image broke many of the stereotypes associated with inspirational leaders. She was soft-spoken and very small. She was frail, and her work with the poor and sick led to many health issues throughout her life. Mother Teresa was not a commanding presence. Yet those who followed her would often remark about the passion in her. "Her dark eyes commanded attention," people said. When we see pictures of Mother Teresa speaking with world leaders, her ability to inspire is apparent. This tiny, unassuming figure could capture and hold anyone's attention.

Like all great leaders, Mother Teresa had her detractors. There were those who accused her of using her aid to coerce religious conversions. Others countered that she did not focus enough on converting those she served. Some criticized that she only addressed the surface problems and not the root cause of the suffering. Many Indians were initially suspicious of her actions, and she faced challenges from the antimissionary policies of the Indian government. Some strict Hindus were concerned that her care for the dying was at odds with Hindu teaching. She never let these obstacles or objections dissuade her.

Regardless of the criticisms, Mother Teresa's life and her calling exposed the power of inspiration. She found her true calling in 1946, and it guided her for the next half century. Mother Teresa had been well into a noble career at the convent and the school, and she had devoted herself to that calling. It would have been wholly understandable for her to be complacent and continue the good work she was doing. But Mother Teresa was inspired, and through her inspiration, she inspired others. She recognized that she had an opportunity to do something important. She saw her opportunity to change the world—and she took it..

MOTHER TERESA TIMELINE: THE ROAD TO INSPIRATIONAL LEADERSHIP

➤ **1910:** Born Agnes Gonxha Bojaxhiu in Skopje, in present-day Macedonia

➤ **1928:** Entered the Sisters of Loreto convent to train to become a Roman Catholic nun; took the name Sister Teresa

➤ **1929:** Arrived in Calcutta, India, to teach geography

➤ **1937:** Took final vows to become a nun

➤ **1946:** On a train to Darjeeling, heard a "calling within a calling" to move from the convent to Calcutta's worst slums to serve the poor

➤ **1948:** Left the Sisters of Loreto; moved to Calcutta to start a school

➤ **1950:** Founded the Missionaries of Charity

- ➤ **1952:** Opened Nirmal Hriday ("pure heart"), a home for the dying

- ➤ **1953:** Opened her first orphanage

- ➤ **1963:** Founded Missionaries of Charity Brothers

- ➤ **1965:** Granted permission by the Catholic Church to organize missions outside India; opened the first of these missions in Venezuela

- ➤ **1976:** Founded Missionaries of Charity Contemplative Sisters branch

- ➤ **1979:** Awarded the Nobel Peace Prize; founded Missionaries of Charity Contemplative Brothers

- ➤ **1984:** Founded Missionaries of Charity Fathers

- ➤ **1985:** Awarded the US Medal of Freedom

- ➤ **1997:** Stepped down as the head of Missionaries of Charity; died in Calcutta at the age of eighty-seven

THE ESSENCE OF INSPIRATION

Inspire means "to influence, move, or guide by divine or supernatural inspiration; to exert an animating, enlivening, or exalting influence on; or to spur on, impel, motivate." Most often in leadership discussions, we refer to the latter definitions. In the case of Mother Teresa, all three definitions are relevant. But more important than the definition of the word is its etymology. *Inspire* is derived from Latin *inspirare*, meaning "to breathe in." Inspiration breathes life into our work. It can turn what might otherwise be drudgery into something interesting, compelling, and even fun. Inspiring leaders create this same type of transformation in those they lead.

In *The Leadership Challenge*, James Kouzes and Barry Posner describe inspiring leadership as speaking "to our need to have meaning and purpose in our lives." They go on to say, "Leaders must uplift their constituents' spirits and give them hope if they're to voluntarily engage in challenging pursuits." The key phrase here is "voluntarily engage." Often our position or reputation can compel others to do as we would like. Real power comes from attracting others to *choose* to follow us. Great leaders make us want to join their causes; they breathe life into our work.

It is important to note, however, that inspirational leaders do more than simply attract others to follow them. Their inspiration also empowers their followers to act. Often those actions are directly related to the leader's cause, so followers extend and expand the cause. At other times, inspirational leaders can motivate their followers to proceed in new and unexpected ways. During her life, Mother Teresa founded five religious orders. Each of these groups developed independently. Their cultures and approaches diverged and evolved independently, but the roots of their inspiration remained the same.

What makes a leader inspirational? We often hear of "natural leaders" whose charisma motivates and inspires. Certainly, people who possess a commanding presence can inspire action, but rarely is that true inspiration. Charisma is to true inspiration what infatuation is to true love. There must be more than charm or physical presence to create lasting inspiration. True inspiration drives those we lead to undertake tasks that seem impossible, to overcome obstacles that stand in the way, and to rebound from the most disappointing setbacks. It withstands the test of time and the challenges we confront.

Leaders like Teddy Roosevelt and Winston Churchill inspired others through the fire in their speech and the passion of their messages. Mother Teresa inspired quietly. The passion behind her eyes came from a deep belief and commitment to her calling.

MOTHER TERESA'S LESSONS

How can we learn to inspire and motivate as she did? Can we lead without inspiration? We can manage without inspiring, but inspiration is essential to leadership. Leadership is about getting others to embrace change, inspiring others to move from the comfortable into the uncertain, and helping them see the possibilities that move offers. What made Mother Teresa so inspirational?

1. *Mother Teresa demonstrated the importance of being inspired before trying to inspire others.* When Sister Teresa decided to leave the convent and live among the poor, she did not ask someone else to do it first or to go with her. She took the plunge on her own. She inspired by showing her personal commitment. For Mother Teresa, this meant real sacrifice. She walked away from a life she knew and loved. She left the comfort and security of a life she had known for almost twenty years. She had little money. She had minimal training. Her plan was only partially defined. Yet she knew what was required of her, and she took action.

   As leaders, our ability to inspire others will come from our own inspiration. Others can tell how committed and passionate we are. They read it in our body language. They see it in our energy level. They hear it in our words. Our ability to effect change requires that we be inspired and personally committed to our cause or mission.

2. *Mother Teresa had the courage to state her beliefs.* She had the ability to look people in the eye and tell them what she wanted and how they could help her reach her goals. With this direct approach, she enlisted the support of some of the most powerful figures of her time. She used her courage to inspire both friends and foes. She encouraged friends, like Pope John Paul II, President Ronald Reagan, and Princess Diana, to provide support. She motivated foes like Fidel Castro and the World Hindu Council to simply get out of her way.

   Those we lead may not want to know about our spiritual or theological beliefs, but they do want to know what matters to us. Often we feel uncomfortable revealing our beliefs and values to others, but doing so reveals what motivates us. This in turn enables us to connect with those we wish to lead.

3. *Mother Teresa shared information that would motivate her followers.* Make no mistake; Mother Teresa never misled her followers. She did withhold some information, but these acts of omission were not for the sake of deceiving or coercing

anyone. Parts of Mother Teresa's personal inspiration were and remain difficult to comprehend. They involved complex theological topics that she was trying to understand fully. Mother Teresa believed that these were best kept to herself. There was also the issue of her wavering faith, but she knew that her mission to help the poor was constant. Certainly, she was inspired in part by her faith, but she also had a motivation that spanned the boundaries between the religious and the secular: the desire to serve others. She remained genuinely inspired by this desire to help those she served. She did not muddy the waters with things that may have been unclear or distracting.

There may be times when we feel uninspired by the work we are doing. We may not be perfectly aligned philosophically with the organization for which we are working. But as long as we remain genuinely inspired by part of the organization's mission, we can lead others by building on our shared values. And if nothing in the organization's mission inspires us, perhaps we are in the wrong place.

4. *Mother Teresa clearly defined the problem she was solving.* Mother Teresa focused on solving a specific problem. She wanted to ease the suffering of the poor and dying. She was accused of not addressing the root cause of poverty—and she was unrepentant about it. Mother Teresa knew her mission. She knew the importance of the work she was doing.

There will be those who criticize us for solving the wrong problem, thinking too big, thinking too small, not thinking about the problem the right way—the list is endless. As leaders, *we* define the change we wish to make. Our views will not always be popular. They may run counter to conventional wisdom. Nonetheless, we must be willing to listen to the feedback we receive from others while making the hard choices and bearing the criticism that comes with it.

5. *Mother Teresa taught that inspiration attracts and empowers those we lead.* By the time of her death in 1997, Mother Teresa

was leading thousands of people in five religious orders. They worked in 500 schools, shelters, and missions in 100 countries. She inspired people to follow her, and she empowered them to act. We can see the power of Mother Teresa's inspiration by the continued growth and success of her organizations. Ten years after her death, her orders were operating more than 600 facilities in 120 nations.

As leaders, our job is to inspire and empower others to act. This doesn't mean simply getting people to make the same decisions we would make. Rather, we must encourage them to think and act independently. At times, this may lead to disagreements or divergent paths—but it can also lead to new and better ways to grow and compete.

Mother Teresa demonstrated the power that an inspired leader can have. She saw a problem, and she committed herself to solving it. She breathed life into the cause of helping the world's poorest and most neglected. She helped open the world's eyes to their plight. Inspired leaders inspire others. As leaders, we must find what inspires us and embrace it. Without that, our ability to truly motivate and effect change will be limited. With it, we can change our world—as Mother Teresa did.

Everyday Inspiration

In 1996, I was asked to take on a job I didn't want. It would take my career in a direction I had no interest in going. In fact, it jeopardized the career path I had chosen to follow. But after withstanding a great deal of arm twisting, I accepted the role of deputy commissioner of the Virginia Department of Social Services. In reality, it wasn't the pressure or the cajoling that convinced me. It was the passion and inspiration of one person, Bob Metcalf, the secretary of Health and Human Resources for Virginia. Secretary Metcalf and others made several attempts to convince me that this was the right decision for me; they tried using facts and logic to show me how great the opportunity was. Finally, Secretary Metcalf invited me to his office and told me why this mattered to *him*. He told me stories about changing lives and breaking the cycle of poverty. He spoke to my heart. He inspired me by revealing his own inspiration. I accepted the position that day, and I have never regretted the decision. Inspiration is rarely a matter of logic and empirical data. We inspire the way Secretary Metcalf did: by helping others feel our passion.

RECOMMENDED RESOURCES

Resources about Mother Teresa:

Mother Teresa: In My Own Words by Mother Teresa and José Luis Gonzalez-Balado
Mother Teresa's Secret Fire: The Encounter That Changed Her Life and How It Can Transform Your Own by Joseph Langford
Mother Teresa: A Complete Authorized Biography by Kathryn Spink

Resources about Inspiration:

How to Win Friends and Influence People by Dale Carnegie
The Story Factor by Annette Simmons and Doug Lipman

CHAPTER 10

John Paul Jones's Courage: The Nerve to Face Your Fears

If you can force your heart and nerve and sinew
To serve your turn long after they are gone

JONES'S COURAGE

John Paul Jones, the father of the United States Navy, secured his place in history on September 23, 1779, at the Battle of Flamborough Head off the northeast coast of England. Flamborough Head was America's greatest naval victory of the American Revolution. Militarily, it was inconsequential. Strategically, it was tremendous. The battle brought the war to Great Britain's shores. It showed the British that its navy was vulnerable. In many ways, Jones's fame was a direct result of leadership failures of his own making. Yet when all else failed him, Jones led by demonstrating one of the most challenging leadership attributes: courage.

John Paul Jones was born John Paul, the son of a Scottish gardener, in 1747. He was raised on the estate of a member of the Scottish nobility. He was intelligent, commanding, and industrious. His disadvantaged birth fostered an ambition and hunger for attention that would prove both a blessing and a curse for much of his life. At the age of thirteen, Jones left the safety and security of home to pursue a career at sea. He aspired to become a British naval officer, but his social status stood in his way. Instead, he joined the British Merchant Navy. He signed on as an apprentice aboard the merchant vessel *Friendship*. Jones's career progressed well over the next eight years. Life at sea was extremely difficult, and sailors often faced physical and emotional hardship. According to his journals, Jones thrived in this environment. In spite of his success, he was not satisfied. He longed to captain a ship. He wanted to lead a ship into combat. His greatest dream was to command a fleet.

In 1768, Jones realized the first of his goals. He became a ship's captain when both the captain and first mate of his ship died of yellow fever. Although he lacked any authority, he assumed command and brought his ship and cargo home safely. The ship's owners rewarded him by giving him his first official command. Jones loved being a captain. The authority, the autonomy, and the prestige all played to his ambition and vanity. His years at sea had prepared him for many of the challenges facing a new captain. He would quickly learn, however, that while he was technically competent, he lacked some basic leadership maturity. His temper and lack of self-control exposed this immaturity, nearly costing him his career and his life. While in port in Jamaica in 1770, Captain Jones put down a mutiny on board his ship. A fight ensued, and Jones killed the mutiny's leader. Jones claimed self-defense. Whether the killing was truly a case of self-defense or not, Jones feared he would not get a fair trial, so he fled. This incident seems to be one of the rare occasions when Jones's courage failed him. Many historians believe that Jones may have feared that this accusation was too similar to an event two years prior in which Jones killed another sailor in another attempted mutiny. In that case, Jones was acquitted, but he may have thought that his luck had run out.

John Paul fled Jamaica and sought refuge in Virginia. When he arrived in Virginia, he adopted Jones as his last name. He quickly became attached to America and decided to make it his home. In 1775, Jones saw an opportunity to serve his new country and to achieve another of his life's goals. He joined the fledgling Continental Navy with visions of commanding a ship in combat. In spite of his experience, Jones did not immediately get a ship of his own. He served as the first officer on the USS *Alfred,* where he experienced his first naval battle. In 1776, he took command of the USS *Providence.*

During the American Revolution, naval battles were decidedly one-sided. General George Washington and the Continental Army were the David facing the British Army's Goliath. Jones and the American navy were like David facing *multiple* Goliaths. During the entire war, America had a total of sixty-five, mostly small and poorly equipped, ships. Their primary duty was to harass the British Royal Navy and raid British merchant ships. In contrast, Great Britain was the most powerful naval power in the world. In 1775 alone, Great Britain had 270 modern, state-of-the-art warships.

Commanding the USS *Providence* and later the USS *Ranger*, Jones established himself as one of the most successful and aggressive captains in the Continental Navy. He also developed other less flattering reputations. First, the British, upon discovering his identity as the accused murderer John Paul, labeled him a pirate. Second, assessments of Jones's leadership skills were mixed. He was fair, but he was also a stern disciplinarian. His hard-driving style caused friction with other captains and discontent among many of his subordinates. His reputation—especially the rumors of piracy—also created an air of mystery about him that Jones used to motivate his crews.

During the Battle of Flamborough Head, Jones showed both his leadership strengths and weaknesses. When Jones engaged the HMS *Serapis*, he faced a superior foe bent on bringing a pirate to justice. His crew was homesick and dispirited, and some of his key officers were insubordinate. Arguably, Jones's force was exhausted and unprepared for the fight ahead of them. This seemed to be a battle that Jones should run from, but he saw an opportunity for an important victory for the American cause. Jones may have been driven by the opportunity for glory, but his crew was motivated by financial gain. The HMS *Serapis* and HMS *Countess of Scarborough* were protecting a fleet of merchant vessels. The officers and crews were entitled to a portion of the value of any ships they captured, so this provided ample motivation for Jones's men.

At this point in the war, no American captain had captured or sunk a British ship as powerful as the HMS *Serapis*. Jones saw the opportunity to be the first. He was not reckless. In fact, he had exhibited on many occasions the sound judgment to avoid fights he could not win. Earlier in the war, while in command of the lightly armed USS *Providence*, Jones had encountered a vastly superior enemy ship. Had he attacked then, his reckless behavior would have uselessly put his ship and crew in danger. On that occasion, Jones showed his wisdom and acted prudently by fleeing.

Despite the danger and personal risk in the Battle of Flamborough

Head, Jones attacked. At the time of the battle, Jones had nominal command of a squadron of seven ships. Jones engaged and defeated the British ships *Serapis* and the *Countess of Scarborough*. At first glance, seven ships defeating two seems like a one-sided fight that Jones should have won without acclaim. In reality, Jones entered this fight at an enormous disadvantage.

First, five of the seven ships deserted him just as he was preparing to engage the enemy. While the desertion likely disappointed Jones, it probably did not surprise him. Jones's authority over the other ships in the squadron was ambiguous. This ambiguity, coupled with the cultural tension between Jones and the other captains (all the other ships' captains and most of their officers were French, and the ships themselves were a combination of American and French naval vessels and French privateers), had created a mood of mutual disrespect and mistrust during the prior six weeks of their mission. Jones's reaction was to use his domineering personality to bring them into line, and his failure to win their trust and respect was a direct contributor to their insubordination at Flamborough Head. His mistake proved almost fatal.

The second challenge Jones faced was the quality of the ships and crews. Jones's ship, the USS *Bonhomme Richard,* was no match for the HMS *Serapis.* The *Serapis* was newer, faster, more maneuverable, and better armed. Jones's other ship, the USS *Vengeance,* was equally matched with the HMS *Countess of Scarborough*, but neither ship played a significant role in the battle. Commodore Jones's adversary, Captain Richard Pearson, was far more experienced than Jones, and Pearson led a better-trained crew. Jones's only advantage was in the size of his crew. His ship had nearly 100 more men than the British ship. Jones recognized the danger he confronted, but he overcame his fear. His courage inspired his men. His reward was victory and a place in American history.

The conflict began at sunset and lasted nearly four hours. It is considered one of the most brilliant sea battles of the American Revolution. Almost immediately, the fight went badly for Jones. The superior British firepower inflicted horrific damage. The *Serapis*'s speed and maneuverability prevented Jones from effectively counterattacking. Jones's most powerful cannons had to be abandoned when one malfunctioned and exploded, killing several of his own sailors. Then, when it seemed nothing else could go wrong, something did. The USS *Alliance*, one of the ships that had deserted Jones just before the battle, entered the fight. Twice, the *Alliance* attacked. Unfortunately, on both occasions she fired indiscriminately and severely damaged both the *Bonhomme Richard* and the *Serapis*.

The *Bonhomme Richard* was dying, and Jones knew it. Most of her cannons had been destroyed, and nearly half of her crew was dead or wounded. To make matters worse, fires raged throughout the ship, threatening to ignite the ship's supply of gunpowder. The captain of the *Serapis* hailed Jones, "Do you surrender?" Jones responded by sending his men to board and capture the *Serapis* and shouting his immortal words, "Surrender? I have not yet begun to fight!" Jones's words revealed his courageous spirit and helped to focus his crew on their goal, in spite of mortal danger, exhaustion, and the imminent loss of their ship. Jones's numerical superiority and his aggressive use of sharpshooters gave him the advantage in the fierce hand-to-hand combat that commenced when Jones and his men boarded the *Serapis*.

Jones won the battle, and his victory boosted the American navy's morale at a critical juncture in the war. Jones proved that the British Navy was vulnerable. He also brought the war home to Great Britain. Jones became a legend within the United States Navy. His courage in the face of a superior enemy has been an inspiration for naval officers for more than 200 years. Jones's words on another occasion demonstrate his courageous spirit and have become the unofficial motto of US naval captains: "I wish to have no connection with any ship that does not sail fast; for I intend to go in harm's way."

JOHN PAUL JONES TIMELINE: THE PATH TO COURAGE

- ➤ **1747:** Born John Paul in Kirkcudbrightshire, Scotland

- ➤ **1759:** Apprenticed aboard merchant ship *Friendship*

- ➤ **1768:** Took command of merchant ship *John* when the captain and mate died of yellow fever; given command upon his return to England; tried and acquitted of murder following the flogging of a sailor aboard *John*

- ➤ **1773:** Commanded merchant ship *Betsy*; killed crewman while putting down a mutiny; fled to Virginia rather than face charges

- ➤ **1775:** American Revolution started; Jones requested appointment to the Continental Navy; took the name John Paul Jones; commissioned as a lieutenant in the Continental Navy; given command of the USS *Alfred*

- ➤ **1776:** Commanded the USS *Providence*; promoted to the rank of captain; captured eight British ships and destroyed eight other ships in seven weeks in command of the *Providence*

- ➤ **1777:** Commanded the USS *Ranger*; ordered to France

- ➤ **1778:** Led campaign to sink, burn, and capture ships along the Irish coast; became the first American vessel to capture a British man-of-war, the HMS *Drake*

- ➤ **1779:** Commanded the USS *Bonhomme Richard*; engaged and defeated the HMS *Serapis* in the Battle of Flamborough Head; commanded the USS *Alliance*

- ➤ **1780:** Commanded the French ship *Ariel* and returned to America

- ➤ **1783:** American Revolution ended

- ➤ **1784:** Jones served as US naval emissary to France

- ➤ **1788:** Left the United States Navy and was appointed rear admiral in the Russian Navy

- ➤ **1792:** Died in Paris at age forty-five

- ➤ **1905:** Exhumed and interred at the US Naval Academy in Annapolis, Maryland

THE NATURE OF COURAGE

What does it mean for us to go in harm's way? Why is it important for today's leaders to demonstrate courage? How is courage different from the boldness required to take risks?

Boldness comes largely from one's head, and courage comes from one's heart. Jefferson's boldness was a function of intellect, objectivity, and rationality. Boldness is cerebral. It is about seeing the opportunities, creating a plan, calculating the exposure, and assessing the danger. Courage is visceral. The potential dangers have become real. For military leaders such as Jones, the dangers are tangible and occasionally life threatening. For most of us, the dangers we face can seem less real. They aren't life and death, but they still require us to show courage. Courage shows up when we jeopardize our status, reputation, financial well-being, or career aspirations. That is what it means to go in harm's way. As we lead, our courage will help give others confidence to do the same.

John Paul Jones was also bold. He had spent a great deal of time and energy prior to his battle with the *Serapis* contemplating such a situation. He had planned. He knew the risks. Even in the hour before the two ships engaged in battle, he had time for further analysis and risk assessment. Jones's courage surpassed his boldness the moment his comrades abandoned him. In that instant, he faced his fear and embraced the danger. Courage requires us to do what is right in spite of the personal dangers we face. Courage occurs in those instinctive fight-or-flight moments. But, as with boldness, courage also requires the wisdom to know when to fight and when to flee. Kipling is not advising recklessness or carelessness. Courage is not mindlessly exposing oneself or others to danger.

When Kipling writes, "If you can force your heart and nerve and sinew to serve your turn long after they are gone," he is not talking about calculating the odds and balancing the risk. He is reminding the reader that when those theoretical risks become reality, a leader does not shy away.

JONES'S LESSONS

General Omar Bradley said, "Courage is doing what you are afraid to do. There can be no courage unless you're scared." Being a leader requires courage, and being courageous underlies many of the other attributes described in this book. How can we become courageous leaders? How can we confront our fears and lead? What lessons does Jones teach us?

1. ***Jones quickly and accurately assessed the situation.*** Jones understood the nature of both boldness and courage. His understanding and appreciation of boldness formed the foundation for his courage. He saw opportunities that others did not. He was also fully aware of his assets and liabilities. He understood the unreliability of the captains under him; so when they abandoned him, he may have been disappointed, but he probably was not surprised. Like Jones, we must objectively assess the situations we find ourselves in. On paper, we may have all of the resources required to deliver a set of results. In reality, one of those resources may be our own *Alliance*. Like Jones, we may have someone abandon us, only to return and create havoc. This highlights the importance of knowing whom we can count on and whom we can't. We may find that some things we considered assets are actually liabilities. Knowing both our strengths and our weaknesses allows us to plan. Assessing a situation often means making decisions or taking actions based on partial data. These leadership moments test our resolve and confidence. Courageous leadership means having the will to make the difficult calls.

2. ***Jones kept himself and his crew focused on the larger goals.*** Most of the crews in Jones's squadron of ships were not Americans. Many were not professional sailors at all; they were mercenaries. The ship's crews were entitled to a portion of the ships and cargo they captured. Jones and many of the officers may have been fighting for country and honor, but most of the crew only cared about money and survival. Jones's crew was not interested in the *Serapis*. Their prize was the more than forty merchant ships that the *Serapis* was protecting. Jones led them by knowing what motivated them. Similarly, we often find ourselves leading teams that are not committed to shared goals. Often the virtual nature of work makes it increasingly likely that part of our team may work for another organization. They may even work for a competitor. Finding

what motivates a disparate team is often challenging, but it is essential.

3. ***Jones led by balancing hope and fear.*** When Jones and his ships attacked the *Serapis*, they had differing and conflicting priorities. Jones wanted a naval victory. His crew was more interested in capturing the forty merchant ships that the *Serapis* and *Countess of Scarborough* were protecting. These merchant ships represented a potential fortune for every sailor under Jones's command. The merchant ships gave the crew sufficient hope to attack a superior enemy. Jones also kept the crew's hopes alive with his bravado. When he shouted, "I have not yet begun to fight," he was speaking to his crew more than to his enemy.

What about the fear? Consider the morale of the crew of the *Bonhomme Richard* as they saw the rest of their squadron sail away from the fight. Did they know how outmatched they were? Fear must have permeated the ship. Jones hated the indignity of being labeled a pirate by the British. At the same time, he used this label to motivate his men. Every sailor knew that by sailing on Jones's ship, they would also be tagged as pirates. They understood that they would possibly hang if they were captured. That fear drove them to fight more fiercely.

Our job is to find the right balance of hope and fear to motivate our followers. Most of us are more comfortable using positive emotions like hope. The bestselling book *How Full Is Your Bucket?* focuses on the power of positive emotions, and it offers outstanding advice for leading with positivity and hope. It also teaches the importance of staying grounded in reality. Others will see a leader who fails to recognize the dangers of a situation as out of touch, or even worse, as a Pollyanna. Leaders can use real danger and the fear it produces to create a sense of urgency and spur action.

4. ***Jones embodied courage by exposing himself to danger.*** Naval officers of Jones's day understood that they must remain visible

to their men. This demanded extraordinary physical courage. In battle, the captain would stand on the quarterdeck, a raised platform at the rear of the ship, exposed to enemy fire. Toward the end of the battle, Jones increased his exposure by personally taking command of one of the cannons. Much of the enemy fire was directed at that gun. His cry "I have not yet begun to fight!" reminded the crew that he was still with them.

How can we lead from the front? One of the most important things we can do is eliminate distractions. Often when a project is at a critical point, stakeholders can become anxious. At these moments, our job is to run interference. By being the focal point of stakeholder anxiety, we give our teams the ability to get the job done. There are times when our teams just need to know we are there. We may not be able to offer anything other than moral support and our appreciation, but often that is enough.

5. ***Jones used innovation to overcome his weaknesses and fears.*** One of the best ways a weaker opponent can prevail is by innovating. One of the most effective weapons of Jones's day was the sharpshooter. Typically, captains would place small numbers of marines and sailors in the ship's rigging to snipe at sailors and officers. They would also throw small bombs at the enemy ship. Most captains used sharpshooters simply to harass the enemy. The conventional wisdom was that too many men in the rigging would increase the risk of igniting their own sails. Jones challenged that thinking by using three to four times the norm. His approach paid off. His sharpshooters quickly eliminated the threat from the *Serapis's* marines, so that Jones's marines could fight in relative safety. This safety also allowed one sailor to climb out over the *Serapis* and drop bombs into an open hatch. Many historians believe this act won the fight.

How can we use innovation to overcome obstacles? We must look for opportunities. We can also solicit ideas from others, especially those on our team. Jones had no idea that one of his sailors would take the initiative that determined the outcome of the battle. The sailor had not asked permission. He saw the opportunity, and he knew his captain would support him. Leaders encourage and welcome this type of impromptu innovation and creativity.

John Paul Jones understood courage and its role in leadership. He recognized that success required him to challenge himself and his crew. To engage and defeat a superior foe, Jones had to embrace danger. More importantly, he had to get others to do the same. What opportunities exist for us to overcome our fears and to lead others to overcome their own? What dangers do those opportunities bring with them? Leaders see the opportunities, and they understand the dangers. Great leaders do the right thing in spite of the danger.

For the firefighters and police officers arriving at the World Trade Center on 9/11, courage meant running into the Towers. Their instinctive reaction revealed their courage. Most of us won't need to show our courage by putting our lives at risk. Our courage will come from putting less tangible things on the line. We may jeopardize our reputations, security, livelihood, or relationships. John Paul Jones knew that maintaining his courage and inspiring his crew to maintain theirs was the key to victory. To do so, he needed his "heart and nerve and sinew to serve" long after they should have been gone. He proved his will, so that those who followed him could maintain their courage and will to hold on. Jones's courage became the foundation of his famous victory and the genesis of his lasting notoriety.

Everyday Courage

Most of us rarely need to display the physical courage of John Paul Jones or the NYFD firefighters on 9/11. What we risk when we show courage is less tangible and far less permanent. We may jeopardize our reputation, our security, our relationships, or our livelihood. Even these mundane demonstrations of courage can be daunting. It can also be difficult to see the lessons or the examples of courage we encounter in our daily lives. Typically, it is only when we recollect situations that we recognize them for what they are.

Several years ago, we took a family vacation to the island of St. Lucia. We were staying on a small resort, and during the week, we had befriended several members of the staff. In particular, we had become very fond of a young man named Kent. He was bright and energetic, and he was delighted to do anything to ensure that our stay was perfect. He was genuinely hospitable, never fawning or submissive. This was his job, and he loved it. That was what made him so good.

On one of the last evenings of our stay, I lost my temper, which was not unusual for me at that point in my life. I responded like many parents do: the more annoyed I was by what my children had done or failed to do, the greater my volume. I was loud enough to be heard by Kent as he was walking past our cottage. He was concerned enough that he knocked on the door to see if everything was alright. He simply asked if there was anything he could do to help.

I'll never know what was going through his mind as he walked up the steps of the cottage, but I can still recall the discomfort in his eyes. While his actions were not confrontational, Kent had no idea how I would react. I could have turned my anger on him or complained to the resort's management. His actions created real risk for him. He showed true courage. Fortunately for both of us, his intervention made me realize I was being unreasonable. I apologized to him for the disturbance. He simply smiled and walked away.

That evening I was glad that Kent had diffused my anger, but I didn't recognize the courage he showed until later. In hindsight, I know that Kent's intervention helped me come to terms with a temper that needed to be controlled. And beyond that, he taught me an important lesson in courageous leadership. He helped me see that there are always opportunities to show courage—to take action when everything is telling us to just keep walking past a problem and let someone else do something about it.

RECOMMENDED RESOURCES

Resources about John Paul Jones:

John Paul Jones: A Sailor's Biography by Samuel Eliot Morison
John Paul Jones: Sailor, Hero, Father of the American Navy by Evan
    Thomas
Six Frigates: The Epic History of the Founding of the U.S. Navy by Ian
    W. Toll

Resources about Courage:

Leadership Courage: Leadership Strategies for Individual and Organizational Success by David Cottrell and Eric Harvey

Courage: The Backbone of Leadership by Gus Lee

The Leadership Moment: Nine True Stories of Triumph and Disaster and Their Lessons for Us All by Michael Useem and Warren G. Bennis

CHAPTER 11

Nelson Mandela's Selflessness: The Strength to Put One's Cause First

Or being hated, don't give way to hating,
And yet don't look too good, nor talk too wise

MANDELA'S SELFLESSNESS

Nelson Mandela spent his entire adult life fighting a system that hated him. The system and the people who supported it did not hate him because of any action or event. They hated him because of the color of his skin. Apartheid was based fundamentally on hatred and mistrust. Those who created it and those who perpetuated it were very open about their personal hatred and disdain for the nonwhite population of South Africa.

Nelson Mandela never allowed others' hatred to infect him. He never hated those who hated him. He hated what they stood for and the system that oppressed him, but he never hated the people. He understood that his struggle was not for vengeance or personal glory, nor was it for the advancement of black South Africans at the expense of whites. His was a selfless struggle to end apartheid and create a true democracy.

Nelson Mandela inherited the title of leader as his birthright, but he became a *great* leader through learning and practice. His leadership style had many influences. Through his studies of Mahatma Gandhi, Mandela learned the power and effectiveness of nonviolence. As a young man, Mandela participated in his tribe's leadership councils, where he observed his father and other leaders exhibiting the tribe's tradition of putting the interests of the people before the interests of their leaders.

In school, he learned positive leadership traits like duty and responsibility from his fellow students and teachers, but he also observed negative traits like abuse of power and arrogance. These were equally important in his development as a leader. Mandela's decision to leave school and move to Johannesburg was a direct result of both positive and negative leadership experiences. One of those lessons involved Mandela's election by his peers to serve on his school's student representative council. He refused to serve on the council, in protest over student living conditions. The headmaster threatened him with expulsion unless he served, but Mandela accepted expulsion rather than be bullied. This act was one of his first public displays of selfless leadership.

Mandela saw that the best way to change society was to work within its legal system. He abandoned his tribal leadership role and moved to Johannesburg to study law. Shortly thereafter, he joined the African National Congress (ANC). His energy, intelligence, and demonstrated abilities quickly propelled him to leadership positions within the ANC. From 1942 until his imprisonment in 1962, Mandela was a prominent ANC leader. He was a founding member of the ANC Youth League. He served on the ANC National Executive Committee, and he was elected deputy president of the organization in 1952. He also cofounded and led Umkhonto we Sizwe (MK), the ANC's military wing.

Unlike many revolutionary leaders of his time, Mandela never desired to drive his oppressors from South Africa. Rather, he sought to work with white South Africans to change the system of government to give all South Africans equal rights. This was a lesson he had learned early in life. One of his tribe's core beliefs was that one's opponents should be allowed to retain their honor, even in defeat.

Prior to his imprisonment, Mandela had spent most of his time and energy working for change through legal action, advocacy, and protests. He was committed to nonviolence. It was only when government actions became increasingly violent and repressive that Mandela resorted to violence. Even then, he championed moderation by insisting that the MK only employ acts of sabotage, which minimized the threat of injury or death. His decision to use violence, build the MK, and undergo military training led to his arrest, conviction, and life sentence for treason. Thus began the most challenging period of Nelson Mandela's life, setting the stage for his greatest acts of selflessness.

To appreciate fully Nelson Mandela's perspective, it is important to understand the system he was fighting. Apartheid was a system based on segregation and discrimination, in which the minority white population dominated and oppressed the majority black and "colored" (the South African term for multiracial people) populations. Key attributes of apartheid included disenfranchisement of nonwhites, prohibition of interracial marriage, suppression of opposition groups and political parties, and the requirement that blacks and coloreds carry travel documents for movement within the country. Even in prison, apartheid established classes and discrimination. White prisoners were treated better than colored prisoners, who were treated better than black prisoners. Political prisoners—especially those deemed to be challenging apartheid—were segregated from common criminals and were treated worse still.

History has shown that the South African government overstated the charges against Mandela and fabricated much of the evidence used to convict him. The resulting twenty-seven years he spent in prison would have given any person reason to hate. Factor in the deprivation, neglect, isolation, and petty bullying that defined the life of a black political prisoner under apartheid and it would have been normal for him to seek to punish his persecutors and to gain compensation for his suffering. Consider just a few details of the mistreatment that Mandela suffered. He was allowed only one thirty-minute visit every six months with no physical contact permitted. He was only allowed to send and receive one letter during this same period. At one point, Mandela waited more than two years between visits with his wife. For most of his imprisonment, he was never permitted to see his children. Even communication among prisoners was limited, and they were frequently prohibited from congregating. Despite this treatment, Mandela never wanted compensation of any form, and he never sought revenge.

Mandela served most of his prison sentence on Robben Island, a windswept island off the coast of Cape Town. In spite of an average winter temperature of 45 degrees, black political prisoners were forced to wear short pants and very thin clothing, and they were forced to sleep on the floor on thin mats with inadequate blankets. White prisoners were issued long pants and warm clothing, and they slept on cots. Political prisoners lived on a subsistence diet of rice, "mealies" (corn gruel that was occasionally cooked with small amounts of meat), and a few vegetables.

Yet Nelson Mandela survived and persevered. When the apartheid government realized that they could not break him, they attempted to bribe him with promises of release if he would renounce violence and the struggle to end apartheid. Eventually the government realized that this approach, too, was misguided.

The government's overtures convinced Mandela that their resolve was weakening. Therefore, despite the ANC policy of nonnegotiation, Mandela began informal discussions with the government in 1985 to end the violence that was ravaging South Africa and to begin the transition to democracy. This move again showed Mandela's selflessness. His willingness to negotiate broke with ANC policy and threatened to alienate him from his closest friends and supporters. He risked appearing to have lost his will and looking like he was being used for government propaganda. This fear of alienation proved to be valid, as many in the ANC accused him of going soft. Even his oldest and closest friend and fellow activist, Oliver Tambo, the exiled head of the ANC, was concerned about the negotiations. Mandela accepted these risks because he recognized that the cause he was fighting for was more important than his own reputation.

The negotiations proved to be bitter and frustrating. They lasted for more than four years, but eventually Mandela prevailed. On February 2, 1990, South African president F. W. de Klerk announced his plans to end apartheid, and on February 10, the government released Mandela from prison. Over the next four years, Mandela resumed his leadership role in the ANC and continued his negotiations with the de Klerk government.

Mandela worked with both supporters and detractors alike to achieve his vision of success—a free and democratic South Africa. He met constant resistance. Many white South Africans were unwilling to end apartheid peacefully, and many in the antiapartheid movement wished to expel whites from South Africa. Despite these obstacles, in 1994, the people of South Africa elected the Government of National Unity, which included Nelson Mandela as president and Thabo Mbeki as first deputy president. The new government also included Mandela's former oppressors and adversaries; F. W. de Klerk served as second deputy president, and a vast majority of the apartheid government leaders and functionaries retained their positions. While this was essential to ensuring that the government continued to function, it also reflected Mandela's philosophy of reconciliation and his desire to move South Africa forward.

President Mandela further proved his selflessness by strongly advocating for racial reconciliation. His strong support for the Truth and Reconciliation Commission helped heal the wounds left by centuries of white domination and decades of apartheid. Because of his personal suffering and sacrifice, Mandela gave legitimacy to the process of reconciliation. While the Truth and Reconciliation Commission had its critics, it was instrumental in the transformation of South Africa.

Mandela's most visible act of selfless leadership was his decision to leave office. He recognized that the key to true democracy was the peaceful transfer of power. In 1999, at the completion of his term as president, Nelson Mandela stepped down. In doing so, he became one of the rare revolutionary leaders to relinquish power voluntarily.

Clearly, South Africa continues to suffer from the lingering effects of apartheid, and its long-term prospects remain uncertain. However, without Nelson Mandela's selfless leadership—in particular his ability to put the needs of his country ahead of himself—the situation in South Africa could have quickly devolved into anarchy, civil war, and ethnic cleansing.

NELSON MANDELA TIMELINE: A TEST OF SELFLESSNESS

➤ **1918:** Born Rolihlahla Dalibhunga Mandela in Mvezo, South Africa

➤ **1937:** Moved to Healdtown to attend Fort Hare University

➤ **1939:** Expelled from Fort Hare for refusing to accept a position on the student representative council; moved to Johannesburg; worked as a clerk at a law firm; began studying law

➤ **1943:** Joined the African National Congress (ANC)

- **1944:** Founded the Youth League of the ANC with Oliver Tambo and Walter Sisulu
- **1952:** Opened the first black legal firm in South Africa with fellow lawyer Oliver Tambo; became active in the ANC's Defiance Campaign
- **1955:** Participated in the creation of the Freedom Charter, which called for equal rights and a program of antiapartheid actions
- **1956:** Accused and acquitted of conspiracy related to his Freedom Charter activities
- **1960:** Led protests of the Sharpeville Massacre, where police killed sixty-nine peaceful protestors; ANC banned; Mandela went into hiding and formed the underground military group, Umkhonto we Sizwe (MK)
- **1962:** Arrested and sentenced to five years in prison for his anti-apartheid activities; went into hiding to avoid prison
- **1964:** Captured; convicted of sabotage and treason; sentenced to life imprisonment
- **1968:** Mandela's mother and son died; Mandela was not permitted to attend either funeral
- **1980:** Oliver Tambo launched an international campaign for Mandela's release
- **1985:** While still in prison, Mandela began negotiations with South African government to free political prisoners and end apartheid
- **1986:** International sanctions against South Africa tightened
- **1990:** Released from prison after twenty-seven years; President de Klerk lifted the ban on the ANC; the ANC and the National Party began talks on forming a multiracial democracy
- **1991:** Elected president of the ANC; International Olympic Committee lifted ban on South Africa
- **1992:** Awarded Nobel Peace Prize with President de Klerk

➤ **1994:** Elected and inaugurated as president of South Africa; appointed de Klerk as deputy president and formed racially mixed Government of National Unity

➤ **1999:** Relinquished the presidency at the end of his term

➤ **2004:** Retired from public life at the age of eighty-five

THE NATURE OF SELFLESSNESS

Nelson Mandela is the epitome of the selfless leader. Whether you call it selfless leadership, altruistic leadership, or servant leadership, the concept is not new. Most religious traditions extol the virtue of selflessness and the need to lead for the benefit of others. The Torah, the Bible, the Koran, and many other religious writings contain myriad references to selflessness. History is full of stories of selfless leaders. The Roman legend of Cincinnatus tells the story of a Roman farmer who abandoned his farm to lead the defense of Rome, only to return to his farm without reward. George Washington's retirement after his second term as president of the United States established the expectation that presidential service was temporary. President Gerald Ford's pardon of Richard Nixon following Watergate contributed to his loss in the 1976 presidential election, but his sacrifice demonstrated his willingness to put the needs of his country ahead of his personal ambitions. All of these leaders did the right thing *because* it was the right thing—not for personal gain or reward—and sometimes with the knowledge that their selflessness would ultimately cost them dearly.

Lately selflessness has not been an attribute that is highly celebrated in leaders. Today's leaders are more often known for the size of their egos and the cults of personality that surround them. Many would-be leaders spend their energies in pursuit of personal rewards and status, rather than focusing on the greater good of those they serve.

Most of the leaders described in this book have demonstrated some degree of selflessness. Leadership is, after all, dependent on one's ability to gain followers, so a leader must give others a reason to choose to follow him or her. Most of us want to follow someone in whom we believe. We want to be part of something worthwhile and meaningful, so we follow leaders who are working for something important.

Love was a primary motivator for Nelson Mandela's actions. He loved his people, his country, and his cause. While we rarely use the word *love* in professional settings, it is the key to selflessness. It is easy to see how selflessness makes us feel good. But is there a business case to justify it? In his book *Love is the Killer App*, Tim Sanders focuses on the power of love and its importance to personal and professional success. In the opening chapter of his book, Sanders celebrates the potential of selflessness. He tells of a conversation he had with a young, brash, selfish subordinate, whom he labeled a Mad Dog, who was trying to change into a "Lovecat," one who grows by helping others grow. Sanders advised the young man, "Offer your wisdom freely. Give away your address book to everyone who wants it. And always be a human." Sanders and the ex–Mad Dog reveal what's in it for us. By acting selflessly, they both succeeded in the hypercompetitive world of Silicon Valley.

Organizations benefit from selflessness as well—in terms of employee satisfaction, employee retention, and customer satisfaction. Many of the companies included on the *Fortune* "100 Best Companies to Work For" list, including Google, Starbucks, Southwest Airlines, and Yahoo, are noted for their focus on selfless leadership.

Mandela's love enabled him to make the sacrifices and endure the hardships that he faced throughout his struggle. His selflessness is evident all through his years as an activist leader. The height of this self-sacrifice was his decision to go underground in 1961, when he was forced to live away from friends and family for more than a year, and his subsequent twenty-seven-year imprisonment. Mandela's self-sacrifice precipitated the end of his first marriage, strained relations with his family, cost him his home, and bankrupted his law practice. Although his absences and failures as a father, husband, son, and colleague weighed heavily upon him, Mandela recognized that South Africa and his cause were more important than his personal suffering.

MANDELA'S LESSONS

So how do we become the Nelson Mandela of our company or organization? The good news is we don't have to spend twenty-seven years in prison, and we don't have to ignore our personal commitments and responsibilities. The bad news is that it still requires a great deal of work and personal sacrifice. Nelson Mandela's life is very instructive for those wishing to embrace selfless leadership.

1. ***Mandela subordinated his personal feelings, needs, and ego to a greater good.*** Mandela described his motivation: "I have always believed that to be a freedom fighter one must suppress many of the personal feelings that make one feel like a separate individual . . . He must subordinate his own feelings to the movement." Obviously, you and I are not freedom fighters or revolutionaries, but we do have choices and trade-offs to make. We can sacrifice our pet project or share our go-to person for the greater good of the organization or the team. We must be willing to ignore the petty slights and interdepartmental bickering that can so easily distract us from creating value.

2. ***Mandela showed that selflessness takes practice.*** Nelson Mandela didn't just decide to forget about the pain and suffering that he had endured under apartheid and reach out to his oppressors. He embraced selflessness early in life and practiced it daily—and not just for the big public events. We have to look for opportunities, both big and small, to practice selflessness. Sometimes others may ignore or be suspicious of our early attempts at selflessness. The greater the change this behavior is, the more proof of our authenticity our colleagues will need. We can start by offering assistance to those who aren't in a position to help us. Do this because it is the right thing to do. Next, we can help a high-potential employee find a new role that advances her career, while solving a bigger organizational problem. Do these things with no expectation of any

results, but don't be surprised when you start to see great outcomes.

3. ***Mandela showed that selflessness requires a strong will and a true sense of self.*** Many may confuse selflessness with weakness or lack of will. On the contrary, selfless leaders often have huge egos and wills of iron. Nelson Mandela knew that his ideas would provide the best path to bring democracy to South Africa. He was confident that he was uniquely qualified to lead the way. He also recognized that his ideas and his cause were more important than himself or any other individual. As leaders we have to remember to keep thinking big and to remain confident, and we must know when and how to put the needs of our organization or cause first.

4. ***Mandela demonstrated the need to understand boundaries and priorities.*** If the cause is great and we believe in our ability to effect change, we should be prepared to make an equally great sacrifice. Mandela was willing to sacrifice his familial duties, his livelihood, his freedom, and even his life to achieve his goals, because the evil of apartheid was so great. As leaders, we must understand our own boundaries. We may jeopardize a big promotion or bonus to do the right thing. We may even put our jobs on the line. We will also make smaller personal sacrifices, like missing family events or bringing the stress of work home with us. Selfless leadership requires us to fully examine our boundaries so that when we confront difficult choices we are prepared to make them.

Anyone can become a selfless leader. Selfless leadership requires hard work, patience, sacrifice, and most of all love. We must love what we do, the people we serve, and our cause. Nelson Mandela led his country to freedom and democracy and ended apartheid through his selflessness and love. His leadership journey was long and challenging—from rural tribal royalty to political activist, from freedom fighter and political prisoner to the first black president of South Africa. His journey is a testament to Kipling's lines "Or being hated, don't give way to hating, and yet don't look too good, nor talk too wise."

Everyday Selflessness

Teaching attracts selfless people. It is a profession that requires people to give of themselves in the service of others. It is an important and difficult job that doesn't pay particularly well. It demands the patience to deal with unruly children, parents who are either overbearing or unsupportive (or often both), and bureaucracies that limit teachers' ability to teach. Despite that, some of the best and most committed professionals enter teaching every year.

One such exceptional teacher was Martha Glennan. She was my teacher in fifth and sixth grades at Hutchison Elementary School in Herndon, Virginia. She was outstanding in many ways. She took genuine interest in learning what each student really needed and ensured that they got it. This level of commitment is challenging under the best of circumstances—but Hutchison Elementary was particularly difficult, thanks to an ill-advised government experiment.

The neighborhoods that fed Hutchison were highly diverse. Half the school was white and middle class. The other half consisted of poor, mostly minority children who lived in a new housing project that the federal government had created. In the name of urban renewal, the Department of Housing and Urban Development had demolished large low-income housing projects in Washington, DC. They then transplanted the displaced residents to suburban projects like this one in Herndon. Unfortunately, the new location lacked the necessities the residents needed to survive, such as jobs, transportation, and social services. Unemployment, crime, and violence were rampant. Racial tensions ran high. All of these factors created a challenging environment for both teaching and learning.

Martha Glennan was undeterred by these challenges and difficulties. She invested herself in the lives of her students. She bridged the racial and socio-economic divides that separated her students. She made learning enjoyable and rewarding. She found interesting and creative ways to teach. She came in early and stayed late to help anyone who needed it. She was like many other great teachers.

What distinguished her from the rest? Martha Glennan also suffered from a painful and degenerative condition that was slowly crippling her. Despite the pain, she was always there.

Her sacrifice and investment changed her students' lives. I know this because she changed mine. For most of my elementary school years, I suffered from severe learning disabilities. I was fortunate to have had several teachers who helped me overcome dyslexia. Others helped me catch up and stay on track with my peers. Mrs. Glennan was the first to help me excel. She saw something in me, and she encouraged me to believe in myself. She gave me my first leadership opportunities. Her years of teaching required her to give part of herself. In 1982, her condition confined her to a wheelchair. Even this didn't deter her. She continued to serve students in an administrative role for the county. She later became an advocate for the disabled.

RECOMMENDED RESOURCES

Resources about Nelson Mandela:

Invictus, 2009 *film*
Long Walk to Freedom by Nelson Mandela
The Nelson Mandela Foundation, http://www.nelsonmandela.org
Mandela: The Authorized Biography by Anthony Sampson

Resrouces about Selflessness

Bhagavad Gita: A New Translation by Stephen Mitchell
*Lead Like Jesus: Lessons from the Greatest Leadership Role Model of
    All Time* by Ken Blanchard and Phil Hodges
The Power of Servant Leadership by Robert K. Greenleaf
Love Is the Killer App: How to Win Business and Influence Friends by
    Tim Sanders

Jim and Louise Mulligan's Stamina: The Will to Hold On When You Have Nothing Left

And so hold on when there is nothing in you
Except the Will which says to them: "Hold on!"

THE MULLIGANS' STAMINA

On October 24, 1965, Commander and Mrs. James Mulligan kissed good-bye for what they expected to be an eight-month separation. Commander Mulligan, an A-4 Skyhawk pilot, was preparing to board the USS *Enterprise*, which was headed to Vietnam. This deployment was nothing new for the Mulligans. Commander Mulligan's naval career had demanded numerous extended separations.

The Mulligans had no way of knowing that nearly seven and a half years would pass before they would see each other again. Five months after their farewell, Commander Mulligan's aircraft was shot down. He would spend the next seven years as a prisoner of war (POW) in North Vietnam. Both Mulligans would endure their own hardships. Their experiences were dissimilar, but they both showed exceptional leadership and stamina.

When I started this chapter, I had intended to write exclusively about Captain Mulligan (the US Navy promoted him to captain while he was a POW; accordingly, I will henceforth refer to him as Captain Mulligan). His stamina and fortitude gave him the strength to lead his fellow POWs. His story is a testament to man's ability to persevere despite absolute physical, emotional, and psychological exhaustion. He demonstrated the ability to endure unimaginable hardship and inspire others to do the same.

As I researched Captain Mulligan's story, I began to see another leadership ordeal. Louise Mulligan's story revealed a different type of stamina. Captain Mulligan overcame abuse and torture. Mrs. Mulligan endured endless government bureaucracy, condescending cultural elitism, and an apathetic American public that had grown weary of the Vietnam War. Her husband and hundreds more like him were languishing in North Vietnam's POW camps, and America seemed both unconcerned and unwilling to bring them home. The Mulligans' respective experiences demonstrated an incredible ability to hold on when there was nothing left.

Captain Mulligan's Story

On March 20, 1966, Commander James Mulligan was shot down while flying a routine mission over North Vietnam. He received severe injuries, including a broken shoulder and ribs, when he ejected from his crippled aircraft and was knocked unconscious. As he regained consciousness, Mulligan was taken prisoner by the North Vietnamese. They immediately began their efforts to break him physically, emotionally, psychologically, and spiritually. For the next 2,522 days, Mulligan endured, spending more than half of that time in solitary confinement.

In many ways, those first days were among the worst. Initially, Mulligan doubted that he would survive even his first day as a POW. His first captors threatened to execute him. They exploited his existing injuries while inflicting new ones. He was bound, blindfolded, and beaten for days. He was denied food and water. The North Vietnamese withheld medical attention for nearly two weeks, despite his severe injuries and the extensive infections caused by his torture and neglect.

Surviving those first weeks was a testament to Mulligan's physical strength and determination. The next seven years proved the mettle of his stamina. All American POWs held by the North Vietnamese suffered unimaginably. They were frequently beaten and tortured. They were malnourished and poorly clothed, and they were regularly deprived of sleep for days on end. They were denied any contact with their families and the outside world for years at a time. Ultimately, the North Vietnamese broke all of the POWs' bodies. To quote Kipling, there was nothing in them "except the Will which says to them: 'Hold on!'" Leaders like Mulligan endured—sustained by faith and will.

Some POWs suffered more than others. The North Vietnamese singled out the prisoners they considered leaders or troublemakers for the most inhumane and brutal treatment. Captain Mulligan was both. He was a senior officer, and he willingly accepted his leadership responsibilities. He understood that he had a duty to lead by example. Mulligan relied on the Code of Conduct for military prisoners of war as the foundation for his actions, and he encouraged other POWs to do the same. The Code of Conduct forbade cooperation with their captors. The North Vietnamese labeled as troublemakers anyone who followed the Code of Conduct or encouraged others to do so.

Mulligan and other leaders quickly learned that leading and resisting carried a high price. The North Vietnamese relentlessly punished Mulligan and other captured leaders. In 1967, he earned the distinction of becoming one of the "Alcatraz Eleven."[1] The Alcatraz Eleven were George Coker, Jeremiah Denton, Harry Jenkins, Sam Johnson, George McKnight, Jim Mulligan, Howard Rutledge, Bob Shumaker, Jim Stockdale, Ron Storz, and Nels Tanner. They were the diehards, and the Vietnamese were determined to break them.

The same resistance and courage that made the Vietnamese view the Alcatraz Eleven as troublemakers made the men leaders among their fellow POWs. These leaders knew that their fellow POWs would gain strength from one another. A sense of community and mutual support were essential to their survival. This required communication, but communication among the POWs was forbidden. Mulligan and his fellow prisoners were constantly evolving and adapting their methods of communication. They created simple codes to exchange messages rapidly. Most frequently, they employed hand signals and

---

1   *Alcatraz* was a name the POWs gave to a small section of a POW camp in Hanoi where the most resistant POWs were kept in solitary confinement. The Alcatraz Eleven was an extraordinary group. Of the eleven, one was awarded the Medal of Honor and became a vice presidential candidate; one became a United States senator; another became a United States congressman; two became presidents of prestigious colleges; one became a CEO for a successful business; and three published books about their POW experience. Ron Storz died in Alcatraz. The remaining ten survived their ordeal and completed successful military careers.

tapping. One of the Alcatraz Eleven, Captain Jeremiah Denton, used Morse code to blink the word *torture* during a television interview the North Vietnamese forced him to do. These and other small POW victories were an ongoing source of frustration for the North Vietnamese.

During his imprisonment, Captain Mulligan made it his duty to keep track of the name of every POW with whom he came in contact. Every day, he would mentally review his memory bank of POW names and whatever pertinent information he could gather. This task, while altruistic in its intent, benefited Mulligan. Mentally, it kept him sharp. Emotionally, it kept him connected to the larger POW community. Spiritually, it reminded him daily that he was *still* a United States naval officer with a duty to his fellow POWs and his country. Upon Mulligan's release, the first thing he did on his flight out of North Vietnam was to dictate the names from his memory bank. There were 459 American POWs on that list.

Mulligan and the rest of the Alcatraz Eleven established and nurtured a leadership structure within the POW community. Their actions served as a beacon for their fellow POWs. Their stamina in the face of unending suffering inspired those POWs whose resolve was wavering. Their courage and fortitude also helped bring five POWs who had been collaborating with the North Vietnamese back into the POW fold. Their leadership saved lives and restored hope.

The abuse and torture these men suffered cannot be adequately described in this short chapter. I encourage you to read Captain Mulligan's book, *The Hanoi Commitment*, so you can truly appreciate the suffering the POWs endured and the stamina they possessed.

JAMES MULLIGAN TIMELINE: A POW'S STAMINA

➤ **1926:** Born in Lawrence, Massachusetts
➤ **1944:** Joined the United States Navy
➤ **1947:** Became a naval aviator
➤ **1948:** Married Louise M. Kolce
➤ **1965:** Assigned as executive officer of VA-36 on board the USS *Enterprise*; departed Norfolk, Virginia, for Vietnam

- **1966:** Scheduled to become commanding officer of VA-36 on April 1; shot down near Vinh, North Vietnam, on March 20; severely injured on ejection

- **1966–1973:**

  - Held as prisoner of war in Hanoi, North Vietnam

  - Imprisoned for almost seven years (2,522 days)

  - Spent almost forty-three months in solitary confinement

  - Spent thirty months in leg irons

  - Labeled a troublemaker by his North Vietnamese captors and became part of the Alcatraz Eleven (1967–1969)

  - February 12, 1973: Released from captivity

  - February 15, 1973: Arrived home to Norfolk, Virginia

- **1975:** Retired from the navy after nearly thirty-two years of service

Mrs. Louise Mulligan's Story

Of the many farewells the Mulligans experienced, Captain Mulligan recalls seeing his wife cry only once: October 1965. As a navy spouse, Louise Mulligan both expected and accepted the sacrifices she and her family would make. Her role was maintaining their family while Captain Mulligan served their country. She understood the separation, loneliness, and difficulties. She had come to terms with the dangers of naval aviation. All of this took on new meaning when Mrs. Mulligan received word in March 1966 that her husband had been shot down, and he was missing in action and presumed captured.

Louise Mulligan spent the next seven years alone, raising six boys and wondering whether they would ever see her husband and their father again. She would have almost no contact with her husband. For months, she did not even know if he was alive.

Initially, Louise Mulligan accepted her role as a navy wife. That meant she was expected to wait patiently and let the United States government obtain her husband's release. She waited for two years, while focusing her energy on raising her sons. It eventually became clear that the government was not making progress. Worse, the American people were ignorant of the POWs' plight, and worse still, the media was spreading misinformation about their condition. Many news reports gave the impression that the American POWs were being treated humanely.

Mrs. Mulligan and several other POWs' wives began to plan and act. Their decision was unprecedented. They broke with long-standing tradition because they saw no alternative. They chose to lead. Louise Mulligan began her work in her local community by organizing the dozens of POW/MIA wives in southeastern Virginia. She became a leader in the League of Families, an organization dedicated to securing the release of Americans held in Vietnam. Mrs. Mulligan was instrumental in making the league a cohesive and unified group, and her work helped cement the league's national reach. While serving as a leader on the league's executive board, she met extensively with senior military and government leaders. She ultimately led delegations to encourage Secretary of State Kissinger and President Nixon to take action.

Louise Mulligan worked tirelessly to bring her husband home. She suffered the frustrations of dealing with a confusing bureaucratic maze. She endured loneliness and misery. She raised six boys by herself. Her stamina carried her through. It enabled her to survive, but it also gave her the strength to lead. She led her family, and she led her fellow spouses. Ultimately, Mrs. Mulligan's actions led her country to change its policy and to bring the POWs home.

THE CONCEPT OF STAMINA

Captain Mulligan believes that everyone has a survival story. This does not have to mean surviving a POW camp. Survival requires stamina. Life is exhausting, and leading others requires that we maintain our energy and overcome exhaustion. Stamina is defined as "the strength or power to endure fatigue, stress, and hardship." It requires that we sustain our physical, emotional, mental, and spiritual energy. All four are essential and interconnected. Captain Mulligan's experience demonstrates the effect that physical and

mental exhaustion can have on one's emotional and spiritual stamina. Mrs. Mulligan's experience shows the physical and mental exhaustion that stems from emotional and spiritual fatigue.

Of the four types of energy—physical, mental, emotional, and
spiritual—physical energy is the most basic. The human body has
certain requisites for survival: food, shelter, water, and sleep. When
we deprive our bodies of any of these, we diminish our energy.
Captain Mulligan and his fellow POWs remained in various states
of extreme physical exhaustion throughout their imprisonment.

Building and maintaining one's physical base is essential. Given
Captain Mulligan's extensive injuries, constant torture, sleep deprivation, malnourishment, disease, and lack of adequate shelter,
his body should have shut down. His physical conditioning before
imprisonment, combined with his mental commitment to rebuild
his broken body, allowed his body to heal and sustain itself in the
most challenging of circumstances. Keeping ourselves healthy is key
to maintaining our energy and stamina. It also prepares us for the
unavoidable crises we regularly encounter that require extra energy
and stamina. As leaders, we must be aware of our own physical energy level, and that of those we lead.

It is hard to compare typical workplace exhaustion with that
suffered by POWs, but many leaders find themselves physically exhausted far too frequently. Certain societal trends contribute to this
exhaustion. Many leaders do not get enough sleep. We eat poorly,
and we don't get adequate exercise. We typically go to the doctor
only when something is wrong. Physical exhaustion, even when it is
well disguised, causes our productivity and effectiveness to suffer.

Our physical exhaustion also affects our mental and emotional
energy. When we are physically tired, our mental performance de-
creases, and our emotional control is diminished. Multitasking and
stress exhaust us mentally and emotionally. Repetition or constant
change can also take their tolls. As leaders, we must look for signs
of exhaustion and help promote energizing behaviors.

Spiritual energy is at the heart of this book. We draw energy by
doing things we believe in and value. Spiritual stamina depends on
our awareness of and adherence to what really matters. By ensuring
that our actions and associations are consistent with our beliefs, we

can maintain high levels of spiritual energy. We promote spiritual stamina by creating open environments where people can discuss their beliefs and values. This starts with our willingness to be open about what we believe and value.

As leaders, our stamina affects our own productivity as well as the productivity of those we lead. When our energy levels are high, we are likely to make better decisions. The Roman philosophy of "a healthy mind in a healthy body" remains true. Fatigue is one of the most common causes cited for bad decision making.

Our actions and behaviors reveal what matters to us. If we model healthy behaviors, others are likely to follow our lead. When we take time from our busy schedules to exercise or recharge, it empowers others to do the same. When we show our personal commitment to maintaining work–life balance, those we lead will start seeing the choices available to them. Our positive actions set an implicit standard. The same is true for unhealthy behaviors.

Captain and Mrs. Mulligan's stories illustrate the power of spiritual energy. Even in the face of absolute physical, mental, and emotional exhaustion, they survived because they knew what they believed and valued. The Mulligans share a powerful faith in God, a belief in their country, and a commitment to family. Their spiritual base gave them the focus and energy to endure.

THE MULLIGANS' LESSONS

Leadership demands stamina. It requires high levels of physical, mental, emotional, and spiritual energy. How do we bolster our own stamina? How can we help others build theirs? Healthy living provides a solid foundation. Enduring extreme difficulties requires us to *build* on that foundation.

1. ***The Mulligans demonstrated the power of giving aid.*** Assisting others builds both physical and emotional stamina. Cynics believe that when things get difficult, we need to look out for ourselves. This was antithetical to the POW culture. The men were committed to taking care of one another. They constantly monitored each other's health, and they took steps

to address each other's physical difficulties. The guards regularly entered POWs' cells to torture or abuse them. Captain Mulligan established a system to discourage these attacks. If any POW heard a guard entering another prisoner's cell, the observing prisoner would shout, "Bao cao!" ("Help!"). This simple act had two benefits. Often, it would stop the attack. Beyond that, it let the POW who was under attack know that he was not alone. How often do we look around to see who needs our help? Those we lead need to know that we are looking out for them. They need to know that we are aware when something is wrong. Most people are uncomfortable admitting they need help. Leaders don't wait to be asked.

2. *The POWs exhibited strength by seeking help when they were exhausted.* The POWs established a succession plan in the event a senior ranking officer (SRO) was unable to lead. If an SRO was isolated or inaccessible, the next ranking officer would step up and assume command. More importantly, if an SRO felt he could not fulfill his duties for any reason, he could relinquish command. This allowed the leaders to recognize their own and each other's exhaustion and take action to restore their energy. It is important to understand what restores our energy and to make time to take care of ourselves. Many people use exercise or meditation. Others develop hobbies. One executive I know has been watching the same soap opera for more than thirty years. Every day he records it and then makes time on the weekend to recharge by watching the week's episodes. Whatever the activity, we need things to help us maintain our energy.

    As leaders, we must recognize when we are incapable of leading because we lack the physical capacity or mental focus required of us. In these situations, we must be prepared to delegate authority or ask for support. We must create a culture where it is safe to ask for help.

3. *The Mulligans knew the importance of maintaining a sense of community.* Our sense of belonging helps build our emotional

stamina. Shortly after Captain Mulligan's capture, Mrs. Mulligan moved her family to Virginia Beach, where she had many friends and colleagues to lean on. They provided the emotional support she needed to endure. This base of support gave her the ability to step up as a leader among the POW families. Her strength fostered the growth and success of the League of Families. This group's strength came in part from their shared burden and the sense of community.

The POWs maintained their sense of community through their communications networks. They were relentless in finding ways to communicate. This mutual support was indispensable to their stamina. As leaders, we must constantly find ways to build a strong sense of team and community among those we lead.

4. **The Mulligans' awareness of their beliefs and values created a foundation for true stamina.** I have known Captain and Mrs. Mulligan for most of my life, and I have always been struck by their strong faith and commitment. Their abiding love for God, country, and family has sustained them. Captain Mulligan once said, "Many people say they couldn't have survived what I went through. I tell them that everyone will be tested." What will enable us to pass these tests? And how can we learn from them? The Mulligans' endurance and stamina show the importance of focusing on what truly matters. Viewing our successes and failures in the context of our overarching values and beliefs allows us to build upon our successes and learn from our failures.

5. **The Mulligans helped set the mood and energy level for those they led.** If our energy is high, others are likely to mirror us. The mutual support, encouragement, and energy of the Alcatraz Eleven restored the energy of those who had given up. Captain Mulligan and the other leaders did many things to sustain the morale of those they led. They established discipline by following and enforcing the Denton Rule. Named for Jeremiah Denton, the rule directed POW conduct: "No

write, no tape, and no read on the radio." This meant that the POWs were to refuse to allow the North Vietnamese to use them as propaganda tools. Captain Mulligan and the other leaders found many ways to lift the POWs' moods. In 1972, the North Vietnamese allowed the Alcatraz Eleven to join a large group of POWs. Mulligan helped arrange an education and entertainment program to keep the POWs engaged. All these efforts helped maintain their energy and stamina.

We set the mood and energy level for those we lead. Unfortunately, we often fail to notice how we might be draining energy rather than creating it. I once had a colleague who was the senior leader in his business unit. He had the habit of working late into the night. He was young and single, and he loved his work. It was his hobby. At night, he would walk the halls, catching up with anyone else who was working late. Everyone in his division soon learned about this behavior, and they all assumed that they too should be burning the midnight oil, regardless of the toll. While working these hours wasn't exhausting for the manager, the schedule was killing his team. Morale plummeted. The most commonly cited reason was the lack of work–life balance. My colleague was shocked to learn that his behavior was at the root of this dysfunction. As leaders, we must be aware of the messages we send—especially the unintentional messages.

During one of my conversations with Captain Mulligan about this book, I told him that I felt absurd comparing his POW experience with the petty trials and tests of everyday leadership. He responded with humility about the gravity of his accomplishment, but he also told me that he wants the POWs' story to help inspire leaders. He wants to ensure that the men's struggle and endurance are not forgotten. His story and the stories of all the POWs teach us powerful lessons about our ability to bear hardship and to maintain our stamina. Kipling's words—"And so hold on when there is nothing in you except the Will which says to them: 'Hold on!'"—remind us of the power and stamina that we possess.

Everyday Stamina

One of the most important leadership roles a person can play is that of parent. Parenting can also be among the most challenging and energy-draining types of leadership. It is demanding in all four ways: physically, intellectually, emotionally, and spiritually. We invest ourselves in helping our children grow and develop. This investment demands a great deal of stamina from all parents.

My sister, Laura, has helped me appreciate the stamina required to be a single parent. She is always on. She helps with homework, she takes my niece and nephew to the doctor, she does the after-school activities, and she is responsible for every meal eaten and every piece of clean clothing worn.

Laura recently described the hardest day she ever experienced. It was Thanksgiving several years ago. Laura was the general manager of a resort, and they were expecting more than 600 guests for Thanksgiving dinner. Early that morning, the resort's chef quit. Laura's original plan had been to work that morning to help the staff prepare for the day. She was then going to spend the afternoon with her children. Instead, Laura had to get one of the resort's housekeepers to watch her children, while Laura stepped in to serve the guests.

When Laura recalled the story, she said, "It killed me!" She had promised her kids a classic Thanksgiving dinner together. Instead, she cooked for strangers while her kids pressed their noses to the window hoping their mom could join them. That day was exhausting on many levels. Physically, Laura was ready for a break. She had anticipated a quiet dinner for three. Instead, she prepared dinner for 600. Emotionally and spiritually, Laura was torn between a family she loved and a career that fulfilled her.

That Thanksgiving, Laura served 603 dinners: 600 strangers and her family. It was eight that night before her children had their meal, but she did it. Laura maintained her stamina as a single parent and as a business leader. Our family now laughs about Laura's crazy Thanksgiving tale—but it has also taught us a powerful leadership lesson.

RECOMMENDED RESOURCES

Resources about Captain Mulligan and Vietnam POWs:

When Hell Was in Session by Admiral Jeremiah Denton

The Hanoi Commitment by Captain James A. Mulligan
The Passing of the Night: My Seven Years as a Prisoner of the North Vietnamese by Robinson Risner

Resources about Stamina:

The Power of Full Engagement: Managing Energy, Not Time, Is the Key to High Performance and Personal Renewal by Jim Loehr and Tony Schwartz
How Full Is Your Bucket?: Positive Strategies for Work and Life by Tom Rath and Donald O. Clifton
Executive Stamina: How to Optimize Time, Energy, and Productivity to Achieve Peak Performance by Marty Seldman and Joshua Seldman
The Energy Project, http://www.theenergyproject.com

Part 3 Summary: Attracting Others

In the previous four chapters, we examined how leadership is dependent on our ability to attract others to follow us and to join our cause. Coming out of this section, you should be better prepared to understand and contemplate the third of the "If" Sixteen Leadership Framework questions: *How can I attract others to choose to follow me?* Simply reading these chapters won't give you the answers to this question. In fact, this section may have raised more questions than it answered. If so, that's good. Each question will help move you forward on your leadership journey.

Our ability to attract others to us and to our causes is not something that happens overnight. We demonstrate the four attributes discussed in the previous four chapters—inspiration, courage, selflessness, and stamina—by repeated patterns of behavior.

PART 3 LESSONS

Inspiration

1. Leaders recognize that they must be inspired before they can inspire others.
2. Inspiration starts with the courage to state our beliefs and to make our goals known.
3. Inspiration means communicating effectively and deliberately to motivate our followers.
4. Inspirational leaders have the ability to clearly define the problems they are solving.
5. Real inspiration has the capacity to both attract and empower those we lead.

Courage

1. Courage requires leaders to quickly and accurately assess situations and dangers they confront.
2. Maintaining our focus and the focus of others on our larger goals helps foster courage.

3. Courage often requires leaders to use a combination of hope and fear.
4. Leaders embody courage by not shying away from danger.
5. Leaders innovate and adapt to situations in order to overcome weaknesses and fears.

Selflessness

1. Selfless leaders subordinate their personal feelings, needs, and egos to the greater good.
2. Selflessness takes practice. When we act selflessly in the little things, we are more easily able to do so when we face the big things.
3. Selfless leadership requires a strong will and a true sense of self.
4. Selflessness demands that leaders have a strong understanding of their boundaries and priorities.

Stamina

1. Leaders understand that maintaining stamina sometimes means giving assistance, and they encourage others to do the same.
2. Leaders encourage those they lead to seek assistance when they are exhausted.
3. Leaders promote stamina and energy by building and maintaining a sense of community.
4. Leaders understand that their beliefs and values create a foundation for emotional and spiritual stamina.
5. Leaders help set the mood and energy level for those they led.

Earning and Retaining the Privilege to Lead

CHAPTER 13:
George Washington's Composure: The Power of Keeping Your Head
CHAPTER 14:
John "Blackjack" Pershing's Patience: When Waiting Counts
CHAPTER 15:
Thomas Edison's Enthusiasm: The Energy to Fill Every Minute
CHAPTER 16:
Golda Meir's Accountability: The Will to Lose and Start Again

Once we know ourselves, we have the ability to apply this awareness to learning and understanding what we want to achieve. Similarly, once we have engaged others and attracted them to follow us and to join our cause, we are better equipped to retain their trust, but we must also constantly work to build and develop that trust. Leadership is a great privilege, and with that privilege comes great responsibility. On a simpler level, those who are attracted to us by our inspiration, courage, selflessness, and stamina will expect— even demand—that we lead them in a manner consistent with that behavior. They will expect us to continue to demonstrate all of the previous attributes, and they will expect more. We should expect more from ourselves because once someone honors us with this great privilege and responsibility, we should feel driven to prove ourselves worthy.

This final section focuses on the attributes that help us retain the trust of those who follow us—and keep them committed and excited. These attributes—composure, patience, enthusiasm, and accountability—can be extraordinarily challenging but are exceptionally important. They reveal our actions and behaviors to our followers on a regular, if not daily, basis. These attributes show how we lead in a full range of settings, from the mundane to the memorable. The chapters in this section will help us answer the fourth and final question of the "If" Sixteen Leadership Framework: *How will I earn and retain the privilege to lead?*

Just as the preceding twelve attributes play a unique and inter-related role in how we lead, composure, patience, enthusiasm, and accountability are distinctly different and individually important. There may be times when these distinctions seem simply semantic; in truth, however, they matter because they allow us to understand and diagnose our specific leadership strengths and challenges. Many of the behaviors and characteristics associated with composure and patience are similar, and they share commonalities with courage, but by distinguishing among them, we can better understand our opportunities to grow and improve as leaders.

Composure

In the first line of "If—" Kipling writes, "If you can keep your head when all about you are losing theirs and blaming it on you." These eighteen words of poetry describe one of the most important tests we must pass as leaders to retain the trust of those who follow us. Our ability to maintain our composure—to keep our heads—is an essential leadership trait, and it can be an all-too-frequent test. From keeping our cool when dealing with the daily annoyances life throws at us, to preventing real panic when things go horribly wrong, our ability to keep our composure will be noted and remembered by those we lead. Even our ability to keep our successes and achievements in perspective will provide proof of our composure. Our ability to lead with composure is not just determined by our reaction to the big events. Rather, our responses to regular and routine events will help instill confidence in those we lead because they reveal how we are likely to respond when something catastrophic happens.

Composure is not stoicism or an unwillingness to show emotions or get excited. It is not the opposite of enthusiasm. Instead, it is an ability to control a situation—including the emotions that it may arouse. Composure is the ability of a leader to prevent the crises that are essential parts of our lives from becoming panics. This is not simple tranquility. The power of composure is self-possession:

our control over our emotions and our presence of mind to deal with a situation deliberately and appropriately.

We distinguish composure from courage, which was discussed in the previous section, by the nature of the external event that a leader is responding to. Courage deals with situations in which risks have manifested themselves into real dangers or problems. Composure may involve danger or risk, but it may also be a response to an unexpected windfall or success. Composure requires leaders to assess situations and determine the appropriate responses. We set the mood and help others internalize the events so they can react in a positive and productive way.

George Washington's response to his defeats in New York and New Jersey in the summer and fall of 1776 provide outstanding illustrations of one leader's ability to maintain composure. To paraphrase Kipling, all about him were losing their heads, and they were blaming it on him. Yet Washington kept his head and prevented a crisis from becoming a panic. His composure allowed him to turn defeat into victory. Washington's composure gave him the confidence to lead, but better still, it reassured his followers that their trust in him was well placed.

Patience

This book is a testament to the patience that is required of leaders. Many of my clients express a degree of frustration when I insist that they start with self-examination and self-awareness before they can begin defining what they want. Others would rather skip self-awareness and discovery of what they want altogether. But real leadership demands the patience to go through all of the steps and to continuously revisit and reassess our capabilities and ourselves.

Merriam-Webster's Dictionary defines *patience* as the capability to "bear pains or trials calmly or without complaint; manifest forbearance under provocation or strain" and "not hasty or impetuous; or steadfast despite opposition, difficulty, or adversity." All four definitions play a part in understanding the role patience plays in leadership. Kipling seemed to understand this: "If you can wait and not be tired by waiting, or being lied about don't deal in lies." Kipling's words reflect a recognition that leadership often requires us to wait. His words also acknowledge that others will not want to wait, and they may respond to our patience with impatience or, worse, frustration and attacks. As leaders, our patience has real value. It gives us the ability to act deliberately and intentionally. It shows our followers that we have the will and ability to persevere and endure. Our patience may frustrate them at times, but it will also reassure them of our commitment and our worthiness.

General John Pershing is an ideal illustration of the concept of leadership patience. He was charged with a seemingly impossible task: to build and prepare an army so America could enter the First World War. He readily and enthusiastically accepted this challenge. After assessing the situation, Pershing devised a plan that would take greatest advantage of the fresh American forces. Unfortunately, his plan conflicted with the opinions of most of those who were considered experts. Rather than cave in to the pressure and change his plan, Pershing displayed extraordinary patience by sticking to it and executing it on his schedule and on his terms. Throughout his preparation, his critics disparaged him for his inflexibility, but his patience proved him right.

Enthusiasm

How do we keep people excited and motivated when the glamorous and high-profile project they have been working on starts to look like it will never end? How do we energize a team whose job is mundane or seemingly holds no prospects for future growth? What keeps people passionate despite all of the things that should be sucking the life out of their work? Enthusiastic leaders can make a difference. They cannot make the mundane interesting or the boring exciting, but they can help us see their relevance and value.

When Kipling writes, "If you can fill the unforgiving minute with sixty seconds' worth of distance run," he speaks to the potential that all leaders face. We can fill our time—and our followers' time—with drudgery or with enthusiasm. This is not about being a vapid cheerleader who can turn any lemon into lemonade. It is about helping create context and connection between our work and something bigger or, if you can't do that, helping people see how the work they are doing today may create opportunities in the future. Enthusiastic leaders cannot be Pollyannaish. Rather, they must be able to create an understanding among their followers about why the work they are leading matters.

We cannot manufacture enthusiasm and excitement. We must draw it out of those we lead by connecting with them and finding what excites them. Our enthusiasm reveals to those we lead that we care enough about them to work to keep them engaged and motivated.

Thomas Alva Edison epitomized enthusiastic leadership. He threw himself into his work, and his passion was contagious. Stories about the long hours he worked and expected others to work are off-set by the stories of his boundless energy and excitement. Edison's 10,000 failures leading up to the creation of the incandescent light bulb revealed his persistence. His response to those failures revealed his limitless enthusiasm. He never saw these 10,000 attempts as failures; rather, he saw them as 10,000 ways not to make a lightbulb.

Accountability

The last leadership attribute in this book is accountability. That was intentional, because ultimately leadership comes down to taking ownership. That is the essence of accountability: a sense of owner-ship. Regardless of what happens, a leader is accountable for the outcome. That means when things fall apart, the leader accepts the blame. When things go well, the leader shares the credit. That is the conundrum. Leadership has more downside risk than upside potential.

In many ways, accountability is the embodiment of all other leadership attributes. Ownership starts with a realization that something matters to us, so without self-awareness there can be no accountability. This same sense of ownership will help us define what we want. All of the attributes associated with attracting oth-ers and retaining their trust demand a willingness on our part to be held to account. Despite the fact that accountability is a part of all of the other attributes, it deserves its own place in the "If"

Sixteen Leadership Framework because it is so critical and often lacking. Accountability is easy to talk about. It is simple and clean, yet it is often so difficult to practice. For these reasons, it is the last attribute.

Golda Meir, Israel's prime minister from 1969 to 1974, was one of those rare political leaders who fully embraced the concept of accountability. In the fall of 1973, Egypt and Syria attacked and nearly defeated Israel in what became known as the Yom Kippur War. A series of military, intelligence, and political failures led to this near disaster, yet an independent commission did not hold Meir responsible for those failures. Despite her exoneration, Meir and her cabinet resigned. She knew that, as leader, *she was accountable*. She also knew that in order to restore the confidence of the Israeli people she had to be held to account.

THE POWER OF EARNING AND RETAINING TRUST

Max De Pree, the former CEO of Herman Miller who became a noted leadership writer, once said, "Earning trust is not easy, nor is it cheap, nor does it happen quickly. Earning trust is hard and demanding work. Trust comes only with genuine effort, never with a lick and a promise." His words reveal an understanding about the tenuous nature of leadership. Followers can be fickle. Our ability to earn and retain their trust will help us keep even the most fickle people following us. All of the "If" Sixteen Leadership Attributes can help us build trust and retain it during difficult times. The next four chapters focus on attributes that are particularly important during the most challenging times: composure, patience, enthusiasm, and accountability. Our ability to keep our heads will give our followers the composure to keep theirs and the confidence to trust our leadership. Our patience to develop and stick with our plans despite the pressure of others will help our followers see that our patience and commitment extend to them as well. Our enthusiasm and passion will help them through difficulty and boredom. Finally, our consistent accountability will reassure our followers that we will not pass the buck when things go badly or take all the credit when things go well. Every time we demonstrate these attributes, we are reminding our followers that their trust and confidence are well placed.

CHAPTER 13

George Washington's Composure: The Power of Keeping Your Head

If you can keep your head when all about you
Are losing theirs and blaming it on you

WASHINGTON'S COMPOSURE

History is full of extraordinary stories of leaders who maintained their composure in the face of large-scale panic and crisis. George Washington's actions during the early years of the American Revolution provide wonderful illustrations of composure in the face of disaster. For most of the early years of the revolution, Washington was in a constant state of crisis management.

Many historians would argue that George Washington was ill prepared to lead the Continental Army. Washington understood his weaknesses better than most. Following the 1775 vote that made him commander in chief of the fledgling Continental Army, Washington expressed his misgivings in a speech before the Continental Congress. He stated, "But lest some unlucky event should happen unfavorable to my reputation, I beg it may be remembered by every Gentleman in the room, that I this day declare with the utmost sincerity, I do not think myself equal to the Command I [am] honored with." These words were not simply false modesty. Washington's correspondence with those closest to him, including his wife and cousin, revealed similar misgivings about his qualifications.

Washington knew that he was in over his head, but he also knew that he had the strong support of the majority of the Continental Congress. He was respected as one of the wealthiest, most successful, and most politically astute men in the colonies. While he had more military experience than any other member of the Continental Congress, Washington had never led a force larger than a regiment. He lacked appropriate experience in many of the essential areas of contemporary military leadership. In spite of these gaps in his experience, Washington was the natural choice. He was probably the only realistic choice because he possessed a basic level of military leadership experience and an understanding of the colonies, their terrain, and their political landscape. All of these factors contributed to his ability to keep his head when things started falling apart.

In spite of his inexperience, Washington enjoyed early success as commander in chief with the siege and capture of Boston, but even this victory had its challenges. His army had a disjointed command structure; it lacked sufficient equipment and supplies; and for much of the Boston campaign, a large number of troops were incapacitated by disease. Nonetheless, this early victory bolstered Washington's confidence and the confidence of both Congress and his army.

Following the American victory at Boston on March 18, 1776, Washington's newfound confidence was tested as things quickly devolved into crisis. Before the end of March, Washington began moving his army to New York to prepare the city's defenses for the British attack that most believed was imminent. As he established his military headquarters in Manhattan, Washington had strong misgivings about the enemy he faced and his army's capabilities. Both the British and Continental armies understood the importance of controlling New York. The British knew that retaking New York would give them the greatest opportunity to crush the nascent rebellion, or at least sever New England from the rest of the colonies, thus dividing and weakening the rebel forces. The Americans knew that New York was a loyalist stronghold and an important base of support for the British Army.

Washington's crisis in New York stemmed from a series of major mistakes. His first mistake was establishing a permanent headquarters that was vulnerable to British naval might. Washington and most of his senior subordinates knew that they could not hold New York if the British made a concerted attack. The battle the Americans faced relied on key capabilities that they lacked: a well-equipped, well-trained professional army and a strong naval presence. Even if Washington had been leading a modern European army, his decision to defend and hold New York would have been risky. England possessed the most powerful navy in the world, and the fact that

Manhattan and Long Island were islands gave the British a decided advantage.

Washington's second mistake was his response to the arrival of the British invasion force on Long Island in August 1776. General William Howe and his brother, Admiral Richard Howe, arrived in New York with a force of 25,000 professional soldiers and almost fifty warships. Washington commanded a force of barely 19,000 untrained and ill-equipped volunteers. When Washington realized that he faced these overwhelming odds, he made the classic blunder of dividing his strength. He sent half of his forces to Long Island and kept half on Manhattan. The British quickly and thoroughly routed the American forces on Long Island. Washington compounded his mistakes by sending more troops to reinforce the trapped defenders at Brooklyn Heights. Fortunately, the weather saved him. A strong wind and dense fog prevented the British warships from surrounding the trapped Americans and gave Washington the opportunity to ferry his army to safety on Manhattan.

Long Island was an absolute defeat, and this defeat intensified the escalating crisis that Washington faced. Did Washington recognize that his situation on Manhattan was hopeless and a potential disaster? Clearly, he anticipated this, as he expressed his concerns in a letter to his cousin Lund Washington written days before the battle. Yet Washington remained committed to his decision to defend Manhattan. Again, the British forces routed his army. As he and his army escaped to New Jersey, he suffered one failure after another. Between August and November 1776, Washington lost almost 40 percent of his troops and most of his artillery. Nearly 7,500 soldiers were killed, wounded, or captured. Washington understood the situation better than anyone, as is evidenced in a letter to John Hancock written in November 1776. Washington wrote, "Our affairs are in a more unpromising way than you seem to comprehend. . . . Your Army . . . is on the eve of its political dissolution." Washington recognized that the crisis had turned to panic, and it was his job to control the panic and save his army.

Throughout this campaign and in spite of the overwhelming failures Washington faced, he never lost his composure. While most around him were panicking, he remained calm. Surely, everyone in

Congress was asking whether Washington was the right person for the job. His troops, officers, and even Washington himself must have questioned his competence. Even his second in command, General Charles Lee, and Washington's closest confidant, Joseph Reed, had expressed their loss of confidence in Washington. Panic was rampant throughout the colonies, Congress, and the Continental Army. Chaos reigned during the summer and fall of 1776. All were losing their heads, and they were blaming Washington. Their blame was justified.

Washington's early mistakes were a result of his inexperience, tactical and strategic miscalculations, and poor judgment. However, when it mattered, he kept his head and led his army to safety across the Delaware River into Pennsylvania. He regrouped and lived to fight another day. By maintaining his composure, Washington saved the bulk of his army. He ultimately reengaged his pursuers with surprise counterattacks at Trenton and Princeton, New Jersey, that resulted in stunning victories. These victories were politically crucial. Militarily, they enabled Washington to halt the British pursuit and put them on the defensive. The victories restored confidence within Washington's forces and within Congress. They must have restored Washington's faith in his own abilities as well. These American victories took the momentum away from the British, who had been on the verge of crushing the American Revolution less than six months after the signing of the Declaration of Independence. The American victories at Trenton and Princeton forced the British back to New York, where General Howe and his army would spend most of the remainder of the war.

The period from the summer of 1775 to December 1776 represented some of the worst times for the Continental Army, yet they were the formative years of the revolution. This was when the odds were stacked against the Americans, and it was up to Washington and the Continental Army to prove to their fellow Americans and the rest of the world that the war was winnable. It was during these early days of the war that Washington established himself as a true leader. This was when he began to build his officer corps. Generals Nathanael Greene and Henry Knox, Colonel Daniel Morgan, and Lieutenant Colonel Alexander Hamilton were just a few of the many leaders to emerge from the early crises. These events also began to reveal to Washington the character flaws and weaknesses of other members of his staff. It became clear that General Charles Lee's personal ambitions and agenda put him at odds with Washington. The disastrous New York campaign marked a critical point in the maturing of the Continental Army, and it demonstrated that General George Washington possessed the composure essential to lead his country through the challenges that lay ahead.

This period also revealed an important characteristic about Washington: his control of his emotions. While Washington's previous military experience had prepared him for the emotional difficulties of war, the New York campaign sorely tested him. At one point, Washington personally witnessed his men pay for his failures with their lives. After the fall of Fort Washington, the British and Hessian troops bayoneted the captured American soldiers. Watching through a telescope from New Jersey, Washington wept at the carnage left in the wake of his defeat. Washington did not ignore his emotions. He recognized that his emotions were essential to who he was, but he also knew it was critical for him to control and manage them and the crisis.

GEORGE WASHINGTON TIMELINE: A LEADER'S ABILITY TO KEEP HIS HEAD

- ➤ **1732:** Born in Westmoreland County, Virginia

- ➤ **1774:** Elected delegate to the First Continental Congress

- ➤ **1775–1781:** American Revolution

- ➤ **1775:** The battles of Lexington and Concord began the American Revolution; Washington was elected a delegate to the Second Continental Congress; elected commander in chief of the Continental Army; assumed command of the siege of Boston

- ➤ **Events of 1776:**

  - ➤ **March:** Forced the British to abandon Boston

  - ➤ **April:** Moved the Continental Army to New York to prepare for an anticipated British attack

- **July:** British forces arrived in New York; the Continental Congress signed the Declaration of Independence; the Congress ordered Washington to hold New York at all cost
- **August:** the Continental Army was routed in the Battle of Long Island
- **September:** British forces captured Manhattan
- **November:** British forces captured Fort Washington and Fort Lee and took almost 3,000 prisoners
- **December:** Washington led the Continental Army to safety by crossing the Delaware River in Pennsylvania; he recrossed the Delaware River and defeated British and Hessian forces at the Battles of Trenton and Princeton; British forces ended pursuit of the Continental Army and returned to New York City, where they spent much of the remainder of the war

- **1781:** Washington defeated General Cornwallis at the Battle of Yorktown, effectively winning the American Revolution
- **1783:** Treaty of Paris officially ended the American Revolution
- **1787:** Elected president of the Constitutional Convention
- **1789:** Elected first president of the United States
- **1793:** Reelected president of the United States
- **1797:** Retired from public life after his second term as president
- **1799:** Died at Mount Vernon, Virginia, at the age of sixty-seven

THE NATURE OF COMPOSURE

Leaders understand that crisis and unexpected events are inevitable. More than that, they know that crisis is a major driver of change, and change is essential to leadership. But crisis can also lead to panic, which can be devastating. Kipling accurately points out that blame is an inevitable part of panic—and leaders know that in the midst of panic the blame will be directed at them.

Composure, the ability to remain calm and self-possessed, was the first of the attributes Kipling described in "If—." He recognized that one's ability to maintain composure, to "keep your head," is one of the greatest leadership challenges. The ability to transform a crisis into positive action is a major determinant in one's success as a leader.

To understand composure, we must understand its opposite: panic. What is panic? For an individual, panic is defined as "a sudden overpowering fright." For a group or organization, the sensation is similar but occurs on a larger scale: "a sudden unreasoning terror often accompanied by mass flight." What causes one individual's fright to become a large-scale panic? There are numerous causes, including a lack of information, conflicting information, imminent danger, and unanticipated adversity.

Some crises we encounter will escalate into panics. The genesis of such a crisis may be a small and immaterial event that quickly spins out of control. However, as leaders we must strive never to allow ourselves to panic. How many crises have turned to panic or even disaster because a would-be leader failed to keep his head? What role does a leader play in controlling panic? Primarily, the leader must assess the situation and share information in a clear and concise way. A leader must always remain calm and demonstrate that he or she is in control. A leader must also exude a positive but realistic attitude.

Why do some individuals keep their heads "when all about them are losing theirs"? Are some people naturally more composed than others? Obviously, some people are more volatile and are not well suited for dealing with panic and crisis. This doesn't mean they are not capable of being outstanding leaders. It does mean that they should avoid roles that are prone to crises and volatility.

While most of us cannot imagine confronting crises like those Washington faced, as leaders we are likely to find ourselves in situations when all about us are losing their heads and blaming it on us. Sometimes, just like Washington, we will deserve the blame thrown our way. We may even find ourselves compounding our mistakes, as Washington did. He could have continued to compound his mistakes, but he was able to maintain his composure, assess his options, and act decisively and effectively. Washington decided to abandon New York. This decision exposed him to more criticism and blame. His critics accused him of running away and failing to follow Congress's orders to defend New York. Despite these daunting setbacks, Washington maintained the composure and confidence to launch his counterattacks across the icy Delaware River. His response to failure became the basis for his eventual triumph.

Go to any newspaper archive and scan the headlines for any period of time, paying close attention to the political or business scandals reported. What could the executives who were responsible for the scandals have done differently? There were probably numerous opportunities for someone to exhibit composure and leadership. Often all it takes to establish control is for one leader to stand up and say, "Stop! What are we doing?" Taking stock of the situation, as Washington did, and recognizing the right thing to do is the first step toward regaining control and averting panic.

WASHINGTON'S LESSONS

There are two distinct sets of lessons for us to learn from Washington's actions: those regarding our choices during crises, and those involving awareness and preparation ahead of them. Washington's choices centered on four critical behaviors:

1. ***Washington chose to take responsibility and control.*** He led by recognizing the situation for what it was: an absolute personal and professional failure. He didn't try to cover up his mistakes by spinning the situation or placing blame. He never allowed others to receive or accept any of the blame for the situation. Washington stoically accepted it, and then he moved forward. Taking responsibility is our first step as well. Our willingness to accept the blame and criticism of others goes a long way toward restoring confidence and control. Surprisingly, many leaders don't do this out of fear of seeming weak, when in fact doing so is an incredible show of strength.

2. ***Washington chose to respond decisively and executed effective contingency plans.*** Any uncertainty or vacillation on his part would have destroyed the confidence that his composure had created. His success reflects his understanding of what was

important and what was urgent. Ultimate victory was the most important goal, but Washington knew that saving his army was his most urgent priority. His actions in the fall of 1776 reflected Washington's singular focus on that priority, while projecting absolute confidence in his ability to achieve it—even if he harbored private doubts. People want to know someone is in charge. One of the best ways to show them is by taking action to stop the bleeding. This is a great opportunity to execute those contingency plans no one thought we would ever use. Lastly, we may need help, so we need to be ready to ask for it.

3. **Washington chose to remain visible to his troops, and he shared information they needed to do their jobs.** He stayed with his troops during the evacuation of Long Island, and he was among the last to board a departing ferry. He also remained visible to Congress by keeping them informed via regular correspondence. Visibility matters because it is how people can see our composure. It doesn't matter how composed we remain in a crisis if people can't see us.

4. **Washington projected a positive attitude.** Historians often use the word gravitas in describing Washington. His seriousness defined him and was at the heart of his composure and positive attitude. Washington did not allow others to see his concern. Even when he inadvertently received a letter from General Lee to Joseph Reed—two of Washington's most trusted subordinates—disparaging his qualifications and courage, Washington simply forwarded the note to Reed and stated that he had not realized it was a private letter. He went on to thank Reed for his "trouble and fatigue." Most of us would have responded to this insult with outrage, but Washington understood that he must maintain his composure at all costs.

Washington's choices reflected an extraordinary level of awareness and preparation for leadership. He was ready when the situations arose. So, what had Washington done to prepare himself for the inevitable crises he faced? How can we emulate him and prepare ourselves for the crises we will inevitably face?

5. **From the beginning, Washington understood the entirety of his situation.** His circumspection helped him to realize that he was in a situation for which he was ill prepared. He also knew that he was the only person who was remotely close to being qualified to undertake the task set before him. Like Washington, we must always objectively take stock of the situations we find ourselves in. The better our understanding of our situations and ourselves, the more effectively we will respond to the crises we confront.

6. **Washington was aware of his strengths and weaknesses.** He understood how unprepared he was for the task before him. He used this understanding to prepare for the crises that he faced. Similarly, we need to be aware of our strengths and weaknesses, so we can facilitate effective contingency planning. We can never plan for every eventuality, but by knowing our strengths and weaknesses, we can build our confidence to respond to the crises we encounter. This awareness also enables us to find others to offset our weaknesses.

7. **Washington was aware of the worst-case scenario that the situation presented.** Washington understood the risk he took in accepting the role as commander in chief of the Continental Army. He risked everything—his family, his wealth, his property, his prestige, and ultimately his life. The punishment for treason was death. He would be drawn and quartered, one of the most horrific forms of execution ever devised. Washington was aware of these risks. As he was planning for the attack on Trenton, he scribbled a note to himself: "Victory or Death" was all it said. Washington was among the first to accept these risks, nearly a year before his colleagues in Congress did the same by signing the Declaration of Independence. By understanding and accepting risks before a crisis arises, we

can focus on resolving the crisis when it comes and not panic about what might happen.

8. **Washington understood how to use crisis to mobilize action.** During the war, Washington and his allies in Congress used the threat of crisis and actual crises as catalysts. Late in the war, Washington used the British successes in the south as a lever to drive action in Congress, stating, "While we have been either slumbering and sleeping or disputing upon trifles . . . the whole strength and resources of the Kingdom [have mobilized] against us." He used this and other arguments to chastise Congress into recognizing the challenges the Continental Army faced and the actions needed to support them. Washington understood that there was a thin line between urgency and crisis, and he used this understanding to create the appropriate sense of urgency while preventing panic. We can see this ability in Washington's efforts to rescue his army by escaping across the Delaware River in late 1776.

9. **Washington was absolutely committed to the cause for which he was fighting.** This wasn't just a job for him. He was fully dedicated, and his decision to lead the Continental Army was not a rash decision. Washington had become increasingly devoted to the American cause in the years leading up to the outbreak of hostilities. His devotion enabled him to accept the risks he faced, and it gave him the strength and fortitude to persevere when crises occurred. Like Washington, we must commit ourselves to the efforts we lead.

General George Washington's actions reveal the importance of composure and the challenges that come with it. This attribute is essential to our success as leaders and to the lives and careers of those we lead. Consider what might have happened if Washington had lost his head. There are innumerable points during the New York campaign when a loss of composure would have resulted in the Continental Army's destruction. Historians agree that this would have ended the American Revolution. Washington and most of the Founding Fathers would have been jailed or executed. The ripple effects would have fundamentally changed the course of history.

The essential lesson to take from this chapter is that leaders control a crisis. They never allow a crisis to control them. Washington showed both the ability to respond effectively when crisis struck and the ability to prepare himself for effective response. As leaders, we must do the same so that we can respond effectively and decisively.

Everyday Composure

During high school and college, I had the best summer job in the world. I was an oceanfront lifeguard. In the summer of 1984, after three years on the beach, I was promoted to lieutenant. That meant I was responsible for a ten-block section of beach. One of the things all lifeguards quickly learn—and that *Baywatch* failed to document—is the most common task we perform: reuniting lost children with their parents. It happened hundreds of times every summer.

We taught every rookie lifeguard an important rule about lost kids. Parents always assume the worst, and many will insist that they last saw their lost child in the water. Many quickly jump to the conclusion that their child has drowned and demand that we start a full-scale search-and-recovery operation. We taught every new guard to ask one simple question: "Where exactly was your child when you saw him go under water and not come up?" Over the years, every time I asked that question, the parent responded with something like, "I didn't." We would always find the child wandering the beach lost and scared.

One day in June of my first summer as a lieutenant, I got a call from one of my rookie guards that a child was lost and the parents believed he had drowned. When I arrived on the scene, everyone—the lifeguard, the parents, the bystanders—was panicked. *Everyone* believed the child had drowned. Unfortunately, my training failed me, and I began to panic as well.

I was just preparing to declare a drowning and start a full-scale search-and-recovery when my boss, Rob Hudome, arrived on the scene. He realized immediately what was happening. He looked at the father and calmly asked that all-important question, "Where exactly was your child when you saw him go under water and not come up?" The father replied just as Rob knew he would: "I didn't." Rob calmly, but emphatically stated, "Sir, your son did not drown. He is simply lost, and we will find him shortly." Within minutes, we had found the child and reunited him with his parents.

Because he kept his head, Rob prevented the crisis from becoming a true panic and restored control. I learned an important lesson that day. Rob taught me the power of composure and the ability of one strong leader to establish control in the midst of chaos.

RECOMMENDED RESOURCES

Resources about George Washington:

His Excellency: George Washington by Joseph J. Ellis
1776 by David G. McCullough
The Real George Washington by Jay A. Parry and Andrew M. Allison

Resources about Composure:

Holding the Center: Sanctuary in a Time of Confusion by Richard
    Strozzi Heckler
*So Smart But...: How Intelligent People Lose Credibility—and How
    They Can Get it Back* by Allen N. Weiner

CHAPTER 14

John "Blackjack" Pershing's Patience: When Waiting Counts

If you can wait and not be tired by waiting,
Or being lied about, don't deal in lies

PERSHING'S PATIENCE

When America declared war on Germany and its allies on April 6, 1917, the United States military was completely unprepared for war. The prewar American military reflected its primary mission of the previous decade, fighting Mexican bandits and putting down Latin American insurrections. It lacked most of the modern weapons of the day. It had no aircraft, tanks, or modern artillery. American industry was exclusively focused on civilian manufacturing, which had to be converted to military production.

President Woodrow Wilson gave General John "Blackjack" Pershing the task of leading America into the war. Pershing understood America's deficiencies. When he took command, America had an army of only 27,000 soldiers. His initial estimates of his needs were for an army of 1.5 million men. By war's end, less than two years later, he would grow the United States Army to more than 2 million soldiers.

When General Pershing and his staff arrived in Paris in June of 1917, soon after Pershing received his charge from the president, a member of his staff was quoted as saying, "Lafayette, we have arrived." This declaration gave a lift to the morale of the war-weary British and French, but their enthusiasm quickly turned to impatience. When the first American troops began arriving in France in June 1917, British and French commanders planned to use them to fill holes in their existing armies. They made a compelling case about their urgent needs. Many Allied leaders believed that without these American reinforcements, the Germans would exploit the weakened lines and defeat the Allies.

However, American soldiers did not join the fight actively until October 1917. It was not until early 1918 that America deployed its troops in meaningful numbers. This was because Pershing insisted that Americans must fight as an intact force under American command, and he refused to succumb to the pressure to split up the American forces to augment the British and French armies. The opposing armies were locked in a deadly stalemate, and Pershing believed this deadlock afforded him the time to transform the raw American troops into an effective game-changing army. Pershing firmly believed America offered more than just soldiers to replace the millions lost in the previous years of the war. He felt America could fundamentally change how the war was being fought, which would help lead to an ultimate allied victory.

Pershing acknowledged that his plan faced one major obstacle: the time needed to recruit, train, equip, and organize America's new army. This meant that Pershing's approach required more time and patience than the Allied leadership was prepared to endure. His plan to overcome this obstacle was two-pronged. America would focus its energy on recruiting, training, and organizing an army as quickly as possible. In parallel, Pershing planned to rely on France and Britain to arm and equip his soldiers. This approach would avoid the delays caused by the inadequacies of America's industrial infrastructure. Even with this approach, best estimates anticipated full American engagement by early 1918. This timetable was unacceptable to the Allies, and they continued to advocate for a piecemeal approach. Under their proposed plan, as troops arrived in France, the Allies would use them as needed.

Pershing, with President Wilson's support, refused. He insisted that the only way for the Allies to defeat Germany and its allies was for the Americans to enter the war as a cohesive fighting force. Pershing believed that this approach would provide the destabilizing pressure needed to win the war more quickly. He was convinced that Allied victory was dependent on learning from the lessons of the preceding three years, and he planned to use the American army to fundamentally change how the war was being fought. This position was reinforced by several Allied military failures in mid-1917. These failures further exposed the need to rethink how the Allies were fighting the war. Pershing recognized that the years of trench war-fare had undermined the morale of the French and British armies. He believed that their low morale would infect the American units if he allowed them to be integrated into the Allied armies.

While Pershing had sound reasons for his convictions, he had to overcome significant objections. Some Allied leaders accused Pershing of being obstinate and overconfident. They felt he was understating the urgency of the situation. Pershing, however, had assessed the level of urgency and the risks his plan posed. While he shared the other Allied leaders' sense of urgency, he felt he had sufficient time to implement his plan. He had learned that there was consensus among the Allied field commanders and some senior military and civilian leaders that the current deadlock could not be broken until mid-1919. The piecemeal addition of US troops would not change the situation. This assessment gave Pershing confidence that he had time to build his army, in spite of the many objections.

By late 1917, the wheels of Pershing's plan were in motion. Fresh American troops were pouring into France to complete their train-ing. By July 4, 1918, more than one million Americans had arrived in France. Pressure continued throughout 1917 and into 1918 for Pershing to abandon his plan. But he held fast while demonstrat-ing appropriate flexibility. On two occasions, he recognized the need to respond to an immediate threat. In March and April 1918, the Germans launched two offensives that threatened to over-whelm the French and jeopardize the entire war effort. Both times, Pershing saw the potential for disaster and altered his plan by send-ing American divisions to reinforce the beleaguered French. He saw these offensives as genuine and legitimate risks, so he responded to the Allies' urgent call for troops.

Pershing used the Allies' impatience to advance his agenda. Late in 1918, when British commanders and political leaders were pressuring him to move faster, he leveraged their urgency to ob-tain more British transport ships to accelerate the movement of US troops across the Atlantic.

By August 1918, Pershing's plan was in full swing as the US First Army came into existence. Pershing's efforts and patience showed immediate and impressive results. The successes at Chateau-Thierry and Belleau Woods proved American fighting abilities and the wisdom of Pershing's plan. In both battles, the American forces under American command won stunning victories. America quickly became the destabilizing force Pershing had anticipated. During the fall, the Allied armies experienced unprecedented success.

On November 11, 1918, Germany signed the armistice. Less than two years after the Americans entered the war, and only three months following the introduction of the Americans as a cohesive fighting force, the war was over. The Allies had won. Did Pershing's plan alone lead to victory? Clearly not. All of the Allied efforts were essential to victory. The Allied armies had paid an awful price in waging a long, brutal war that bled Germany dry. Great Britain, France, and their allies had sacrificed more than 20 million soldiers during the preceding four years. The Royal Navy's blockade cut off Germany from its sources of military and civilian supply, thus undermining Germany's will and ability to fight. Pershing's approach to fighting the First World War, however, has been widely recognized as a deciding factor in the speed of victory. Had Pershing succumbed to pressure, many historians believe the war could have dragged on for at least another year, costing hundreds of thousands more lives.

JOHN "BLACKJACK" PERSHING TIMELINE: LEADING WITH PATIENCE

- ➤ **1860:** Born near Laclede, Mississippi
- ➤ **1882:** Sworn in as a West Point cadet
- ➤ **1886:** Graduated from West Point and commissioned second lieutenant in the United States Army
- ➤ **1895:** Commanded a troop of the Tenth Cavalry
- ➤ **1897:** Appointed an instructor at West Point; given the nickname Blackjack as a derogatory reference to his leadership of African American soldiers
- ➤ **1898:** Served with distinction in the Spanish-American War
- ➤ **1905:** Promoted to brigadier general by President Theodore Roosevelt

- ➤ **1914:** First World War began
- ➤ **1916:** Pershing commanded US forces to capture Mexican revolutionary leader Pancho Villa; Pershing's wife and three daughters killed in a house fire; Pershing was promoted to major general
- ➤ **Events of 1917:**
    - ➤ **April:** America entered First World War
    - ➤ **May:** Pershing appointed by President Wilson to command the American Expeditionary Force (AEF), an army of less than 30,000 that needed to grow to more than 2 million soldiers; promoted from major general to general; departed United States for France
    - ➤ **June:** Arrived in France with a small force of 14,000 soldiers and headquarters staff
    - ➤ **July:** Proposed initial plans for the AEF and insisted that forces remain under American command; established training facilities for AEF soldiers
    - ➤ **October:** AEF grew to 100,000 soldiers; US First Division arrived at the front
- ➤ **Events of 1918:**
    - ➤ **May:** AEF reached one million soldiers in France, with 500,000 on the front lines
    - ➤ **July:** First American engagements, the Battle of Hamel and the Second Battle of the Marne, took place
    - ➤ **September:** AEF engaged in the first distinctly American offensive, the Battle of Saint Mihiel; Battle of Meuse-Argonne launched; Allied victories forced German armistice
    - ➤ **November:** Armistice signed, ending hostilities; AEF grows to 2 million soldiers
- ➤ **1919:** Pershing promoted to general of the Army (the first time in US history that this rank was awarded)
- ➤ **1924:** Retired from army
- ➤ **1948:** Died in Washington, DC

THE ESSENCE OF PATIENCE

Patience is a virtue. This pearl of wisdom has been a bone in the throat of even the most patient leader. Patience is an easy thing to talk about, but it is extremely difficult to practice. Most of us think of patience as a construct of time, but Kipling addresses the broader definitions. He refers to the patience required to bear the nagging and sniping that often accompany a decision to wait.

Patience is a quality often lacking among today's leaders. Society expects those in charge to take action quickly and decisively. True leaders recognize that patience enables them to take stock of a situation, to understand what is required, and to wait while they build the capacity to take appropriate and effective action. Patience requires composure and character. Societal pressures for action may cause others to criticize and condemn a leader's perceived inaction or lack of speed. Our stakeholders will first demand quick and decisive action. Then they will demand equally quick results. The greater the crisis, the greater the impatience. But by demonstrating patience, leaders reinforce the importance of focusing on the long-term outcomes. Patience does not mean ignoring the interim milestones or short-term deliverables. It does mean keeping them in context.

Many tasks associated with leadership require patience: strategic planning, complex negotiations, people development, and program management. The bigger the issue and the longer the planning horizon, the greater the patience required to remain committed. For example, strategic plans typically have a long-term time horizon and address the big issues that affect an organization. It is easy for a leader to see the desired end state and want to jump ahead without exercising the patience needed for long-term success. Leadership means understanding that patience may require sacrificing short-term accomplishments for long-term results.

Patience has contributed to many great leadership successes, and impatience has led to many failures. Benjamin Franklin's successful negotiation with France to support the American Revolution was a great test of his patience. It required years of hard work and sacrifice, but in the end, it was instrumental in securing American independence. Gandhi exhibited extraordinary patience in working for an independent India. For more than thirty years, Gandhi worked, never varying from his commitment to nonviolence. His patience resulted in a free India.

Many encouraged Franklin and Gandhi to give up or to compromise, but their successes relied on their patience. Most of us think about the patience required to wait months to build the capability to take action. Franklin and Gandhi recognized that they must work and wait for years or even decades before they could succeed.

Impatience was at the heart of the international financial crisis that led to the recession that began in 2008. Many attribute the source of the crisis to greed and regulatory failures. I would argue that the root of the problem was impatience on the part of investors, consumers, lenders, and regulators. Everyone wanted immediate results. Too many people lacked the patience required to create long-term value. This impatience led to disaster.

PERSHING'S LESSONS

General John "Blackjack" Pershing's extraordinary patience during the First World War helped him and the Allies to achieve great success. Our successes as leaders require patience as well, even if our challenges pale in comparison to building, training, and equipping an army of 2 million men. The patience that Pershing showed was a function of extraordinary leadership.

1. ***Pershing assessed the situation and established the facts.*** A patient leader understands the situation. How important is this problem? How urgent is its resolution? If we are facing a challenge that is both important and urgent, patience may be a luxury we cannot afford. In the previous chapter, Washington didn't have time to contemplate all of his options and to develop a comprehensive plan to defeat the British. The situation required immediate and decisive action. Once his army was safe and the crisis had passed, Washington was able to formulate his plan. Pershing, on the other hand, had ample time. He accumulated sufficient data to make an informed

and grounded assessment. He surrounded himself with a team of trusted experts. He asked questions of those who had already faced this challenge. Finally, he relied on his own expertise, skills, and abilities. President Woodrow Wilson chose Pershing because he was the best person to handle the job. As leaders, we must recognize that we are chosen for our own expertise, skills, and abilities—and we must trust these. Similarly, we must be willing to ask others for their opinions and rely on their expertise.

2. ***Pershing had the patience and discipline to create a robust plan.*** Patience requires us to know what we are going to do. As leaders we must each create a plan that aligns with our vision and our principles. A thorough and well-articulated plan can take many forms and can follow a variety of methodologies. A plan's effectiveness comes down to managing three things: scope, schedule, and budget. What are we going to do? When are we going to do it? What will it cost? There are many details, but they all fit into those three buckets. Planning is a critical management function that helps leaders to build stakeholder confidence. The complexity and comprehensiveness of a plan should reflect the nature of the problem we are solving.

3. ***Pershing understood the importance of building support and getting the right backing.*** Any good program manager knows that having a powerful and engaged champion is the best way to relieve the pressure from impatient stakeholders. President Woodrow Wilson's support gave General Pershing the confidence he needed to withstand intense pressure. Pershing also built and maintained a broad base of support in Washington, but Wilson remained the key. Pershing understood the importance of effective communication. He kept Wilson appropriately informed throughout the war. Leaders learn to understand and respond to stakeholder and sponsor needs. Knowing how, when, and what to communicate is essential to maintaining the support that allows us to "wait and not be tired by waiting."

4. *Pershing had the determination and discipline to execute his plan on his schedule.* Pershing understood that his greatest constraint was time. He needed time to recruit, train, equip, and fully prepare his army. Had he succumbed to the Allies' pressure, the American troops would have faced the same fate as their British and French counterparts. They would have fought and died using the same failed approach that the Allies had used for years. Instead, Pershing stuck to his plan, and the United States Army entered the war as a destabilizing force that brought about a speedy victory.

We have all heard this advice: "Undercommit and over-deliver." Our patience as leaders will be tested by the anxieties of others. The best way to allay their anxieties is to deliver results. If the key to building support for our plan is communication, then the key to retaining that support is doing what we promised. Pershing knew this, so he held himself and his army to the highest standard. Great leaders realize the importance of maintaining the same high standard.

5. *Pershing prepared to respond to the unexpected.* There is an old military saying, "No plan survives the first shot of battle." Nothing ever goes as planned, and our patience can be sorely tested by this fact. The sign of a good plan and a great leader lies in the ability to respond effectively when things do not go according to plan. Unforeseen events always undermine our plan and our patience. Pershing's plans did not anticipate the success of the German offensives in March and April 1918, but his plans were fluid enough for him to respond decisively and effectively. He responded to the unexpected threat without jeopardizing his overall plan. We know that unanticipated events will occur. Our plans should have the flexibility to allow us to respond when they do.

Leaders often face challenges for which they are unprepared. Having the patience to plan and respond deliberately may cause others to attack us. Leadership means enduring their attacks. America entered the First World War unprepared. In less than two years,

General Pershing built an army from nothing and created a force that decided the Allied victory. Pershing's patience was the key to that victory.

Often the greatest threat to a leader's success is his or her unwillingness to bear the affliction. To "wait and not be tired by waiting" can test even the most patient leader. With careful assessment and planning, patience can lead to victory over our own leadership challenges.

Everyday Patience

Youth sports can be a great test of patience. My eleven-year-old son's soccer team is no different. Mike Zohab, or Coach Mike, is one of the most patient and composed leaders I have ever met. Over the past four years, I have observed his extraordinary leadership skills on the soccer field, and I've also witnessed the way those skills carry over into Mike's everyday and professional life.

Mike experiences all of the usual challenges associated with youth sports—unruly kids, demanding parents, real injuries, fake injuries, overly competitive fellow coaches, questionable calls made by the refs—and takes it all in stride. Physically, Mike looks the part of coach: big, imposing, and powerful. He is a police captain in Richmond, Virginia. If you don't know him, he can be intimidating.

Like any good coach, Mike starts the season by assessing his team's overall strengths and challenges. He also assesses each individual player. He uses this assessment to formulate his plan. Many of the boys have played for Mike for multiple seasons, so his plans have a multiyear time horizon. He thinks in terms of how he can develop lifelong soccer players.

Mike comes to practice knowing which specific skills need development, but he also has the ability to read the team in the moment and respond to their needs. During a recent practice, the boys were distracted and unfocused. Mike sensed that they needed to blow off some steam, so he asked them what they wanted to do that day. They wanted to scrimmage, so he let them. While that practice was a diversion from his plan, it was what they needed. On another day, the team was acting in a rebellious and disrespectful manner. Mike sensed that they needed a firm hand, so he modified his plan to include push-ups and running. As usual, he maintained control, and he never lost his temper. After practice, I complimented him on his ability to remain patient and flexible. He replied, "I get very impatient—I just don't show it."

Mike's patience is legendary during soccer games. Unlike many youth coaches, he doesn't give constant direction to the team. He makes appropriate comments and gives encouragement, but he never yells. No matter what happens, he uses a calm yet commanding voice, always including a "please" or a "thank you." The contrast between Mike and other coaches is striking. My son recently said, "All the other coaches yell too much. Coach Mike gets us to do stuff by being nice."

Maybe Mike's ability to bear anything calmly comes from his career in law enforcement, where patience can avert potentially lethal situations. But I think Mike's leadership patience is rooted more deeply; it comes from his awareness of what really matters and his choice to keep things in perspective.

RECOMMENDED RESOURCES

Resources about Pershing:

Pershing by Jim Lacey
World War I by S. L. A. Marshall

Resources about Patience:

Choosing Civility: The Twenty-Five Rules of Considerate Conduct by
    P. M. Forni
Wherever You Go, There You Are by Jon Kabat-Zinn
The Highway to Leadership by Margaret Slattery

CHAPTER 15

Thomas Edison's Enthusiasm: The Energy to Fill Every Minute

If you can fill the unforgiving minute
With sixty seconds' worth of distance run

EDISON'S ENTHUSIASM

Many people criticized Thomas Alva Edison for his numerous unsuccessful attempts to invent a commercially viable lightbulb. Edison's response revealed the most important characteristic that contributed to making him history's greatest inventor: his enthusiasm. He said, "Results? Why, man, I have gotten lots of results! If I find ten thousand ways something won't work, I haven't failed. I am not discouraged, because every wrong attempt discarded is often a step forward." His enthusiasm kept him motivated. He saw every setback as a step on the path to ultimate success.

True, Edison is without rival as an inventor, and his scientific and engineering advances changed the world. Yet he was more than this. He was an entrepreneur who founded companies that have become American icons. He was also a visionary and transformational leader. He saw opportunities others missed. He solved problems that had stumped many other great thinkers for decades. What made Edison different? What set him apart as a leader?

Were Edison's innovation and creativity simply a matter of his extraordinary intelligence, curiosity, and good luck? While all three played important roles in his success as an inventor, his greatest attribute was his enthusiasm. Enthusiasm enabled Edison to fill every minute "with sixty seconds' worth of distance run." He once said, "The three great essentials to achieve anything worthwhile are: Hard work, Stick-to-itiveness, and Common sense." Two of these, hard work and stick-to-itiveness, were products of his enthusiasm. Edison's enthusiasm gave him the energy to work hard and the patience and fortitude to stick to whatever he undertook.

And his enthusiasm paid off. In his lifetime, Thomas Edison received 1,093 US patents, the most patents awarded to any one person. He also received numerous Canadian and British patents. His inventions and innovations made him famous, wealthy, and powerful.

For much of his early life, Edison's enthusiasm and intelligence were his only true assets. He lacked many of the characteristics and opportunities typical of an outstanding engineer, scientist, or inventor. His upbringing was unusual in that his formal education was very limited. Edison's family did not make school a priority. His father was virtually illiterate. While Edison's mother was reasonably well educated, she was generally ignorant of the subjects most important for Edison's future: mathematics and science.

Edison frustrated many authority figures—teachers, employers, and investors—because his approach to problem solving often challenged conventional thinking. Some questioned his intellectual ability. (One teacher called him "addled.") Much of this trouble stemmed from Edison's curiosity and enthusiasm. Many who thought him unintelligent simply could not see what he saw, understand his interests, or comprehend his questions.

Throughout his life, Edison learned quickly, and he often became bored. This led to frequent daydreaming. He was impatient to do things, rather than read about or study them. He once said books could "show the theory of things . . ., [but] doing the thing is what counts." He constantly sought to understand how things worked. His curiosity was a lifelong source of creativity, but it led to an endless stream of questions that frustrated all who knew him.

This curiosity, combined with his inexhaustible enthusiasm, defined Edison as an inventor. These two characteristics drove him to solve some of the most perplexing technical challenges of his day. The sheer number of Edison's inventions—as well as the variety of disciplines in which he worked—proved how extraordinary he was. He is best known for his work with electricity, entertainment, and telecommunications, but he also worked in mining, construction, chemical engineering, medical technology, and botany. He often bounced among the various domains of research at once. Edison relied heavily on his team of assistants and engineers to achieve his results. His passion and excitement drove his own efforts—and his passion and excitement energized and motivated others.

Even Edison's catastrophic failures revealed his unflagging passion. Edison spent more than a decade and much of his fortune attempting to improve iron-ore processing. While he was never successful, he never lost his passion for the project. Many of his critics called this effort "Edison's folly." He believed, however, it was important work. He felt he could revolutionize an industry. While Edison recognized that this would be a difficult and costly undertaking, he believed that he had the ability to make it a success. Ultimately, the iron-ore project almost bankrupted Edison. Years later, he responded to a colleague's lamentations about the money and time they had spent on the project, "Yes, but we had a hell of a good time spending it."

In 1914, Edison's Menlo Park laboratory, which he called the Invention Factory, was virtually destroyed by fire. The fire consumed more than just the buildings and equipment. Much of Edison's research and many of his most important papers also burned. Edison would not allow his loss to stifle his enthusiasm. While Edison's children looked on in dismay, he calmly watched the fire. He shouted to his son, "Charles, where's your mother? Find her. Bring her here. She will never see anything like this as long as she lives." While he was surveying the damage, Edison remarked, "There is great value in disaster. All our mistakes are burned up. Thank God we can start anew."

Edison's enthusiasm touched all aspects of his life. His passion as an inventor and scientist are well known. He was also an enthusiastic business leader and industrialist. He founded numerous companies that commercialized his inventions. Edison used his creativity to support the American war effort during the First World War. Even this endeavor reflects Edison's enthusiasm. His strong personal moral and spiritual beliefs compelled him to nonviolence, yet his love for his country drove him to action. Ultimately, he reconciled these passions by inventing defensive weapons only. After the war he said, "I am proud of the fact that I never invented weapons to kill."

Edison has been called history's greatest inventor. His ability to define and solve problems led to his unprecedented success. The lightbulb exemplifies his essence as an inventor. Just as the incandescent bulb harnesses electricity to illuminate and reveal, Edison's enthusiasm, intelligence, and curiosity illuminated and revealed thousands of inventions and ideas.

THOMAS EDISON TIMELINE: THE SPARKS OF ENTHUSIASM

- ➤ **1847:** Born in Milan, Ohio
- ➤ **1859:** Lost most of his hearing (the cause is unknown)
- ➤ **1868:** Filed his first patent application for the automatic vote recorder
- ➤ **1869:** Patented several telegraph devices
- ➤ **1871:** Devised improvements in stock-ticker technology; married Mary Stilwell
- ➤ **1874:** Invented the quadruplex telegraph for Western Union, which transmitted four messages simultaneously
- ➤ **1876:** Moved to Menlo Park, New Jersey, and established his first full-scale industrial research laboratory
- ➤ **1877:** Invented the carbon transmitter (a crucial improvement in telephone technology) and the phonograph
- ➤ **1879:** Invented the carbon-filament lamp and a direct-current generator for incandescent electric lighting
- ➤ **1881:** Constructed the first permanent central power station
- ➤ **1884:** Mary Edison, his wife, died
- ➤ **1886:** Married Mina Miller, his second wife
- ➤ **1887:** Moved laboratory to West Orange, New Jersey; established the Invention Factory
- ➤ **1892:** Embarked on decade-long failed effort to develop a method for processing low-grade iron ore; nearly went bankrupt
- ➤ **1893:** Demonstrated a system for making and showing motion pictures

- ➤ **1900:** Organized the first modern research-and-development laboratory
- ➤ **1909:** Marketed the alkaline storage battery
- ➤ **1912:** Introduced the Kinetophone, or talking motion picture
- ➤ **1914:** The Invention Factory was destroyed by fire
- ➤ **1916–1917:** Worked with the US military to design defensive weapons and tools
- ➤ **1920s:** Collaborated with Henry Ford and Harvey Firestone to find domestic alternatives to rubber
- ➤ **1931:** Died in Llewellyn Park, New Jersey

THE NATURE OF ENTHUSIASM

Have you ever known anyone who was as enthusiastic as Thomas Edison? Someone who believed that attempting something 10,000 times unsuccessfully isn't a failure? Many people would consider this type of unbridled enthusiasm to be outrageous. It is definitely an anomaly—but it is also worth exploring. Imagine how empowering working for someone like Edison would be. We would likely be more willing to take chances and work harder. Certainly, we would experience more failures, but each of those setbacks would be learning opportunities.

Enthusiasm was at the heart of Edison's innovation and risk taking. What is enthusiasm? How is it different from inspiration? Like boldness and courage, these two attributes are interconnected. Enthusiasm is defined as "a strong excitement of feeling (ardor); something inspiring zeal or fervor." Inspiration breathes life into an idea. Mother Teresa's calling inspired change. Enthusiasm is the sustained energy that fuels creativity and action. Edison's enthusiasm was the fuel that kept his Invention Factory functioning.

Is it a coincidence that success often comes to those leaders who are enthusiastic and upbeat? Enthusiasm is what can make the difference between reaching our goals and giving up. How many great ideas have failed because we lacked the passion to get started? How many more failed because our enthusiasm waned when things got tough?

Great leaders understand the importance of remaining enthusiastic. They know that innovation and change can be unsettling. They know getting and keeping stakeholders on board is impossible without enthusiastic leadership. Enthusiastic leaders tend to be more optimistic. They are more likely to see opportunities that others may miss.

Of course, enthusiasm has its risks and drawbacks. It is easy for enthusiastic leaders to become overly optimistic. Their positive attitudes may cloud their views, causing them to miss threats or issues. They may lose their objectivity and perspective. Our enthusiasm should excite those we lead; our ideas and passion should draw others to follow us. But they must remain grounded in reality.

Remaining positive and demonstrating passion for our ideas and undertakings give those we lead the confidence to follow us. Enthusiastic leaders ground this confidence by proving and sharing their ability to find solutions to the obstacles that they encounter.

Enthusiasm has real value for us as leaders and for those we lead. People want to be around others who are positive; they want to work for leaders who are positive. Edison was a demanding taskmaster who often took credit for the work of others, yet many of the best minds of his day competed for the opportunity to work for him. His enthusiasm attracted and motivated them.

Companies spend billions of dollars to motivate and energize their employees. They spend this money because they know that engaged and enthusiastic employees deliver greater value. Our enthusiasm can attract and inspire people to follow us, and our enthusiastic leadership can help them to achieve more and deliver better results.

For many leaders, enthusiasm comes very naturally. For some professionals—sports coaches, clergy, and politicians, for example—enthusiasm is expected, even demanded. For many of us, however, enthusiasm can seem fake or inauthentic. That may be a reflection of how we feel about the work we are doing, or it may be an indication of our personal commitment. Edison loved what he did. It was never work for him. Similarly, when we truly enjoy our work, we become genuinely enthusiastic.

EDISON'S LESSONS

Edison's life and success show clearly the power an enthusiastic leader can wield. Our ability to harness and use our own enthusiasm may determine our success as leaders. Everyone can feel enthusiastic about something. It is simply a matter of finding the right thing.

1. ***Enthusiasm is an invaluable asset.*** Thomas Edison knew this because he started with nothing except intelligence, curiosity, and enthusiasm. He once said, "If the only thing we leave our kids is the quality of enthusiasm, we will have given them an estate of incalculable value." The same is true of those we lead. If we can instill in them the type of passion Edison showed in all his endeavors, we can unleash limitless potential. Edison knew that his enthusiasm was also important in promoting his inventions and ideas. He invested significant time and ingenuity in making sure that people understood and valued each new invention. As leaders, we must recognize that our ideas and the changes they precipitate may take time to catch on. Remember the old adage, "Enthusiasm is contagious." Our enthusiasm will generate excitement for our ideas and attract followers.

2. ***Edison demonstrated the power of doing what he loved.*** He spent his life focusing his enthusiasm and creativity on things that mattered most to him. Edison once said, "Genius is 1 percent inspiration and 99 percent perspiration." He showed that success requires focus, hard work, and dedication. His enthusiasm was the key to maintaining all three. The source of Edison's enthusiasm was his belief in and passion for his work. He dealt with the drudgery and tedium of invention by remaining focused on his objectives.

    As leaders, we help others stay focused on what matters most. Often, when we undertake a new endeavor, it is difficult to contain people's passion. Soon, even the most exciting projects start to become routine. As leaders we create and maintain enthusiasm by establishing a line of sight between our actions and our ultimate objectives. We help our teams see the difference between activity and action. Simple activity didn't matter to Edison. He said, "Being busy does not always mean real work. The object of all work is production or accomplishment and to either of these ends there must be forethought, system, planning, intelligence, and honest purpose, as well as perspiration. Seeming to do is not doing."

3. *Competition (and much more) motivated Edison.* He saw opportunities everywhere he looked, from the work of competitors to historic successes and failures. Contrary to popular belief, Edison didn't invent the lightbulb. Many other scientists had experimented with early lightbulbs. Humphry Davy created the first incandescent lightbulb in 1802. Several inventors created working lightbulbs in the mid-1800s. The problem was that none was commercially viable. Edison was motivated by his desire to beat his competition to market with a commercially viable lamp. His success was partly driven by the failure of others. Edison understood that his competitors' focus on a particular problem reflected that problem's importance and commercial potential.

How can we use competition to motivate others and ourselves? A crowded competitive field may create greater risk. It may also show us where the opportunities lie. By knowing what the competition is doing, we can generate enthusiasm and excitement. We can harness competitive knowledge, while maintaining our focus on our long-term goals and objectives. This awareness of self and others will enable us to differentiate ourselves from our competitors.

4. *Edison understood the power of fun.* Edison enjoyed life. He enjoyed work. He once said, "I never worked a day in my life. It was all fun." One of the things he liked best about his Invention Factory in Menlo Park was the camaraderie and

practical jokes he and his team shared. Much of Edison's innovation depended on the work and contribution of others. He needed to build an environment that fostered collaboration and collegiality. He needed others to enthusiastically give and receive feedback. Edison knew that often his initial ideas were raw and needed refining. His open working environment allowed others to improve on and expand on his ideas, inventions, and innovations. Open communication and willing cooperation were essential to this process.

How can we spark more creativity and openness among those we lead? Is fun a part of how we work? Many entrepreneurs understand and appreciate the importance of fun. The idea of making work fun was a key element of the dotcom boom of the 1990s. Although some firms may have taken it too far, most companies began to see the practical value in creating a fun work environment. Like Edison, leaders at firms like SAS, Google, and DreamWorks have found ways to combine fun and profitability. Every leader has the same opportunity to use fun to increase creativity and productivity.

5. ***Edison saw obstacles as opportunities.*** Not all of Edison's inventions and innovations were demand driven. Many of his innovations originated from problems he encountered while working on completely unrelated issues. For example, his work with iron-ore refining stemmed from his frustration about the cost of the high-quality steel needed to produce generators and other equipment. Similarly, as leaders we will experience obstacles regularly. Often we seek to work around them. Yet how can our enthusiasm help us see the opportunity that these challenges present? What innovations can come from them?

Some of the obstacles Edison faced were organizational, societal, or cultural. His ability to overcome these was rooted in his enthusiastic spirit, which manifested itself in a variety of ways. Edison believed in maintaining a healthy irreverence about his work and life in general. This went along with having fun, but it was also important in eliminating obstacles.

He liked to challenge conventional thinking. Sometimes that meant breaking rules. Edison once said, "Hell, there are no rules here—we're trying to accomplish something." As leaders, we need to see what rules are interfering with our team's ability to "accomplish something." What can we do to change or eliminate those rules that interfere with delivering value?

The name Thomas Alva Edison is synonymous with inventor and innovator. His creativity and genius forever changed the world. His enthusiasm drove him to think big and to achieve greatness. As enthusiastic leaders, we can also make meaningful change that affects those we work with and lead. Edison chose to see the challenges and problems around him as opportunities. He chose to embrace even the most difficult challenges. He chose to act with enthusiasm and passion and to generate enthusiasm in others. Many of the quotations attributed to Edison reflect his unwillingness to give up—his enthusiasm. We can choose to be like Edison. He once said, "Our greatest weakness lies in giving up. The most certain way to succeed is always to try just one more time." How we tackle the problems, challenges, and choices we face is entirely up to us. Our success depends on maintaining the enthusiasm to try just one more time.

Everyday Enthusiasm

Thomas Edison's advice to parents about instilling enthusiasm in their children made me think of my own children and their passion and enthusiasm for life. Children's enthusiasm stems from the novelty of everything around them. Too soon, our excitement and enthusiasm begin to fade. Somewhere in early adulthood, we stop being amazed by the new and different things we confront. Some people retain their childlike enthusiasm, but most of us lose most or all of it as we grow up.

My son, Max, is a great example of the power of youthful enthusiasm. When he was four years old, as he was playing with one of his friends, he proposed an outlandish idea for making furniture out of paper. His friend looked at him with a furrowed brow and asked incredulously, "Max, when are you going to stop trying to do things that are impossible?" Max responded with equal incredulity, "Never! Someday it'll be possible."

Max has always been a passionate idea guy. In fourth grade, Max told his teacher about an idea he had for curing cancer. She responded with perfect sincerity, "That makes sense. I wonder why no one has ever tried that." When an idea guy is given a little encouragement, he's unstoppable. Curing cancer became *the* topic of conversation for the next month. Max talked about it at the dinner table, in the car on his way to soccer practice, while he was doing his homework—just about everywhere. Enthusiasm can be exhausting—even exasperating—but at the end of the day, I wish I could bottle Max's youthful enthusiasm and give it to everyone I know. It is an extraordinary gift.

RECOMMENDED RESOURCES

Resources about Thomas Edison:

Edison: A Life of Invention by Paul Israel
The Wizard of Menlo Park: How Thomas Alva Edison Invented the Modern World by Randall E. Stross

Resources about Enthusiasm:

Flow: The Psychology of Optimal Experience by Mihaly Csikszentmihalyi
The Wisdom of Crowds: Why the Many Are Smarter Than the Few and How Collective Wisdom Shapes Business, Economies, Societies and Nations by James Surowiecki

CHAPTER 16

Golda Meir's Accountability: The Will to Lose and Start Again

And lose, and start again at your beginnings
And never breathe a word about your loss

MEIR'S ACCOUNTABILITY

On Yom Kippur 1973, Egypt and Syria attacked and nearly destroyed Israel. For most of the prior twenty-five years since Israel's creation, Israel and its Arab neighbors had been in a near-constant state of conflict. During that time, Israel had emerged victorious in the three declared wars, and it had dominated most of the border clashes. Most military experts believed that the Israel Defense Force (IDF) was equipped and trained to continue this trend. So, what led to this near defeat in 1973? And how did Israel emerge victorious?

One of the most important figures of the Yom Kippur War was Israeli prime minister Golda Meir. Her leadership and accountability were instrumental in averting disaster. Ultimate accountability for the mistakes that led to the Yom Kippur War rested with Meir and her government. During the war and the months that followed, Meir never shied away from this accountability, leading her country through one of its darkest periods.

To fully appreciate Meir's leadership, one must understand her life and her relationship to Israel. Meir's story and modern Israel's history are intertwined. Serving her country was the focal point of most of her life. She became active in Zionism, the effort to return Jews to Palestine, as a teen. In 1921, at the age of nineteen, Meir emigrated from the United States to Palestine. She entered politics in the 1930s, helping to establish a political infrastructure for the future Israel.

Following the Second World War, Meir became a leader in the creation of a Jewish state in Palestine. She led the negotiations with the British government, which had legal authority over much of the

Middle East, including the territory that would later become Israel. She also raised tens of millions of dollars to purchase arms and sup-plies in anticipation of Israel's defense. On May 14, 1948, Golda Meir became one of twenty-four signatories to the Israeli Declaration of Independence. She had worked most of her life to achieve this goal. Over the next eighteen years, she held many posts in the Israeli government, including labor minister and foreign minister. Meir left government in 1966 after she was diagnosed with lymphoma.

In 1969, Meir returned to public life to become Israel's third prime minister. During this tumultuous period, Israel faced both internal and external threats. The greatest threats came from its Arab neighbors, who were determined to destroy Israel.

In the summer and fall of 1973, tensions were mounting. Egypt and Syria wanted to avenge their previous losses, especially those of the Six-Day War of 1967, when Israel had decimated them. On October 6, 1973, they launched coordinated attacks against Israeli positions in the Sinai Peninsula and the Golan Heights. The at-tacks caught Israel by complete surprise and proved to be the great-est threat to its survival since Israel's 1948 War of Independence. Accountability for Israel's surprise lay with Meir and Israel's govern-ment, military, and intelligence leaders.

Three issues led to Israel's surprise: overconfidence, intelligence failures, and poor planning. Israel's string of victories had made it overconfident. Its intelligence apparatus had identified the threat, but its leadership had failed to comprehend the danger it posed. Finally, the Israel Defense Force (IDF) and Israel Air Force (IAF) were not prepared for war when it came. Israel's leaders, its military establishment, and its people all believed they were invincible. In the previous three wars, Israel had been vastly outnumbered, yet it had prevailed. During the Six-Day War, Israel lost no tanks and fewer than fifty combat aircraft. Within the first forty-eight hours of the Yom Kippur War, Israel lost nearly 300 tanks and 100 air-planes. During the first week of the war, the situation became so dire that Moshe Dayan, Israel's defense minister, advised Meir to make plans to surrender. This was a situation to which Israel was unaccustomed.

Many of Meir's cabinet ministers called for her to discipline or replace the military and intelligence leaders who had failed to prepare for war. She understood that there would be ample time for assessing blame after the war was over. She also knew that it would be disastrous to try to replace leaders, given the changing conditions and volatility. Some of the most pressing problems involved leaders who were not capable of dealing with the situation. Meir did not even replace those leaders. Rather, she leveraged other more experienced leaders who had the skills needed to buttress those who did not.

Although Egypt and Syria enjoyed early successes, Israel was able to rally and reverse its losses. By the end of hostilities on October 26, Israel had invaded Egypt and was less than eighty miles from Cairo. Israel's success against Syria was even greater. Israel was able to repel the Syrian attack, and the IDF ultimately captured the remainder of the strategically critical Golan Heights. Meir's leadership was an essential component of Israel's victory. She rallied the IDF and the Israeli people. She took decisive action. She took huge political and military risks. She maintained her composure and helped others maintain theirs. Her leadership reflected her overarching sense of accountability.

Israel's victory came at an enormous cost. Its military casualties were staggering. More Israeli soldiers were killed than in any other war since the 1948 War of Independence. Israel lost nearly twenty percent of its airplanes and tanks. The Israeli people lost confidence and began to feel vulnerable. The hubris felt throughout the country prior to the war was replaced by outrage and fear. Israelis were shocked and angered by the military and intelligence failures.

Meir understood the anger, fear, and loss that her people felt. She immediately took accountability. She realized the importance of restoring confidence, and she recognized that accepting accountability was the critical first step in regaining trust. Ultimately, she and her cabinet resigned. This selfless act demonstrated Meir's sense of personal ownership, and it enabled Israel to start rebuilding and restoring its faith in its government.

GOLDA MEIR TIMELINE: LEADING WITH ACCOUNTABILITY

- **1898:** Born Golda Mabovitz in Kiev, Russia

- **1906:** Immigrated with her family to Milwaukee, Wisconsin

- **1917:** Graduated from Milwaukee State Normal School (now called the University of Wisconsin–Milwaukee); married Morris Myerson; became active in the Zionist movement

- **1921:** Moved to Palestine; held key positions in the Jewish Agency and in the World Zionist organization

- **1928:** Entered Zionist politics

- **1948:** Israel created; Meir among signers of the declaration of independence; Meir appointed ambassador to the Soviet Union; Israel was invaded Arab countries, starting the first Arab-Israeli War

- **1949:** Elected to Knesset; appointed minister of labor; first Arab-Israeli War ended

- **1956:** Became minister of foreign affairs; Suez Canal Crisis began

- **1966:** Became secretary general for the Labor Party

- **1967:** Israel seized the Gaza Strip, Sinai Peninsula, and Golan Heights during the Six-Day War

- **1969:** Meir elected prime minister of Israel

- **1973:** Yom Kippur War

  - **September:** King Hussein of Jordan warned Meir of imminent attack; Israeli military and intelligence refused to believe threat was real

  - **October 6:** Meir mobilized the Israeli military at 8:00 a.m.; at 2:00 p.m., Egypt and Syria attacked, causing significant Israeli losses; Israel fought a defensive battle; Meir requested American aid

  - **October 8:** Israeli forces stopped and reversed Syrian attack

  - **October 14:** Israeli forces began to reverse early Egyptian gains; American military supplies began to arrive

➤ **October 25:** Hostilities ended

➤ **1974:** Agranat Commission investigated events that led to the Yom Kippur War; Meir cleared of culpability but resigned as prime minister

➤ **1978:** Died of cancer in Jerusalem, Israel

THE MEANING OF ACCOUNTABILITY

In Chapter 7 on boldness, Jefferson's actions illustrate the benefits that come when you "make one heap of all your winnings" and win. Accountability, on the other hand, is often most important when we lose. Accountability is about starting again. It is about picking up the pieces. It is about rebuilding. Mostly, it is about taking ownership and living with and learning from the consequences of one's choices.

Accountability is defined as an obligation or willingness to accept responsibility or account for one's actions. At its heart, accountability is about a sense of ownership. When we are accountable, we feel that whatever happens, good or bad, is a direct reflection on us. We feel an ownership of and connection to the outcome. Accountability is a very personal matter. Others can hold us responsible for our actions, but only we can take accountability for these same actions. Accountability means we own the decisions that we make and the actions we take. Legend has it that an ancient Roman tradition required the engineer who was accountable for the building of a bridge to stand under it as the capstone was put in place. That action demonstrated his sense of ownership and personal commitment to his work and its outcome.

Leaders must have the strength and confidence to be accountable. Accountability involves a high degree of awareness, honesty, and trust, as well as an orientation toward action. Accountability requires leaders to take action and move decisively. As leaders, others expect us to know what to do next. Accountable leaders articulate a plan, empower others to act, and clear obstacles. Beyond that, accountability requires a commitment to a set of principles that will guide action.

MEIR'S LESSONS

The Yom Kippur War and Golda Meir's responses to it provide great leadership lessons. Of course, most of us cannot imagine facing the type of challenge that confronted her. Meir exhibited accountability in her tactical and strategic leadership. Tactically, she had to stop the bleeding. Egyptian and Syrian forces were streaming across Israel's borders, and it wasn't clear if the IDF and IAF could stop them. Once the crisis was averted, Meir had to attempt to regain lost ground. Strategically, once the war was won, she needed to restore confidence and trust among the Israeli people.

1. ***Golda Meir focused on the problem, not the people.*** During the first two days of the war, it was hard to find anything that had gone right for the Israelis. There was plenty of blame to go around, but accountability is not about blame. Rather, it is about addressing what went wrong and correcting it. During the war and the subsequent investigations into culpability, Golda Meir remained focused on the problem, not the people. As leaders, we must keep in mind that it is easy to focus on who failed rather than focus on the processes that broke down or caused the failure. We may find that part of the problem does involve people's failure to do their duties. In those cases, we may need to take disciplinary action. Meir ultimately removed several senior leaders following the war. Conversely, she also recognized that many mid-level and lower-level people had performed their jobs exceedingly well but that their superiors had ignored their warnings. Meir took steps to recognize and acknowledge them and to include them in lessons learned. When things go wrong, we need to act similarly. Too often, we want to put an incident behind us, so we ignore anyone involved—including those people who were trying their best to warn us.

2. ***Meir took action to restore confidence.*** One of the most effective ways to restore confidence in a crisis is for a leader to assert her accountability. During the disastrous first days of the war,

Meir took public action to regain control. She spoke directly to the Israeli people and assured them that Israel would be victorious. Meir did not downplay the criticality of Israel's situation, but she also did not share all of the facts with the public either. She knew that the citizens were on the verge of panic, so she only told them what they absolutely needed to know.

Leaders are expected to take decisive action. Often this isn't a problem. Most leaders tend to be people of action, so the key challenge is determining what action to take. Sometimes the right action to take is to do nothing, to simply let things continue to progress. Other times, we need to make bold moves, as Meir did. Some in Meir's cabinet were troubled by her decision to only tell the Israeli people what "they needed to know." As a leader, you must know how and when it is appropriate to filter information to others. Confidence can be quickly destroyed by releasing too much information. On the other hand, it can also be destroyed by a perception that you are withholding necessary information.

This does not mean that leaders can lie or deceive others. The argument that the lie or omission is for a good cause can be a slippery slope. Knowing when to filter information can present difficult ethical challenges. The key is ensuring that the whole truth is ultimately told, regardless of the personal pain or discomfort. Once the war was over, Golda Meir revealed all of the facts, and that honesty led to her resignation.

3. *Meir delegated to and empowered others, creating leverage while building confidence.* As prime minister, Golda Meir was commander in chief of the IDF and IAF, but she had no personal military experience. She recognized that she could do the most good by leaving the military decisions in the hands of her defense minister and generals. That didn't mean that she abdicated her accountability for this function. Meir remained actively engaged in the prosecution of the war, and she inserted herself into those decisions that had broader political and international implications. For example, when Moshe

Dayan, the Israeli defense minister, became increasingly vocal about the threat to Israel's survival, she convinced him not to speak publicly. Meir recognized that she could also help the military situation by personally negotiating with the United States to establish an airlift of critical war supplies. She authorized the transfer of resources from the Egyptian front to the Syrian front when it became clear that the situation required it. Throughout the war and the ensuing investigation, Meir always maintained ultimate accountability, whether it was for her own actions or the actions of those she had empowered.

One of the most important skills leaders can possess is the ability to delegate effectively. Knowing when to delegate and when to retain control is essential. Equally important is knowing whom to trust. Delegation can be one of the greatest tests of our accountability. Regardless of the outcome, we are always accountable.

4. **Golda Meir took the blame for the failures and asked for forgiveness.** Once the fighting was over and the immediate threat had passed, she publicly apologized for the failures that led to war and the excessive losses Israel suffered. Meir knew that there was ample blame to be shared, but she would not allow others to take the blame that she believed was hers. Several observers during the Agranat Commission, the independent commission that investigated the events surrounding the war, commented that Meir never tried to defend her actions. She accepted full responsibility. According to one commission member, "She accepted the full burden." The commission exonerated her, but she recognized that public confidence in her and her government was still shaken. On April 10, 1974, just eight days after the Agranat Commission interim report was released, Golda Meir and her cabinet resigned. As a final act of accountability, she agreed to remain in office until June, in order for the new government to be formed.

Golda Meir's life mirrors the story of modern Israel. She was, and remains, one of the best-loved leaders in Israel's history, and she revealed her love and commitment to her country through continued acts of accountability. She served Israel for most of her adult life, even after she had earned a leisurely retirement. Instead, at the age of seventy-one and in poor health, Meir agreed to be prime minister. As prime minister, she led Israel through one of its darkest moments. After resigning from office in 1974, she continued to serve. She used her charisma and strong will to help Israel further its goals. Meir died on December 8, 1978, less than two months after seeing one of her dreams achieved. Israel had made peace with one of its greatest enemies. While she would receive no credit, Golda Meir's leadership laid the foundation for the Camp David Accords and peace between Israel and Egypt.

Robert Slater's biography calls Golda Meir the uncrowned queen of Israel. Although she was not a monarch, her actions showed the accountability of one. Monarchs and the states they lead are often considered inseparable. The same could be said of Golda Meir and Israel.

Everyday Accountability

Accountability is one of the attributes we get many opportunities to practice. We are constantly confronted with decisions and choices that test us. Several years ago, a promising young leader named Mark Hugel was working in my organization. He had performed exceptionally well as a thought leader and as a peer leader, and my colleagues and I were confident in his ability to succeed at the next level. Less than a week before we were going to promote him, Mark came to his direct manager with a problem. Mark had discovered an error in a project that he had recently completed. If this mistake had gone uncorrected, it would have created significant problems that would have affected a large number of customers. By fixing it then, it simply cost us time, but the timing could not have been worse. It was less than two weeks before Christmas, and many of the people whom we needed to fix the mistake were either on vacation or about to leave for vacation. Mark's project was also up for a high-profile award, so he had every reason to just sit on the problem and hope no one noticed it.

Mark's manager was conflicted. He felt that we should proceed with Mark's promotion, but he also knew that several key stakeholders were advocating disciplinary action, not promotion. When we heard the whole story, the project's sponsor and I insisted on proceeding with Mark's promotion for one simple reason. He had done the right thing, even though he knew that it might jeopardize his well-earned promotion. There was one more fact that silenced even his strongest critics: we learned that it was highly likely that no one would have ever known that Mark had caused the problem, and he knew it. He was accountable for his work. He owned it. He also had the integrity to do the right thing, even though no one would have ever known if he had not.

RECOMMENDED RESOURCES

Resources about Golda Meir:

Golda by Elinor Burkett

The Yom Kippur War: The Epic Encounter That Transformed the Middle East by Abraham Rabinovich

Golda, the Uncrowned Queen of Israel: A Pictorial Biography by Robert Slater

Women in Power: The Personalities and Leadership Styles of Indira Gandhi, Golda Meir, and Margaret Thatcher by Blema S. Steinberg

Resources about Accountability:

It's Your Ship: Management Techniques from the Best Damn Ship in the Navy by Captain D. Michael Abrashoff

Teamwork Is An Individual Skill: Getting Your Work Done When Sharing Responsibility by Christopher Avery

Good to Great: Why Some Companies Make the Leap . . . and Others Don't by Jim Collins

Part 4 Summary: Earning and Retaining Trust

In the previous four chapters, we examined how leadership is dependent on our ability to earn and retain the trust of those we lead. This section of the book focused on the privilege and responsibility that leadership carries. All of the "If" Sixteen Leadership Attributes help us earn and retain trust, and composure, patience, enthusiasm, and accountability are particularly important. Now that you have read this section, you should be better prepared to understand the challenges associated with answering the fourth of the "If" Sixteen Leadership Framework questions: *How can you earn and retain the privilege to lead?*

Now consider the final leadership attributes: composure, patience, enthusiasm, and accountability. What have you learned about the distinctions among them? How will their interconnectedness affect how you choose to lead?

PART 4 LESSONS

Composure

1. In the face of the unexpected, leaders step up, take responsibility, and exert control.
2. Leaders respond decisively and execute effective contingency plans.
3. In a crisis, leaders remain visible and share the information others need to do their jobs.
4. Leaders recognize the importance of projecting a positive attitude.
5. Leaders maintain their composure by maintaining perspective.
6. Awareness of their own strengths and weaknesses helps leaders maintain perspective.
7. Leaders don't wait for a crisis to anticipate risks and potential outcomes.
8. Leaders know how to use a crisis to mobilize action.
9. Leaders recognize that commitment is a precursor to composure.

Patience

1. Leading with patience requires that we understand a given situation and establish the facts.
2. Leading with patience starts with having the rigor and discipline to create a robust plan appropriate to the situation we confront.
3. Leading with patience means building support and getting the right backing for our plans.
4. As leaders we must have the determination and discipline to execute our plans on a suitable schedule.
5. Leading with patience means having the foresight and wisdom to anticipate the unexpected and showing the resolve to respond appropriately.

Enthusiasm

1. Leaders recognize that enthusiasm is an invaluable asset.
2. Leaders acknowledge the power of people doing what they love.
3. Leading with enthusiasm means finding motivation in a variety of areas.
4. Leaders recognize that nothing builds excitement and passion better than doing work in a fun environment.
5. Leaders build enthusiasm by turning obstacles into new opportunities.

Accountability

1. Accountable leaders focus on fixing a problem, not placing the blame.
2. Accountable leaders move aggressively to restore confidence.
3. Accountable leaders create leverage and build confidence by delegating and empowering others.
4. Accountability means taking the blame for failures and then asking for forgiveness.

Will You Choose to Lead?

Frequently, people ask why I chose the title *If You Will Lead*. They challenge that the title indicates a degree of uncertainty. My response often surprises them. I tell them, "Good. It is supposed to. Leadership is never certain." I believe that everyone can be a leader. More than that, I believe that everyone *is* a leader at some point or in some situations, but we have a choice about how well we lead.

The greatest uncertainties associated with leadership are how we use the skills and abilities we have, how hard we work to acquire and build those we don't, and how well we create positive change by inspiring and motivating others. We reduce the uncertainty by becoming more *aware* of what it takes to lead well. We reduce uncertainty further by *choosing* to invest and commit ourselves to our development. That means a great deal of hard work.

This book has centered on four simple questions that form the foundation of real leadership and are the basis for the "If" Sixteen Leadership Framework. The preceding chapters examined the attributes we must possess to answer these questions and to become the best leaders we can be. Our ability to answer them will go a long way in determining how effectively we lead:

- Who am I, and what do I believe?
- What do I want?
- How can I attract and motivate others?
- How will I earn and retain the privilege to lead?

While these are simple questions, our ability to answer them completely and honestly is extremely difficult. They are critical to understanding our personal leadership journey, and our willingness to continuously ask and answer them will promote constant growth.

LEARNING WHO YOU ARE AND WHAT YOU BELIEVE

The consistent characteristic that each of the leaders in this book shared was a deep awareness of self. When they were at their best, their actions reflected this awareness. When they slipped or failed, their self-awareness had first slipped or failed as well. The same is true for us.

The "If" Sixteen Leaders all demonstrated the four attributes that most support self-awareness:

- character
- authenticity
- integrity
- self-efficacy

Imagine knowing yourself so completely that you can trust yourself, even when everyone else doubts you and believes you are wrong. Imagine being comfortable enough with who you are that you can be *yourself* regardless of the situation. How would it feel to have the integrity to always seek and defend the truth, regardless of how unpopular it is? What would it be like to have the self-efficacy to confidently take on any task set before you?

This level of self-awareness would be incredibly liberating. It would empower us to act based on what is right, without worrying about what others think. It would allow us to live without fear of judgment. Of course, we might still be wrong or misguided, and there will always be consequences for our actions. We might still fear those consequences.

What would it be like to work for someone like this? She would probably foster these same behaviors and trust in those around her. She would likely encourage her followers to increase their own self-awareness. She would neither fear new or unorthodox ideas, nor would she feel threatened by values or beliefs that conflicted with her own.

Unfortunately, far too few leaders are like this. They may fear conflict. They may seek homogeneity and conformity as a means of minimizing or controlling dissent. Their insecurity may prevent them from encouraging self-awareness among those they lead.

Which type of leader is more appealing? Whom do you want to follow? Most of us would welcome the opportunity to follow someone who is self-aware. Research shows that many of the attributes and characteristics people most admire in leaders reflect a high degree of self-knowledge and self-awareness. In their book *The Leadership Challenge*, James Kouzes and Barry Posner identify the twenty most admired leadership characteristics. Of the twenty, seven relate directly to self-awareness. In their book *Primal Leadership*, Goleman, McKee, and Boyatzis identify self-awareness as one of four domains of emotional intelligence.

The importance of self-awareness is a constant. Consider these thoughts on self-awareness:

> "Knowing others is intelligence; knowing yourself is true wisdom. Mastering others is strength; mastering yourself is true power." (Lao-tzu)

> "Look well into thyself; there is a source of strength which will always spring up if thou wilt always look there." (Marcus Aurelius)

> "As human beings, our greatness lies not so much in being able to remake the world . . . as in being able to remake ourselves." (Mahatma Gandhi)

> "What lies behind us, and what lies before us, are tiny matters compared to what lies within us." (Oliver Wendell Holmes)

It is easy to believe that we are already highly self-aware. In reality, most of us have only scratched the surface of understanding our beliefs and values. Self-exploration and examination are difficult, complex, and often painful. They call for a significant investment of time, thought, and emotional energy. The process requires a willingness to take a step back from our day-to-day tasks. It also necessitates our recognition that this effort has value because we are worth this level of investment. It requires a degree of self-love.

Self-awareness also demands a level of vulnerability that many find disconcerting. I regularly ask clients to inventory and prioritize their values and beliefs. Typically, most people find the process of listing the values that matter most to them easy. What becomes challenging is prioritizing those values. Deciding what truly matters most can be very uncomfortable. Some would argue it's like picking one's favorite child.

Personally, I found this process to be very revealing, yet also troubling. As I contemplated my list of prioritized values, I began to realize that my actions didn't reflect these values. Things that I said were most important to me were too often given a backseat. I wasn't consistently living my values.

This type of realization can lead to self-criticism and recrimination. However, if we move beyond these feelings, we can begin to explore how to make our lives and actions reflect our values. Our increased awareness expands our options and choices. Make no mistake, moving past the self-criticism is very difficult. It can be one of our biggest personal and leadership obstacles. The book *Taming Your Gremlin* by Richard David Carson is a great resource to start with.

Most people want to follow truly self-aware leaders. Most people would like to be more self-aware themselves. How do we go about gaining a greater understanding of our beliefs, our values, and ourselves? How do we better understand and develop our character, authenticity, integrity, and self-efficacy?

There are countless exercises and tools that can help build our self-knowledge and self-awareness. Here are a few to try:

1. ***Values Identification and Prioritization.*** This is a great first step. Appendix 1 lists 130 values. Start by sorting them into two categories: important and unimportant. Take some time to contemplate the two lists. What patterns do you see? Does anything strike you as inconsistent with how you act? Next, start prioritizing your "Important" list. Divide it into two equal lists: more important and less important. Keep doing this until you have a list of your three to five most important values. Now comes the hard part. Pick the value that matters most—the one value that is most important to you.

2. *Values and Behavior Alignment.* Once you have completed the exercise, start looking at how you spend your time. How are you dividing your day? What choices are you making? For example, if you said that family was a top value for you, how does your time reflect this? The problem for many of us is that the boundary between work and home has become less distinct. Our personal and professional lives are more intermingled than ever before. So, when you are making trade-offs between work and family, which one typically wins? How do you spend your money? Does your personal budget reveal what truly matters to you? Next, start examining your affiliations. How do your relationships reflect your values? Do you share the same core values as your employer, friends, religious institution, and so on?

    If the answers to these questions reveal strong alignment between your actions and your values, keep doing what you're doing. If they don't, start exploring what this misalignment means. When I have done this, I have found two common trends. First, I wanted certain values to be important but found that, in reality, they were not. More commonly, my problem was a failure to recognize the choices I was making and those I was not. I would realize that by choosing one path or action over another I was unwittingly prioritizing one value over another. This awareness doesn't make the choices easier, but it does help us recognize that it is up to us to choose.

3. *River of Life Exercise.* This exercise is most often used as a team-building exercise. It can also be useful for self-examination and self-discovery. It uses a river as a metaphor for one's life. It helps visually document your life history. Using a flip chart or butcher paper, draw a river to represent your life. Your river should show changes in direction (bends and curves), major events (streams and other rivers feeding your river), obstacles (waterfalls, rapids, and obstructions), and periods of calm. Next to the river, draw symbols to illustrate important life events. Include personal and professional events or issues. Document successes and failures. Don't worry about

the quality of the drawing. Focus on the subtle messages the exercise reveals. Spend as much time as you need on this. Put it aside for a week, and then revisit the drawing. Once you feel the history is complete, add a section of river to describe your future. Where is your river heading? What does the drawing tell you about who you are and what really matters to you? The final step in this exercise is to share it with those who are important to you.

If these exercises don't work for you, there are many more available. Simply type "self-awareness exercises" into your search engine. You will be amazed at the number and diversity of tools available. Regardless of how we get there, understanding who we are and what we believe is the first step in achieving our leadership potential.

KNOWING WHAT YOU WANT

Abraham Lincoln, Martin Luther King, Jr., Thomas Jefferson, and Harriet Tubman were great leaders not only because they knew themselves but also because they knew what they wanted. They showed clarity of purpose that enabled them to effect incredible change. They lived the four attributes most closely aligned with knowing what we want:

- ambition
- vision
- boldness
- resilience

These four leaders all had strong a desire to achieve goals that were important to them. They described compelling visions of the future that excited others and themselves. Their ambition and vision encouraged them to act boldly and gave them the resilience to overcome obstacles. Collectively, these attributes drove these leaders to define, describe, and achieve extraordinary results.

In the book *Alice's Adventures in Wonderland*, Alice's conversation with the Cheshire Cat illustrates what happens to those who don't know what they want and where they want to go.

Alice asked, "Would you tell me, please, which way I ought to go from here?"

"That depends a good deal on where you want to get to," said the Cat.

"I don't much care where," said Alice.

"Then it doesn't matter which way you go," said the Cat.

Like Alice, if we don't know where we are going—or what we want to achieve when we get there—then what we choose really doesn't matter either. Our individual decisions may matter in the short term, and collectively they will take us somewhere. The problem is that the outcome of our choices will be unpredictable. We are unlikely to effect meaningful change. We may also find ourselves doing things we don't like or want to do.

Early in my career, I had vague ambitions and goals. As a result, many of my actions and decisions were tactical in nature. Lacking a coherent plan and objective, my choices often had unintended consequences. Once I began to understand and articulate my goals and dreams, I began to see how my individual actions and decisions could help me achieve my long-term goals.

Great leaders effect great change for a variety of reasons. One important reason is that they aim extraordinarily high. Some may even exceed their own audacious expectations. Lincoln never envisioned his level of success or the profound impact he would continue to have. His ambitions were great, and they propelled him beyond his wildest dreams. But what happens to those leaders who aim high and fall short? Many still achieve exceptional results. Some may become frustrated or disappointed. Others recognize that their success—while not as great as they had hoped—has enduring value.

How do we build our ambition, vision, boldness, and resilience? There are numerous tools and exercises that can help us discover and define what we want. Here are three that you may wish to try:

1. ***Write Your Own Eulogy.*** As I was finishing this book, my father passed away. I had the privilege of giving the eulogy at his funeral. This proved to be exceedingly difficult. The hardest part

was distilling all of the stories and anecdotes about him into a comprehensive message. As I thought about the stories, I began to see the themes that defined his life. The events collectively painted a picture of what he had achieved.

Similarly, our lives contain many events and accomplishments. Try writing your eulogy now. If you can't get past the strangeness or morbidity of writing your own eulogy, try writing your own retirement speech. This exercise gives you the opportunity to catalog the things you have already achieved, while starting to identify those things you still want to accomplish. These ambitions and goals should reflect your beliefs and values. As you document the past and predict your future, you may begin to see patterns, trends, and themes. You may start to see and understand what really matters. The last part of this exercise is to pick the one thing you feel is most important to accomplish in your life. It may be simple, or it may be audacious. Whatever it is, by identifying it now, you can begin working to achieve it immediately.

2. **Create a Strategic Plan for Yourself.** Strategic plans are powerful tools that help organizations expand their thinking and focus their efforts. They allow us to step back and contemplate the future objectively and dispassionately, whether we are individuals or organizations. Go through the entire strategic-planning process. Define your personal mission. You can use the self-awareness exercises described on pages 236–238 to help. Articulate a set of measurable objectives that will help you attain the mission over the next ten to twenty years. Assess where you are right now. Look back at what you have accomplished in the past five to ten years. Conduct a SWOT (strengths, weaknesses, opportunities, and threats) assessment.

Using the information you collect, begin formulating a strategy and creating an implementation plan. These should include a list of those capabilities you need to acquire and milestones you must pass to achieve your goals and objectives. The key to success with strategic planning is balancing audacity with realism. Your plan should push you to accomplish more than you believe possible, yet it must be rooted in reality. Share your plan with colleagues, friends, and family. Ask them to provide critical feedback.

3. **Go to the Movies.** I find that movies can be great sources for leadership wisdom. Several movies are particularly helpful in illustrating the power of leaders who know what they want. *Remember the Titans* is an outstanding example of leaders achieving and overcoming seemingly insurmountable obstacles by coming to understand what they truly want. *Braveheart* and *The Pursuit of Happyness* are also good examples. As you watch these movies, notice how the leaders learn about themselves and what they truly want. All of these films highlight that the process of understanding what we want takes time. Our understanding evolves as we become more aware.

   Movies can be used to help you better understand all of the "If" Sixteen Leadership Attributes. John Clemens and Melora Wolff's book, *Movies to Manage By,* is a great resource. All of the films mentioned in their book provide enlightening leadership lessons.

   Whatever you do, figure out what you really want. Be ambitious. Set your sights to achieve something bigger than yourself. Set your goals and pick a path. Be ready to adjust as you learn and grow. Articulate a vision that paints a picture that excites you and others. Act boldly and be prepared to respond to the obstacles that you will confront.

ATTRACTING AND MOTIVATING OTHERS

Only after we know who we are and what we want can we begin to attract others to join us on our journeys. Leaders like Mother Teresa, Nelson Mandela, John Paul Jones, and Jim and Louise Mulligan drew others to them. They made themselves compelling leaders by demonstrating the four attributes that attract and motivate others to follow:

- inspiration
- courage
- selflessness
- stamina

Great leaders draw people to them and to their causes. Their inspirational messages, selfless behaviors, acts of courage, and extraordinary stamina and endurance give people the confidence to engage and commit. Great leaders know that individuals have choices as to whom they follow. People also choose how committed and passionate they will be about the people and causes they follow.

In this section, we began to examine the relationship between the leader and the led. Mother Teresa showed that a leader must first be inspired before she inspires others. John Paul Jones taught that we must face down our own fears before we can instill courage and confidence in others. Nelson Mandela showed the power of self-less leadership. He drew people to him by proving his willingness to put his cause ahead of himself. The Mulligans showed the benefits of maintaining their own energy. Their stamina strengthened and motivated those who followed them.

The following exercises will help you develop the "If" Sixteen Leadership Attributes linked to engaging and motivating others. Again, a variety of tools are available to build these capabilities. Try these, or find others that work for you.

1. ***Write a Newspaper Article Describing a Future Success.*** Fortunately, not all the news we read is bad. Some of the best news articles are those that highlight or celebrate successes. These articles can motivate and inspire those connected with the success, as well as those with no association at all. So why not start with a celebration of the success you will enjoy if your wildest ambitions come to fruition? Picture what it would take to make whatever you are working on truly newsworthy. What would it take to get it on the front page of the *Wall Street Journal* or the *New York Times*?

    Focus your article on behaviors that would attract and motivate people to follow you. How would you describe the success in a way that made readers feel your selflessness, inspiration, courage, and stamina? As you write the article, pay attention to how it makes you feel. When you reread it, does it get your blood pumping? Remember, you must be inspired before you can inspire others. Share the article with one or two trusted colleagues to gauge others' reactions. How do they respond? If you don't get the response you are looking for, consider what it would take to energize them.

2. **Start Noticing Behaviors.** Increase your awareness of behaviors that attract and motivate others. During each of the next four weeks, take note of actions that reflect inspiration, selflessness, courage, and stamina. For example, spend a week noting every selfless act you encounter. Include everything from small acts of politeness to public figures' newsworthy deeds. Pay particular attention to where these behaviors show up and where they don't. Are people more likely to act selflessly in one type of situation than another? Reflect on your own selfless acts. Do you behave differently around some people? Are you more likely to act selflessly in certain situations?

At the end of each week, review the list. What patterns do you see? Whose behavior surprised you, whether positively or negatively? What was your reaction when you witnessed or experienced the different attributes? How often did you find yourself behaving in ways that were inconsistent with the attribute you were noticing that week? How did that make you feel?

At the end of the four weeks, look for patterns and trends. What are you more aware of? What choices and opportunities does this awareness present? Which behaviors do you want to demonstrate more often?

3. **Dissect Heroes and Villains.** It is easy to look at successful leaders and want to imitate them. The problem is that we may pick up bad behavior unintentionally. This is where the dissection comes in. By examining other leaders' specific behaviors,

we can start distinguishing between those that attract followers and those that repel them.

Make a list of the three to five leaders you most admire. These can be people you know personally, or they can be leaders you have read about or studied. Now make a list of three to five poor leaders. List the behaviors that make the first group admirable. Be specific. What behaviors drew others to follow or admire them? Now consider the ineffective leaders. What did they do that drove others away? You should be able to compile an extensive list. What specific actions or behaviors revealed attributes like inspiration, courage, selflessness, or stamina? What other attributes may have made these leaders more or less attractive to follow? Now consider your own behaviors. Are there things you could be doing that would make you a more appealing leader? Are there things that you could stop doing?

Causing others to want to follow us is essential to powerful and effective leadership. That doesn't mean that we must be charismatic. Real-world leadership isn't a popularity contest, despite what we may have experienced in middle school or seen on TV. True leaders attract and motivate followers by proving their accountability to the causes or organizations they lead. They work hard and selflessly, putting their causes ahead of themselves. They show the courage to confront their fears and the stamina to achieve difficult results.

EARNING AND RETAINING THE PRIVILEGE TO LEAD

Great leaders recognize that leadership is a privilege. They understand that the key to this privilege is earning and retaining the trust of those they lead. When things are going well, this can seem quite easy. The real tests come when things are falling apart. Washington proved his greatness by having the composure to save his army. Pershing's ability to wait until America was ready to fight altered the balance of power in the First World War. Edison's 10,000 failures never discouraged him. Meir's accountability during one of Israel's darkest moments prevented disaster.

Washington, Edison, Pershing, and Meir recognized that leadership matters most when things are at their worst. Earning the privilege to lead and retaining the trust of those who follow us demand that we possess these essential attributes:

- composure
- patience
- enthusiasm
- accountability

These traits keep people following us during both adversity and success. They help us keep others from panicking in a crisis. They allow us to follow our plans, even when others want to take shortcuts or rush ahead. They can turn drudgery into meaningful and important work. They can give our followers the confidence to take initiative.

How can we act in ways that keep others following us in good times and bad? Here are some exercises to help you develop the qualities that will earn and retain the trust of those who follow you:

1. **Reapply for Your Own Job.** At the end of the year (or after a major milestone of some sort), pretend that you are your own boss and your current position is vacant. Now, interview yourself for the job. Focus on assessing your competence as a leader. Write your answers to the following behavioral interview questions:

   ➤ Tell me about a time when you used a failure or setback to motivate others to achieve a desired result.

   ➤ Tell me about a time when you took accountability for a failure.

   ➤ Describe a time when you were being pressured to deliver results before you were prepared. How did you handle the pressure?

   ➤ Tell me about some demanding situations in which you managed to remain calm and composed.

Make up other questions as you see fit. Whenever possible, use recent examples. As you answer the questions, think about what you did well in the scenarios you describe. Objectively assess ways you could have been more effective. What were the results of your behavior?

After completing your mock interview, decide whether you would hire yourself. Regardless of the answer, use the results of this process to help you build and acquire key competencies and attributes.

2. ***Become a Feedback Junkie.*** Someone once told me, "Feedback is a gift." I responded, "That's why sometimes it feels like a pair of socks or an ugly tie." In reality, the value of the feedback we receive is often a function of our curiosity and interest. That's what distinguishes the socks and ties from the gems. When we are curious and interested, we seek genuine and sincere feedback—both constructive and critical. We ask questions that invite others to tell us the good and the bad. We are enthusiastic about learning our strengths and our weaknesses.

Regardless of whether or not your organization has a formal 360-degree feedback process, cultivate your own feedback loops. Start soliciting feedback from key stakeholders, such as subordinates, peers, customers, and managers. Let them know that you are truly interested in learning what they think. Don't make this a once-a-year event. Make feedback an ongoing process. Seek timely opportunities to ask their opinions about how you can improve, such as after reaching a project milestone or completing a major deliverable, after a failure or setback, or immediately after an important presentation. Insist on specifics about how well or poorly you are exhibiting specific leadership attributes. Ask for one or two things they would like to see you do differently. Whatever feedback they provide, do something with it. If it is well grounded and appropriate, you may decide to incorporate it into your development plan. If it isn't, thank them for the feedback anyway. You may also want to tell them why you aren't going to act on it.

3. *Become a Storyteller.* Earning and retaining others' trust requires that we truly connect. This means speaking to people's hearts. Public speakers know this. That's why they are so adept at storytelling. Great leaders like Abraham Lincoln and Ronald Reagan were legendary for their ability to tell stories that both entertained their audiences and solidified their leadership positions. They told stories about themselves and about others.

Becoming a good storyteller requires practice. It also means becoming a collector of stories to tell. I am often surprised to hear leaders say they don't have motivational stories to tell. I encourage them to learn by listening to the stories of public figures. The best stories aren't about big, memorable events. Typically, they are about funny or poignant minor incidents that reinforce an important message.

Start noticing the daily events that catch your attention. Keep a list and review it regularly. Notice the types of events that attract your attention. Look for opportunities to weave stories into your conversations. Be aware of how others react to the various stories. Find stories that ennoble the work your team is doing or that celebrate successes. Never use stories that embarrass or discomfort anyone—except stories about you. Everyone always enjoys hearing the boss make fun of himself.

Retaining the mantle of leadership can be more challenging than earning it. Leadership isn't always sexy or exciting. Neither is the work done by those we lead. It can be boring and frustrating. Things can—and do—go wrong. Our job as leaders is to remind those we lead of what really matters. We can help them to remain excited about a never-ending project by showing how important it is to the organization's mission. We can put problems and failures in their proper context, so crises don't become panics. Leadership means keeping things moving forward regardless of the difficulties and challenges we face.

NOW, WILL YOU LEAD?

Awareness and choice: these two concepts form the foundation of leadership. They enable us to truly understand ourselves and the world around us. Awareness and choice are at the core of the "If" Sixteen Leadership Framework and each of the attributes that it contains.

As I was writing this book, new and troubling leadership failures filled the headlines. It is likely that, as you were reading this book, you read about and watched reports on similar events in the news. This awareness can easily become disheartening, even depressing.

I have chosen to look for encouragement and motivation in the news, even the bad news. I see the opportunities that these problems and failures create for leaders who choose to rise to the challenges they present. Even more, I am encouraged by the countless stories that go unreported. I am motivated by the stories I've heard about the outstanding leaders who work quietly and effectively. I am motivated by the well-led and thriving organizations that don't make headlines. There *is* good news. We just have to be aware of it. For every headline that announces failure, there are dozens of stories of leaders doing the right thing and leading honorably and effectively.

Rudyard Kipling published "If—" 100 years before I wrote this book. Kipling's words and wisdom remain relevant. They aren't a prescription for becoming a powerful leader. Neither is this book. The poem and this book are simply tools intended to guide those who choose to lead. The only prescription is hard work, dedication, and experience.

In his book *Outliers*, Malcolm Gladwell writes about the importance of hard work and practice. He asserts that truly world-class performance only occurs when someone exceeds 10,000 hours of deliberate practice in a given discipline. His research addressed musicians, artists, computer programmers, and a variety of other individual endeavors. I would argue that leadership is no different.

To put 10,000 hours into context, it would take five years of working full time to accumulate 10,000 hours. It is virtually impossible for anyone to devote 100 percent of his or her time to leading.

In reality, most of us spend more time managing, administering, and doing than leading. As we grow into positions that are more senior, the percentage of leadership time goes up, but no one spends 100 percent of his or her working hours leading.

Most of us will never acquire 10,000 hours of dedicated practice leading. Does that mean we should accept mediocrity? No, because every minute of practice we put in will make us better. Every experience can be a learning event. Every learning event increases our awareness and our ability to choose effectively. The fact is that it will take most of us an entire career to reach our full leadership potential.

Awareness reveals choices, and choices generate greater awareness. The cycle is virtuous and perpetual. We have the opportunity to choose to lead. The choice is ours. Those we lead choose as well. They choose whom they will follow. If they choose us, we must honor their choice by making ourselves worthy of their trust.

Now, will you lead?

What Else We Need to Know

Throughout the process of writing this book, I regularly solicited feedback from leaders about the "If" Sixteen Leadership Framework. I specifically asked, "What's missing?" The feedback I received helped me in two ways. First, it allowed me to see opportunities to enhance the descriptions of several of the "If" Sixteen Attributes. Second, it helped me recognize that there are some attributes worthy of note beyond the "If" Sixteen. That recognition led to this list, the Next Sixteen.

For most of us, once we finish a book like this, the last thing we want is another list of things to learn. For our purposes, the Next Sixteen are simply complementary to the "If" Sixteen. They provide enhanced precision in our leadership development. On the other hand, those of you who are gluttons or overachievers may be wondering, "What else do I need to know?" For you, the Next Sixteen list provides an opportunity to keep digging and exploring. However, before you move on too quickly, I encourage you to take a moment to reflect on one question: What else can I glean from this book and the "If" Sixteen Leadership Framework? I applaud anyone who recognizes that there will always be more to learn about leading and being an effective leader. No single list, book, or framework will capture all of the nuances and subtleties of leadership. Nevertheless, the beauty and power of this framework is that it provides a perpetual cycle for development and learning. By constantly asking and answering the four "If" Sixteen Leadership Framework questions, you can gain a lifetime of leadership growth.

As you review the Next Sixteen Attributes, consider how they fit into your leadership style. How are they related to the "If" Sixteen Attributes? Many of these are closely linked to one or more of them. I arranged the following list alphabetically to minimize the temptation to infer any priority or significance to their order.

Action Orientation. Why is it that leaders are often geared toward taking action? As leaders, others expect us to execute. Action orientation is a key component in boldness and courage. Frequently, being action oriented means proceeding based on only partial data, intuition, and/or instincts. General George Patton was one such leader who exemplified this quality. He was so inclined to act that he often failed to fully consider the repercussions of his actions; however, this predisposition was also the source of many of Patton's greatest successes.

Adaptability. As leaders we must have the ability to respond to the changing circumstances we confront. Adaptability is an important component in character, authenticity, integrity, boldness, and courage. Because adaptability is integral to so many other attributes, it is important that we understand it and develop it. James Madison, the fourth president of the United States, is a perfect example. Schoolchildren know him as the father of the US Constitution, and it was Madison's adaptability that enabled him to orchestrate the ratification of one of the most enduring political documents of all time.

Assertiveness. Our ability to clearly, forcefully, and unambiguously make our expectations known can mean the difference between effective and mediocre leadership. In order to obtain real results, we must be assertive, and we must develop assertiveness in those we lead. One of the primary drivers of visionary and bold leadership is the willingness and ability to tell people what we want. Pope John Paul II led the Catholic Church during a period of huge social change and turmoil by asserting his will and expectations. His assertive leadership made him instrumental in the collapse of communism and the strengthening of relations between the Catholic Church and other religious groups.

Creativity. Not all leaders are creative, but we all must promote creativity. Leaders push others to transcend traditional ideas, rules, patterns, and relationships that define how things are. They unleash the creativity in themselves and others to define how things *could* be, whether that means finding solutions to troubling problems, addressing a social ill, inventing a world-changing product, or making a breakthrough discovery. Creativity is an essential part of leadership. When asked "Who invented the automobile?" it's amazing how many people respond, "Henry Ford." While Ford didn't invent it, he did revolutionize how automobiles—and everything else—are manufactured. By developing and refining the assembly line and modern mass-production processes, he changed the world.

Dedication. One of the most important functions of a leader is getting others to invest whatever time or energy is necessary to accomplish a task. We do this by demonstrating our personal dedication to our work and our organization. Dedication means making trade-offs and sacrifices, and it is often the key differentiator between success and failure. While it shares a great deal in common with stamina, resilience, inspiration, and patience, dedication is a frequently cited leadership attribute. Christopher Columbus was exceedingly dedicated. He tried and failed numerous times to launch his expedition that led to the discovery of America. His dedication served him as he pushed his crews to keep moving forward. His sacrifices enabled him to achieve his dreams.

Empathy. One of the signs of superior leadership is the ability to be aware of and sensitive to others' feelings, thoughts, and experiences. Our empathy strengthens our connections and bonds with those we lead. Empathy demands that we truly listen to others. Queen Elizabeth I, who ruled England from 1558 to 1603, was one of its most powerful and successful monarchs. Her exceptional empathy was one of her greatest assets. It gave her the ability to connect with a wide variety of people.

Fairness. People want to know that their leaders are going to act consistently and justly. We are often required to make decisions that benefit one party while harming another. Leadership means accurately and honestly weighing the facts before passing judgment. We earn loyalty and trust by leading fairly and creating fairness throughout our organizations. The role of judge is fundamentally about fairness. Some of the greatest Supreme Court justices earned their places in history because of their commitment to fairness. Chief Justice Earl Warren oversaw sweeping changes in America. Many of his court's greatest decisions, like *Brown v. Board of Education*, overturned patently unfair laws.

Humility. People often ignore humility as an important

leadership trait, because it is frequently misunderstood. We confuse it with meekness or uncertainty. Rather, humility is accepting and embracing our talents, positions, and power—without ever caring about them for their own sake. Humble leaders don't deny their gifts, but they don't dwell on them either. In his book *Good to Great*, Jim Collins describes an exceptionally successful type of leader, what he calls "Level 5" leaders. One of their most important characteristics is their humility. They are also confident and aware of their strengths (which are often extraordinary), and they acknowledge their weaknesses. Their leadership strength comes from their ability to recognize their gifts and put them to use serving those they lead. Mahatma Gandhi epitomized leading with humility. His work was never about him. He never focused on his many extraordinary abilities, nor did he ever deny them.

Humor. We all think we have a sense of humor; unfortunately, many leaders lose theirs as they advance. We begin to take ourselves far too seriously. Effective leaders recognize the importance of using humor to energize followers. Humor helps keep things in context and provides effective ways to release stress and anxiety. Humor can also be dangerous. Leaders must always use humor to build others up, not tear them down. Politicians and comedians use humor to draw attention to important issues of their day. President Harry Truman was adept at using it to soften difficult issues or highlight problems that needed to be solved.

Intellect. Those we lead want to know that we have basic intellectual capacity. They want to know that we can think clearly and that we are bright enough to solve the problems that confront us. This doesn't mean that they expect each of us to be the smartest person in an organization, but they do want us to be sharp enough to find and empower those who are. Madame Marie Curie, a pioneer in physics and the study of radioactivity, was both brilliant and capable of seeing brilliance in others. Curie's intelligence and perseverance allowed her to become a leader in her male-dominated field of work. Her intellect also earned her the distinction of being the first person to receive two Nobel Prizes.

Magnanimity. Aristotle called magnanimity "the crowning virtue." In his book *Virtuous Leadership*, Alexandre Havard identifies it as a foundational virtue of leadership. Magnanimous leaders see the potential greatness in those they lead or wish to lead. The word *magnanimous* is derived from the Latin *magnus* ("great") and *animus* ("mind"). Like wisdom, it goes far beyond intellect. Robert Schuman, father of the European Union, represents leading with magnanimity. Following the carnage of two world wars, most French leaders wanted to see Germany rendered impotent. Schuman knew that long-term European peace and success depended on unity and cooperation, and this relied on Franco-German harmony. This type of magnanimity required seeing potential greatness, despite the destruction, misery, hatred, and desire for revenge.

Openness/Approachability. Great leaders must be willing to hear and consider new ideas. But what happens if no one brings us new ideas? Leaders must create inviting and welcoming environments to encourage those they lead to step forward and share their thoughts. One of Colin Powell's rules of leadership is, "The day soldiers stop bringing you their problems is the day you stopped leading them. They have either lost confidence that you can help them or concluded that you do not care. Either case is a failure of leadership." Whether those we lead are bringing us problems or the next great idea, our openness is essential to effective leadership.

Optimism. Laura Olle, one of my favorite bosses, used to say, "When someone asks you how you are, always answer, 'Great.'" She was reminding us that most people don't want to hear our problems. However, they do want to help us solve interesting and challenging problems. She knew that optimism was contagious, but beyond that she knew that her positive attitude would attract others to want to help her. Optimism is a critical component associated with several of the "If" Sixteen Leadership Attributes: resilience, ambition, enthusiasm, and inspiration. Helen Keller, despite her extraordinary disabilities and adversity, never lost her optimism. She once said, "Optimism is the faith that leads to achievement. Nothing can be done without hope and confidence."

Persuasion. Leadership is often defined as the ability to persuade or influence others to do something they might not do otherwise. The ability to influence others and cause them to move in a particular direction is essential to leadership. Our ability to persuade is tightly coupled with our ability to build trust. It is also closely linked to our ability to communicate clearly and effectively. Mustafa Kemal Atatürk was the founder of the Republic of Turkey and its first president. Atatürk's persuasive leadership transformed the former Ottoman Empire into a modern and secular nation-state.

Rigor/Discipline. Rigorous leaders create the structures and processes that help people do their jobs. Leaders recognize that some discipline helps organizations achieve their missions, while too much discipline actually undermines their ability to do so. Rigorous leaders promote the former and eliminate the latter. Sports teams provide great examples of the importance of rigor. Precise execution can mean the difference between a great team and a mediocre one. Don Shula, former head coach of the Miami Dolphins, holds the NFL record for most career victories. Precision and rigor were essential to his coaching and leadership philosophies. In his book *Everyone's a Coach*, Shula writes, "Perfection only happens when the mechanics are automatic." His rigor as a coach helped his players seek perfection.

Wisdom. There is a line from a Christmas carol that goes, "It's in every one of us to be wise. . . . We can all know everything without ever knowing why." Knowing why is the essence of wisdom. Having the intellectual horsepower to solve the world's problems without knowing *why* we are doing what we are doing can lead to horrible mistakes. Wisdom means knowing what is true or right, combined with the moral judgment to take action. Benjamin Franklin was both intelligent and wise. His great contribution to the founding of the United States was the wisdom he showed during some of the nation's most difficult challenges.

To paraphrase Wolfgang Amadeus Mozart: there you have it— too many attributes. Now you have thirty-two things to focus on to become a successful and effective leader. Remember that this list, just like the original sixteen, is intended as a guide to help identify areas on which you can choose to focus. It is not a to-do list. Don't try to fix everything at once. Work on a few things at a time, and go after them with vigor. When you have achieved a level of mastery on those, work on a few more. This is a marathon, not a sprint.

You may have noticed that in addition to adding sixteen new

attributes, I have added sixteen new leaders. Learn more about them. Read their biographies, and see how they led. Each used an approach that best suited him or her and the situations he or she confronted.

Now, put yourself in my shoes. Whom would you have picked? Who are your "If" Sixteen Leaders? Who are your Next Sixteen Leaders? Share your lists with the *If You Will Lead* community by posting them at www.ifyouwilllead.com. While you're at it, tell the community what leadership attributes you would have included or left out. Which attributes do you view as most important to successful leadership? Developing leadership skills is a dynamic and interactive process: the more information we share, the better we all become. Thank you in advance for your participation.

APPENDIX 1

Values List for Self-Awareness Exercise 1

Accountability	Dependability
Adventure	Discipline
Altruism	Diversity
Ambition	Empathy
Appearance	Empowerment
Approval	Enthusiasm
Authenticity	Environment
Authority	Equality
Autonomy	Excellence
Awareness	Expertise
Beauty	Exploration
Boldness	Fairness
Career	Faith
Challenge	Fame
Character	Family
Choice	Financial Security
Clarity	Flexibility
Collaboration	Focus
Comfort	Freedom
Commitment	Friendship
Communication	Fulfillment
Community	Fun
Competence	Generosity
Competition	Gratitude
Composure	Growth
Connectedness	Happiness
Contentment	Harmony
Contribution	Health
Control	Honesty
Courage	Hope
Creativity	Humility
Curiosity	Humor

Independence

Innovation

Inspiration

Integrity

Intelligence

Intimacy

Joy

Knowledge Sharing

Leadership

Leading

Learning

Legacy

Leisure

Love

Loyalty

Making a Difference

Meaning

Nature

Nurturing

Openness

Orderliness

Participation

Partnership

Patience

Peace

Performance

Pleasure

Popularity

Power

Privacy

Productivity

Professionalism

Prosperity

Quality

Recognition

Relationships

Religion

Reputation

Resilience

Respect

Romance

Security

Self-awareness

Self-efficacy

Selflessness

Self-love

Sensuality

Service

Simplicity

Spirituality

Stamina/Energy

Status

Strength

Success

Teaching

Teamwork

Tradition

Trust

Truth

Variety

Vision

Wealth

Wisdom

APPENDIX 2

The "If" Sixteen Leadership Framework

KNOW WHO YOU ARE

- **Character**—The Wisdom to Know and Trust Yourself
- **Authenticity**—The Resolve Always to Be Yourself
- **Integrity**—The Wisdom to Know the Truth and the Strength to Defend It
- **Self-Efficacy**—The Confidence to Gain from Triumph and Disaster

KNOW WHAT YOU WANT

- **Ambition**—The Will to Make the World What You Want It to Be
- **Vision**—The Power of Having and Sharing a Dream
- **Boldness**—The Ability to See and Seize Opportunities
- **Resilience**—The Ability to Bounce Back from Adversity

ATTRACT OTHERS

- **Inspiration**—The Ability to Connect with and Motivate Friends and Foes
- **Courage**—The Ability to Face the Dangers When They Become Real
- **Selflessness**—The Ability to Put Your Cause and Beliefs Ahead of Yourself
- **Stamina**—The Will and Energy to Hold On

RETAIN TRUST

- **Composure**—The Power to Keep Your Head
- **Patience**—The Strength and Will to Endure and Wait
- **Enthusiasm**—The Energy to Fill Every Minute
- **Accountability**—The Will to Take Ownership Regardless of the Outcome

◢

The "If" Sixteen Leadership Attributes Summary

THE *WHO AM I?* ATTRIBUTES

➤ **Character**, at its most basic, involves cataloging and understanding the traits and features that define us. Character means knowing who we are and what we believe and value. It means acting in ways that demonstrate these beliefs and values. Leading with character means willingly sharing our values, beliefs, and traits with those around us.

- Character matters. Leadership means investing the time and energy to know ourselves.
- Character means grounding our beliefs in principles and morality.
- Character requires us to align our actions and decisions with our beliefs and values.
- True character is tested. We must recognize and address misalignments between our actions and our values.
- Leading with character means more than having character. It requires us to be open and public about our beliefs and values.

➤ **Authenticity** means recognizing and embracing the fact that leaders must remain themselves regardless of the situations they confront. We play many roles, and each role demands a different combination of the traits that define our character. By living and acting according to our beliefs, values, and principles, we can lead from positions of strength and power.

- We build authenticity on a solid foundation—our character.

- Authenticity means knowing who we are at any given moment.
- Authentic leadership means knowing who we are not.
- Authenticity requires a great deal of commitment.
- Leading and living authentically are essential to building solid relationships.

➤ **Integrity** is about having the wisdom to learn the truth and then choosing to defend it. Speaking and defending the truth reveals who we are. But integrity goes far beyond truth. Integrity also involves remaining whole. Leading with integrity means that we remain true to ourselves in our many roles. It means leading with an awareness of the potential for conflict or contention among our various roles.

- Integrity means seeking the truth and changing our positions when we gain better perspective.
- Integrity requires leaders to accept the consequences of speaking and defending the truth.
- Integrity may mean that others twist our words and manipulate the truth.
- Leading with integrity means having the ability to anticipate what will prevent others from accepting the truth.
- Integrity means having the patience to repeat the truth so others might understand it.

➤ **Self-efficacy** means that we must have the humility and confidence to learn from both triumphs and disasters. Self-awareness and self-knowledge give us the confidence and wisdom to learn and grow from every experience.

- Leading with self-efficacy means learning continuously and teaching those we lead.
- Self-efficacious leaders model positive responses to triumphs and disasters.
- Self-efficacy requires us to embrace the value of both praise and criticism.

- People with high levels of self-efficacy constantly prepare to achieve the results they know they are capable of.

THE *WHAT DO I WANT?* ATTRIBUTES

➤ **Ambition** is our desire for achievement and accomplishment. We should distinguish between societal and personal ambitions, recognizing that the two can be complementary. Our own ambitions (or our organizations' ambitions) form the foundation for understanding what we want to achieve.

- Ambition builds on the investment we make in learning who we are so we can then understand what we truly want.
- Real power comes from connecting personal ambition with societal ambition.
- Achieving our ambition means exploiting our talents and acquiring new skills.
- Ambition sometimes means surpassing others who appear to be more qualified.
- Leadership demands that we enlist both friends and foes to help us achieve our ambitions.

➤ **Vision** is the external manifestation of character and ambition. Vision starts with telling the world what we believe and then what we want to accomplish. We do this by describing a world that reflects our ambitions and aspirations. Publicizing and repeating our vision is essential to leadership.

- Leaders understand that a compelling vision allows others to see what we see.
- Our visions have power when they reflect our values, beliefs, and principles.
- Our visions must speak to both our core supporters and our extended stakeholders.
- Powerful visions balance audacity with credibility.

- Clarity matters. Leaders understand the power of simple messages repeated with conviction.

➤ **Boldness** is our ability to see opportunities that others don't—and it promotes the willingness to seize those opportunities, even when others say we should not. Effective risk taking and strategic boldness are essential to effective leadership.

- Boldness starts with seeing things others miss.
- Boldness means assessing the relative strengths and weaknesses of our options.
- Leaders act to seize the opportunities presented to them.
- Leaders recognize that boldness depends on leveraging others and empowering them to act.
- Leaders act despite the ambiguity they may confront.

➤ **Resilience** is the ability to bounce back from setbacks. Leading by knowing what we want means anticipating challenges and recognizing and overcoming the obstacles we encounter.

- Leading with resilience means maintaining a positive outlook. Leaders keep looking forward.
- Resilience requires us to be creative problem solvers.
- Resilient leaders remain focused on their end goals.
- Leaders acknowledge the weaknesses or failings of others without allowing those factors to discourage or dissuade them.
- Resilience means accepting and using the resources we have.

THE ATTRIBUTES THAT HELP ATTRACT OTHERS

➤ **Inspiration** is the ability to connect with and motivate others—both friends and foes. Our actions and words can inspire others to achieve extraordinary accomplishments. Inspiration is the catalyzing force that instigates change.

- Leaders recognize that they must be inspired before they can inspire others.
- Inspiration starts with the courage to state our beliefs and to make our goals known.
- Inspiration means communicating effectively and deliberately to motivate our followers.
- Inspirational leaders have the ability to clearly define the problems they are solving.
- Real inspiration has the capacity to attract and empower those we lead.

➤ **Courage** is how leaders respond when the risks they anticipate become reality. These difficult situations can be make-or-break moments for leaders. Courage requires leaders to "force their heart and nerve" and to put themselves in harm's way.

- Courage requires leaders to quickly and accurately assess situations and dangers they confront.
- Maintaining our focus and the focus of others on our larger goals helps foster courage.
- Courage often requires leaders to use a combination of hope and fear.
- Leaders embody courage by not shying away from danger.
- Leaders innovate and adapt to the situation in order to overcome weaknesses and fears.

➤ **Selflessness** means putting our people and our causes ahead of our own interests. This requires a deep awareness, and it often requires difficult choices.

- Selfless leaders subordinate their personal feelings, needs, and egos to the greater good.
- Selflessness takes practice. When we act selflessly in the little things, we are more easily able to do so when we face the big things.
- Selfless leadership requires a strong will and a true sense of self.

- Selflessness demands that leaders have strong understandings of their boundaries and priorities.

➤ **Stamina** is what enables us to survive and thrive despite the exhausting nature of leadership. Leading can be draining—physically, psychologically, emotionally, and spiritually. Our focus on maintaining our energy and persevering will inspire those we lead and facilitate their doing the same.

- Leaders understand that maintaining stamina sometimes means giving assistance, and they encourage others to do the same.
- Leaders encourage those they lead to seek assistance when they are exhausted.
- Leaders promote stamina and energy by building and maintaining a sense of community.
- Leaders understand that their beliefs and values create a foundation for emotional and spiritual stamina. Leaders help set the mood and energy level for those they lead.

THE ATTRIBUTES THAT ENABLE LEADERS TO RETAIN AND EARN TRUST

➤ Through **composure** a leader is able to transform the energy of a crisis into positive action. Leaders do this by keeping their heads. Composure requires us to be fully aware of the situations we face. At the same time, composure is about making choices and taking action to restore calm.

- In the face of the unexpected, leaders step up, take responsibility, and exert control.
- Leaders respond decisively and execute effective contingency plans.
- In a crisis, leaders remain visible and share the information others need to do their jobs.
- Leaders recognize the importance of projecting a positive attitude.

- Leaders maintain their composure by maintaining perspective.
- Awareness of their own strengths and weaknesses helps leaders maintain perspective.
- Leaders don't wait for a crisis to anticipate risks and potential outcomes.
- Leaders know how to use a crisis to mobilize action.
- Leaders recognize that commitment is a precursor to composure.

➤ **Patience** is the ability to know when we should act and when we should wait. Patience often means choosing to wait when others are pushing us to move.

- Leading with patience requires that we understand a given situation and establish the facts.
- Leading with patience starts with having the discipline to create a robust plan appropriate to each situation we confront.
- Leading with patience means building support and getting the right backing for our plans.
- Leaders must have the determination and discipline to execute their plans on a suitable schedule.
- Leading with patience means having the wisdom to anticipate and respond to the unexpected.

➤ **Enthusiasm** is the positive energy and passion at the heart of innovation, creativity, and exceptional performance. Leaders who produce great ideas often possess extraordinary enthusiasm.

- Leaders recognize that enthusiasm is an invaluable asset.
- Leaders acknowledge the power of people doing what they love.
- Leading with enthusiasm means finding motivation in a variety of areas.
- Leaders recognize that nothing builds excitement and passion better than doing work in a fun environment.

- Leaders build enthusiasm by turning obstacles into new opportunities.

➤ **Accountability** means choosing to take ownership, regardless of how things turn out. Our decision to be accountable helps define us as leaders. A leader's trustworthiness is often determined by his or her willingness to be held to account.

- Accountable leaders focus on fixing a problem, not placing the blame.
- Accountable leaders move aggressively to restore confidence.
- Accountable leaders create leverage and build confidence by delegating and empowering others.
- Accountability means taking the blame for failures and asking for forgiveness.

BIBLIOGRAPHY

Abrashoff, D. M. *It's Your Ship: Management Techniques from the Best Damn Ship in the Navy.* New York: Warner Books, 2002.

Avery, C. M. *Teamwork Is an Individual Skill: Getting Your Work Done When Sharing Responsibility.* San Francisco: Berret-Koehler Publishers, 2001.

Badaracco, J., Jr. *Defining Moments: When Managers Must Choose Between Right and Right.* Boston: Harvard Business Press, 1997.

Badaracco, J., Jr. and Ellsworth, R.R. *Leadership and the Quest for Integrity.* Boston: Harvard Business Press, 1993.

Badaracco, J., Jr. *Questions of Character: Illuminating the Heart of Literature Through Leadership.* Boston: Harvard Business Press, 2006.

Bandura, A. *Self-Efficacy in Changing Societies.* Cambridge: Cambridge University Press, 1995.

Bandura, A. *Self-Efficacy: The Exercise of Control.* New York: Worth Publishing, 1997.

Bernstein, R. B. *Thomas Jefferson.* New York: Oxford University Press, 2003.

Bernstein, P. L. *Against the Gods: The Remarkable Story of Risk.* New York: Wiley and Sons, 1996.

Blanchard, K., and Hodges, P. *Lead Like Jesus: Lessons from the Greatest Leadership Role Model of All Time.* Nashville: Thomas Nelson, 2005.

Blanchard, K., and Shula, D. *Everyone's a Coach.* New York: Harper Business, 1995.

Branch, T. *Parting the Waters: America in the King Years, 1954–1963.* New York: Simon and Schuster, 1988.

Bronson, P. *What Should I Do with My Life?: The True Story of People Who Answered the Ultimate Question.* New York: Random House, 2002.

Brooks, R., and Goldstein, S. *The Power of Resilience: Achieving Balance, Confidence, and Personal Strength in Your Life.* New York: McGraw Hill, 2004.

Burkett, E. *Golda.* New York: Harper, 2008.

Burns, J. M. *Transforming Leadership.* New York: Atlantic Monthly Press, 2003.

Carnegie, D. *How to Win Friends and Influence People.* New York: Simon and Schuster, 1981.

Carson, R. D. *Taming Your Gremlin.* New York: Quill, 2003.

Cerami, C. A. *Jefferson's Great Gamble: The Remarkable Story of Jefferson, Napoleon and the Men Behind the Louisiana Purchase.* Naperville, IL: Sourcebooks, 2003.

Christensen, C. M. *The Innovator's Dilemma: When New Technologies Cause Great Firms to Fail.* Boston: Harvard Business School Press, 1997.

Churchill, W. *Never Give In!: The Best of Winston Churchill.* New York: Hyperion, 2003.

Clemens, J., and Wolff, M. *Movies to Manage By.* New York: Contemporary Books, 1999.

Clinton, C. *Harriet Tubman: The Road to Freedom.* Boston: Back Bay Books, 2005.

Collins, J. *Good to Great: Why Some Companies Make the Leap . . . and Others Don't.* New York: Harper Business, 2001.

Coogan, T. P. *Michael Collins: The Man Who Made Ireland.* London: Hutchison, 1990.

Cottrell, D., and Harvey, E. *Leadership Courage: Leadership Strategies for Individual and Organizational Success.* Dallas: The Walk the Talk Company, 2005.

Covey, S. *The 7 Habits of Highly Effective People: Powerful Lessons in Personal Change.* New York: Simon and Schuster, 1989.

Crossan, M., Fry, J., Killing, P. J., and Rouse, M. *Strategic Analysis and Action,* 5th ed. Toronto: Prentice Hall, 2002.

Csikszentmihalyi, M. *Flow: The Psychology of Optimal Experience.* New York: Harper Perennial Modern Classics, 2008.

Denton, J. *When Hell Was in Session,* 7th ed. Washington, DC: WND Books, 2009.

De Pree, M. *Leadership Is an Art.* New York: Doubleday Business, 1989.

Donald, D. H. *Lincoln.* New York: Simon and Schuster, 1996.

D'Souza, D. *Ronald Reagan: How an Ordinary Man Became an Extraordinary Leader.* New York: Free Press, 1999.

Dwyer, T. R. *Michael Collins: The Man Who Won the War.* Dublin: Mercier Press, 2009.

Elliot, T. S. *The Uses of Poetry and the Uses of Criticism.* Boston: Harvard University Press, 1967.

Ellis, J. J. *American Sphinx: The Character of Thomas Jefferson.* New York: Random House Value Publishing, 1998.

Ellis, J. J. *His Excellency: George Washington.* New York: Alfred A. Knopf, 2004.

Forni, P. M. *Choosing Civility: The Twenty-Five Rules of Considerate Conduct.* New York: St. Martin's Griffin, 2002.

Fortune magazine. "100 Best Companies to Work For." *Fortune,* February 4, 2008.

Frederick J. Ryan, J. *Ronald Reagan: The Wisdom and Humor of the Great Communicator.* San Francisco: Collins Publishing, 1995.

George, B. *Authentic Leadership: Rediscovering the Secrets to Creating Lasting Value.* San Francisco: Jossey-Bass, 2003.

George, B. *True North: Discovering the Secrets to Creating Lasting Value.* San Francisco: Jossey-Bass, 2007.

Gilbert, M. *Churchill: A Life.* New York: Henry Holt and Company, 1991.

Gilmour, D. *The Long Recessional: The Imperial Life of Rudyard Kipling.* New York: Farrar, Straus, and Giroux, 2003.

Gladwell, M. *Outliers.* New York: Little, Brown and Company, 2008.

Goleman, D., and McKee, A. *Primal Leadership: Realizing the Power of Emotional Intelligence.* Boston: Harvard Business School Press, 2002.

Goodwin, D. K. *Team of Rivals: The Political Genius of Abraham Lincoln.* New York: Simon and Schuster, 2005.

Greenleaf, R. K. *The Power of Servant Leadership.* San Francisco: Barrett-Koehler Publishing, 1998.

Harvard Business School Press. *Harvard Business Review On Change.* Cambridge MA: Harvard Business School Press, 1998.

Havard, A. *Virtuous Leadership.* New York: Scepter Publishers, 2007.

Heath, C., and Heath, D. *Made to Stick: Why Some Ideas Survive and Others Die.* New York: Random House, 2007.

Heckler, R. S. *Holding the Center: Sanctuary in a Time of Confusion.* Berkeley CA: Frog, Ltd., 1997.

Hillman, J. *The Force of Character: And the Lasting Life.* New York: Random House, 1999.

Israel, P. *Edison: A Life of Invention.* New York: Wiley and Sons, 1998.

Joiner, B., and Josephs, S. *Leadership Agility: Five Levels of Mastery for Anticipating and Initiating Change.* San Francisco: Jossey-Bass, 2007.

Kabat-Zinn, J. *Wherever You Go, There You Are.* New York: Hyperion, 1994.

King, Martin Luther, Jr., and Carson, C. *The Autobiography of Martin Luther King, Jr.* New York: Grand Central Publishing, 2001.

King, Martin Luther, Jr., edited by Washington, J. M. *I Have a Dream: Writing and Speeches that Changed the World.* San Francisco: HarperSanFrancisco, 1992.

Kituku, V. M. W. *Overcoming Buffaloes at Work and in Life: What You Need to Increase Productivity, Overcome Setbacks and Stay Motivated Without Leaving Your Life Behind.* Boise, ID: Vincent Muli Wa Kituku, 2008.

Kouzes, J. M., and Posner, B. Z. *The Leadership Challenge*. San Francisco: Jossey-Bass, 2002.

Lacey, J. *Pershing*. New York: Palgrave MacMillan, 2008.

Langford, J. *Mother Teresa's Secret Fire: The Encounter That Changed Her Life and How It Can Transform Your Own*. Huntington: Our Sunday Visitor, 2008.

Larson, K. C. *Bound for the Promised Land: Harriet Tubman: Portrait of an American Hero*. New York: Old World/Ballantine, 2004.

Lee, G. *Courage: The Backbone of Leadership*. San Francisco: Jossey-Bass, 2005.

Lind, M. *What Lincoln Believed: The Values and Convictions of America's Greatest President*. New York: Doubleday, 2004.

Loehr, J., and Schwartz, T. *The Power of Full Engagement: Managing Energy, Not Time, Is the Key to High Performance and Personal Renewal*. New York: Free Press, 2003.

Lowery, B. *Harriet Tubman: Imagining a Life*. New York: Anchor, 2008.

Manchester, W. *The Last Lion: Winston Spencer Churchill: Alone, 1932–1940*. Boston: Little, Brown and Company, 1998.

Mandela, N. *Long Walk to Freedom*. New York: Little, Brown and Company, 1994.

Marshall, S. L. A. *World War I*. New York: Mariner Books, 2001.

McCullough, D. *1776*. New York: Simon and Schuster, 2005.

Millard, C. *The River of Doubt: Theodore Roosevelt's Darkest Journey*. New York: Doubleday, 2005.

Mitchell, S. *Bhagavad Gita: A New Translation*. New York: Three Rivers Press, 2000.

Moir, P. *I Was Winston Churchill's Private Secretary*. Wilfred Funk, 1941.

Morison, S. E. *John Paul Jones: A Sailor's Biography*. Annapolis, MD: US Naval Institute Press, 1999.

Morris, E. *Theodore Rex*. New York: Random House, 2001.

Mukherjee, B. "*Time 100 Most Important People of the Century: Mother Teresa*." Time, June 14, 1999.

Mulligan, J. A. *The Hanoi Commitment*. Virginia Beach: RFI Marketing, 1981.

Noonan, P. *When Character Was King: A Story of Ronald Reagan*. New York: Penguin, 2002.

O'Connor, F. *The Big Fellow: Michael Collins and the Irish Revolution*. Dublin: Poolbeg, 1998.

Parry, J. A., and Allison, A. M. *The Real George Washington*. Malta: National Center for Constitutional Studies, 1991.

Peabody, B. *Lucky or Smart?: Fifty Pages for the First-Time Entrepreneur*. New York: Random House, 2004.

Pearce, T. *Leading Out Loud: Inspiring Change Through Authentic Communications*. San Francisco: Jossey-Bass, 2003.

Peck, M. S. *The Road Less Traveled: A New Psychology of Love, Traditional Values, and Spiritual Growth*. New York: Touchstone, 1998.

Phillips, D. T. *Martin Luther King, Jr., on Leadership: Inspiration and Wisdom for Challenging Times*. New York: Business Plus, 2006.

Pomeranz, D. *It's in Every One of Us*. Arista Records, 1975.

Rabinovich, A. *The Yom Kippur War: The Epic Encounter That Transformed the Middle East*. New York: Schocken Books, 2004.

Rath, T., and Clifton, D. O. *How Full Is Your Bucket? Positive Strategies for Work and Life* New York: Gallup Press, 2004.

Reagan, R. W., and Ryan, F. J. *Ronald Reagan: The Wisdom and Humor of The Great Communicator*. San Francisco: Colins Publishers, 1995.

Reagan, R. *The Reagan Diaries*, edited by D. Brinkley. New York: HarperCollins, 2007.

Reivich, K., and Shatte, A. *The Resilience Factor: 7 Keys to Finding Your Inner Strength and Overcoming Life's Hurdles.* New York: Broadway, 2003.

Ricketts, H. *Rudyard Kipling: A Life.* New York: Da Capo Press, 2001.

Risner, R. *The Passing of the Night: My Seven Years as a Prisoner of the North Vietnamese.* Old Saybrook: Konecky and Konecky, 2004.

Roosevelt, T. *The Man in the Arena: Selected Writings of Theodore Roosevelt: A Reader.* New York: Forge Books, 2003.

Rubin, G. *Forty Ways to Look at Winston Churchill: A Brief Account of a Long Life.* New York: Ballantine Books, 2003.

Fredrick, F. J. *Ronald Reagan: The Wisdom and Humor of the Great Communicator*

Sampson, A. *Mandela: The Authorized Biography.* New York: Vintage Books, 1999.

Sanders, T. *Love Is the Killer App: How to Win Business and Influence Friends.* New York: Three Rivers Press, 2002.

Schweitzer, P. *Reagan's War: The Epic Story of His Forty-Year Struggle and Final Triumph Over Communism.* New York: Doubleday, 2003.

Seldman, M., and Seldman, J. *Executive Stamina: How to Optimize Time, Energy, and Productivity to Achieve Peak Performance.* Hoboken, NJ: Wiley, 2008.

Seuss, Dr. *Oh, The Places You'll Go.* New York: Random House, 1990.

Simmons, A., and Lipman, D. *The Story Factor.* New York: Basic Books, 2006.

Slater, R. *Golda, The Uncrowned Queen of Israel: A Pictorial Biography.* New York: Jonathan David Publishing, 1982.

Slattery, M. *The Highway to Leadership.* Boston: Kessinger Publishing, 2007.

Spink, K. *Mother Teresa: A Complete Authorized Biography.* San Francisco: HarperOne, 1998.

Steinberg, B. S. *Women in Power: The Personalities and Leadership Styles of Indira Ghandi.* Montreal: McGill-Queen's University Press, 2008.

Stern, S. "Kipling's 'If—' Has a Message for Today's Corporate Leaders." *Financial Times*, April 29, 2008.

Stross, R. E. *The Wizard of Menlo Park: How Thomas Alva Edison Invented the Modern World.* New York: Three Rivers Press, 2007.

Strozzi-Heckler, R. *Holding the Center: Sanctuary in a Time of Confusion.* Berkeley, CA: Frog, Ltd., 1997.

Surowiecki, J. *The Wisdom of Crowds: Why the Many Are Smarter Than the Few and How Collective Wisdom Shapes Business, Economies, Societies and Nations.* New York: Anchor, 2005.

Teresa, Mother, and Gonzales-Balado, J. L. *Mother Teresa: In My Own Words.* New York: Gramercy Book, 1998.

Thomas, E. *John Paul Jones: Sailor, Hero, Father of the American Navy.* New York: Simon and Schuster, 2003.

Tichy, N. M., and McGill, A. *The Ethical Challenge: How to Lead with Unyielding Integrity.* San Francisco: Jossey-Bass, 2003.

Toll, I. W. *Six Frigates: The Epic History of the Founding of the U.S. Navy.* New York: W.W. Norton and Company, 2008.

United States Department of Defense. *Military Code of Conduct.* Washington, DC: US Government, 1955.

Useem, M., and Bennis, W. G. *The Leadership Moment: Nine True Stories of Triumph and Disaster and Their Lessons for Us All.* New York: Three Rivers Press, 1999.

Wagenknecht, E. *The Seven Worlds of Theodore Roosevelt.* Guilford: The Lyons Press, 2008.

Watson, T. J., and Brown, C. C. *A Business and Its Beliefs: The Ideas that Helped Build IBM.* New York: McGraw-Hill, 2003.

Weiner, A. N. *So Smart But . . . :How Intelligent People Lose Credibility—and How They Can Get it Back.* San Francisco: Jossey-Bass, 2006.

INDEX

About the Author

Doug Moran has more than twenty-five years of leadership experience in a variety of industries. He has worked for Verizon and Capital One (where he was CIO of the financial services division), and served the governor of the Commonwealth of Virginia as deputy secretary of health and human resources, chief operating officer of the department of social services, and telecommunications director. His leadership consultancy, If You Will Lead LLC, focuses on leadership development, executive coaching, organization excellence, and infrastructure strategy. He is certified by the International Coach Federation, received his professional training from Georgetown University, and earned a bachelor degree from James Madison University. Married and the father of two children, Moran lives in Richmond, Virginia, and serves on the board of the Better Housing Coalition.